THE CHINESE
TAO OF BUSINESS:
THE LOGIC OF
SUCCESSFUL BUSINESS
STRATEGY

THE CHINESE TAO OF BUSINESS:
THE LOGIC OF SUCCESSFUL BUSINESS STRATEGY

George T. Haley
Usha C. V. Haley
Chin Tiong Tan

John Wiley & Sons (Asia) Pte Ltd

■ Other Wiley Editorial Offices:
John Wiley & Sons, Inc., 111 River Street, Hoboken, NJ 07030, USA
John Wiley & Sons Ltd, The Atrium, Southern Gate, Chichester,
PO19 8SQ, England
John Wiley & Sons (Canada) Ltd, 22 Worcester Road, Rexdale,
Ontario M9W 1L1, Canada
John Wiley & Sons Australia Ltd, PO Box 174, North Ryde, NSW 2113, Australia
Wiley - VCH, Boschstrasse 12, 69469 Weinheim, Germany

■ Library of Congress Cataloging in Publication Data
ISBN 0470-82059-4

Typeset in 10.5 points, Palatino by Paul Lim.
Printed in Singapore by Saik Wah Press Ltd.
10 9 8 7 6 5 4 3 2 1

We dedicate this book to those
who instructed us in the "Way":
Helen Basila Haley, James B. Haley
and Sarah Basila;
Nandini Venkatesan and Dr. C. Venkatesan;
Indira Bellare and Vasudevrao Bellare;
Khoo Loo Eng and Tan Thye Bee

acknowledgments

GEORGE T. HALEY,
USHA C. V. HALEY, AND
CHIN TIONG TAN
USA & SINGAPORE
JULY 2004

A book of this nature requires the support and co-operation of several people. In particular, an international group of senior managers gave us considerable time and valuable insights; to these managers (listed in Appendix A), we extend our sincere thanks.

We owe an enormous debt, too, to the businesspeople, colleagues and students with whom we have discussed and refined the ideas in this book. We thank them all, particularly Csaaba Soos (formerly of Artesyn Technologies) Frank-Jürgen Richter (Director for Asia, World Economic Forum), and Indra Nooyi (President and Chief Financial Officer, Pepsico). Winnie Hu and Austin C. T. Hu (Deputy Chief of Mission, The World Bank Office, Beijing) provided enormous assistance for our interviews in Beijing.

We also owe sincere thanks to Nick Wallwork, Malar Manoharan and David Sharp of John Wiley & Sons Publishing. Without their faith, patient support, encouragement and occasional nagging, we would never have completed this project.

This project was funded by a grant from the Scholarly Research Grant Program of the University of Tennessee, Knoxville, and we thank Oscar Fowler and David Schumann for providing this support.

Tan Poh Lin, at the Singapore Management University, provided efficient help by transcribing interviews with managers.

This book went through several iterations and required co-operation of numerous people across myriad time zones — in Hong Kong, China, Singapore and the USA. We owe a deep debt to our families, and heartfelt thanks to our friends and colleagues, as well as George and Usha's cats, Comet Baby and Marmalade, for easing strain, making life enjoyable, and for their support and patience when deadlines loomed and tempers frayed.

Finally, we owe an intellectual and emotional debt to our parents and grandparents for showing us the Way, the foundation for a meaningful life; to our ancestors, we dedicate this book.

about the authors

GEORGE T. HALEY

George T. Haley, Ph.D. (University of Texas at Austin) is Professor of Marketing and International Business at the University of New Haven where he teaches in the graduate and executive programs. He has also taught on the faculties of other top universities, including the Instituto Tecnologico y de Estudios Superiores de Monterrey, the National University of Singapore, Queensland University of Technology, Thammasat University and the Harvard University Economics Department's Summer Program – and presented seminars to academics, businessmen and government policy makers in Vietnam, Thailand, India, Singapore, Mexico, Australia and New Zealand. He is a frequent public speaker for corporate executives and government policy-makers worldwide, and an award-winning author, with over 90 book chapters, journal articles, research reports and books. He previously co-authored *New Asian Emperors: The Overseas Chinese, their Strategies and Competitive Advantages*, the top-selling book on Asian business strategies worldwide in 1999. He is on the Review and Advisory boards of several US and European journals including *International Marketing Review (IMR)*, *Industrial Marketing Management (IMM)*, *Journal of Business & Industrial Marketing (JBIM)*, *Marketing Intelligence & Planning (MIP)*, and is a member of the PeerNet Review Board of the *Journal of Management Development (JMD)*, where he lends his expertise on Asia and other emerging economies; additionally, he has guest edited several journal special issues on business in emerging economies and on Internet-Based B2B Marketing. Please contact him at gthaley@asia-pacific.com.

Usha C. V. Haley

Usha C. V. Haley (PhD, Stern School of Business, New York University) is a Professor of Management, focusing on Strategic Management and International Business, in the College of Business Administration at the University of New Haven. She has more than 90 books, journal articles, book chapters and research presentations on international strategic management. Her latest books include *New Asian Emperors: The Overseas Chinese, their Strategies and Competitive Advantages* (Butterworth-Heinemann); *Strategic Management in the Asia Pacific: Harnessing Regional and Organizational Change for Competitive Advantage* (Butterworth-Heinemann); *Multinational Corporations in Political Environments: Ethics, Values and Strategies* (World Scientific) and, *Asian Post-Crisis Management: Corporate and Governmental Strategies for Sustainable Competitive Advantage* (Macmillan/Palgrave). She has taught International Business and Strategic Management at major universities in the United States (including Harvard University), Singapore (at the National University of Singapore), Australia (at the Australian National University), and Mexico (at ITESM, Monterrey Campus). She has also taught in major executive-development programs in the United States, Australia, Russia, Mexico, Vietnam, Italy, India and Singapore. She consults on strategic management and foreign direct investment for several multinational corporations, sits on several journal editorial boards and serves as Regional Editor (Asia Pacific) for three academic journals. Her research on China and the Asia Pacific has been covered extensively in the media and business publications including the *Wall Street Journal*, *Wall Street Journal (Europe)*, *Forbes*, the *Economist*, *Barron's*, *Red Herring*, the *San Francisco Chronicle*, the *Salt Lake City Tribune*, CNN, PBS's *WideAngle*, Voice of America, *Asahi Shimbun*, *The China Post*, *The Australian*, the *Sydney Morning Herald*, *The Hindustan Times*, *The Guardian*, *Business 2.0* and several others. In 2003, Usha received a Life-time Achievement award in Management from the Literati Club (UK) and a panel of businesspersons, policy makers and academics, for her contributions to the understanding of business in the Asia Pacific. She is listed in *Who's Who in America*. Please contact her at uhaley@asia-pacific.com.

CHIN TIONG TAN

Chin Tiong Tan (PhD, Pennsylvania State University) is the Provost of Singapore Management University. He spent 20 years of his career at the National University of Singapore where he was Professor of Marketing, Chairman of Executive Programs of the Faculty of Business Administration, Co-Director of the Stanford-National University of Singapore Executive Program and Director of the NUS Office for Continuing Education.

He is active in management development and consulting. He is a sought after speaker and had designed and taught in executive programs in the US, Europe, Australia, New Zealand, Asia and South Africa. Prof Tan was the Academic Advisor to Singapore Airline's Management Development Centre for 10 years. Other organisations that he worked with include the Standard Chartered Bank, Swiss Bank Corporation, Citicorp, Singapore Telecom, Inchcape, Sime Darby Singapore, Avon Products (US), James Segwick (Australia), ACE Daikin, Carrier, Hewlett-Packard, Acer Computer, Altron Group (South Africa), Motorola (Asia Pacific), Cultur (Finland), Akzo Nobel (The Netherlands), and others. He is on the Board of Directors of several listed companies and served as strategic and business advisor to many organisations. He is Past President and Chairman of Senate of the Marketing Institute of Singapore.

Prof Tan published his research in many international journals including the *Journal of Consumer Research, International Journal of Bank Marketing, Marketing and Psychology, International Journal of Marketing, Journal of International Business Studies, Research in Marketing, International Marketing Review, Journal of the Academy of Marketing Science, Marketing Intelligence & Planning, European Journal of Marketing* and others. He sits on the editorial boards of several international journals. Dr Tan has chaired and organised several international conferences for international professional associations such as the American Marketing Association, Association for Consumer Research and Academy of International Business.

He is also the co-author of Philip Kotler's *Marketing Management: An Asian Perspective* (3rd Edition, 2003, Prentice Hall),

John Quelch's *Strategic Marketing Cases for 21ˢᵗ Century Asia* (2000, Prentice Hall), *Marketing in the New Asia* (2001, McGraw-Hill), *New Asian Emperors: The Overseas Chinese, Their Strategies and Competitive Advantages* (1998, Butterworth-Heinemann), and *Marketing Insights for the Asia Pacific*, (1996, Heinemann Asia).

Part I

THE
CIVILIZATION
CHASM

1

UNDERSTANDING THE CIVILIZATION CHASM

"Hence, look at the person through the person;
look at the family through the family;
look at the hamlet through the hamlet;
look at the state through the state;
look at the empire through the empire."

Tao Te Ching

Book 2, Chapter 54, Stanza 124

INTRODUCTION

The small town of Camden, South Carolina, with about 8,000 people, has a heavy Southern drawl. Locals shop at the Wal-Mart, Kmart and Piggly Wiggly. Fried chicken and steak, grits and biscuits dominate the local restaurant fare. Here, a pioneering Chinese-owned factory is establishing its presence. As the first units roll off the line at the 300,000-square-foot, state-of-the-art refrigerator factory owned by the Qingdao-based Haier Group, one wonders whether Haier will fit well with provincial Camden. The Camden plant's Chinese and US managers say they often struggle to communicate with one another, and much of this difficulty centers on cultural issues and assumptions. "I think it's a learning situation for the Chinese on how to manage Americans, especially Southerners," said Nelson Lindsay, the Kershaw County Economic Development Office's director. "The Chinese had plenty of questions for local officials concerning employee recruitment and benefits," he said.[1] Yet the Chinese appear more comfortable than early Japanese arrivals in delegating day-to-day operations to US managers. Bernie Tymkiw, the factory's highest-ranking US manager, with about three decades in the home-appliance industry, and its human-resource director, Gerald Reeves, said they have wide latitude to manage as they see fit.[2] Understanding the civilizational chasm appears the first order of business.

To remove workers who might clash with Haier's corporate culture, prospective employees must undergo a 40-hour initiation program before Haier hires them. The program stresses teamwork, safety and the importance of quality, as well as an understanding of Chinese history, culture and philosophy. In 2001, Haier flew 10 workers to China for a two-week training program to instill its corporate values. This trip included climbing the Great Wall.

This book provides insights for effective management by Westerners in China as well as Chinese in the West. This first chapter introduces the *Tao Te Ching*, which offers an understanding of ancient power relationships and their acceptance in modern China. The next section outlines Chinese moral, social and legal philosophies on which later chapters will elaborate. The ensuing section delineates differences between Western and Chinese cognitive styles. Finally, the last section sketches how China's history has taken a unique trajectory because of these philosophical and cognitive differences.

THE *TAO TE CHING*

"Not to honor men of worth
will keep the people from contention;
not to value goods which are hard to come by
will keep them from theft;
not to display what is desirable
will keep them (the people) from being unsettled of mind."
Tao Te Ching
Book 1, Chapter 3, Stanza 8

"Heaven and earth are ruthless,
and treat the myriad creatures as straw dogs;
the sage is ruthless,
and treats the people as straw dogs."
Tao Te Ching
Book 1, Chapter 5, Stanza 14

These two opening statements provide the essence of the *Tao Te Ching* and Chinese philosophy as well as a prism to understand the ancient, civilizational chasm between Chinese and Western philosophical thought. The *Tao* literally means the "road" or the "Way"; yet, over the millennia of Chinese history, this word has come to represent a spiritual and moral pathway. In the West, Confucius and his philosophical ideals serve as China's cultural trademark. However, in modern-day China, and because of historical circumstances, Lao Tzu and his philosophical ideals communicated through the *Tao Te Ching* have far more daily relevance; Lao Tzu's *Tao Te Ching* comprises the most-translated and most-read of all Chinese books. Indeed, while Confucianism served as the philosophy of the ruling classes and elites, Taoism emerged historically as the ideology of the common people. Confucian scholars filled China's imperial courts, providing guidance and education to the aloof aristocrats and their children; Taoist scholars and hermits lived in China's villages and caves, providing guidance and education to the villagers and their children.

The opening statement demonstrates the Chinese elites' negative historical attitudes towards the creation and distribution of wealth. It provides justification for the subsistence economic system that Chinese governments have followed from ancient times, not just since the Communist Party seized control in 1949. It explains why the Chinese and Russians have reacted differently to communist liberalization programs.

The second statement presents the traditional Chinese perspective on useful people and tools. The importance of individuals and ideas derives from functional uses, and not from subjective evaluations of personal worth. "Straw dogs" comprised straw figures that the Chinese traditionally offered to the gods. Prior to making these offerings, the Chinese cared assiduously for the straw figures; after making the offerings, the supplicants crushed the straw dogs under their feet. Similarly, Chinese philosophy urges nurturing something or someone that serves a purpose; but once they serve that purpose, it advocates ruthlessly discarding or crushing the now useless tool or potentially dangerous individual. Despite the many ruthless tyrants in Western history, and several contrarian philosophers on power (such as Machiavelli), Western Judeo/Christian/Islamic philosophic dogmas and moral codes shunned the ruthless, routine use of power. In China, the philosophy of power and rule forms the center of Confucian and Taoist philosophies and their offshoots. Consequently, Communist dogma and China's traditional philosophy viewed as acceptable the crushing of pro-democracy protesters at Beijing's Tiananmen Square — though the West saw these actions as shocking. Confucius saw no justification for challenging the rulers' power and stability, regardless of whether the rulers proved to be tyrants, abused power and ruled poorly. As he stated, "Be ready to die for the good of 'the Way'. Do not enter a state that pursues dangerous courses, nor stay in one where the people have rebelled."[3]

Pursuit of behaviors in accordance with "the Way" served as the primary goal under Confucian and Taoist philosophies. Hence, by admonishing his disciples not to enter a state where the people had rebelled, Confucius was identifying rebellion as an unacceptable behavior under "the Way". Confucius and Lao Tzu would have concurred that the Communist government reacted appropriately to the Tiananmen protesters. The protesters should not have challenged the government, but should have packed their belongings and left the country — a move which was somewhat easier before passports and immigration laws, of course.

CONFUCIUS[4]: MASTER K'UNG

Confucius is traditionally considered to have been born in 551 BC, in the state of Lu during the Zhou dynasty, and to have died in 479 BC. His father died in Confucius' infancy and his mother raised him. Though he encountered severe constraints and poverty, he seemed to have early success in his career as he obtained modest public offices within the bureaucracy. Unfortunately, the Zhou dynasty was in serious decline and the constant ebb and flow of the political situation served to disrupt his career and aspirations. His home state of Lu was lost to the empire when three influential and wealthy families joined together to wrest control of the state away from the center. Once his career as a mandarin bureaucrat stalled, Confucius lived as an itinerant teacher and bureaucrat in search of his next posting. During the Confucian era, bureaucrats could travel from state to state in search of employment. At one time, Confucius, in desperation, considered leaving China to seek service in barbarian countries. His difficulties and apparent frustration in gaining material success in his civilized homeland may have led to two traits in Confucian philosophy. First, and most importantly, he exhibited open disdain for personal gain or profit — something, he argued, that the true gentleman never sought. Second, he expressed dissatisfaction with civilized society and he idealized the "Noble Savage"

The Analects, in Chinese the *Lun Yu*, forms the primary body of his philosophy that has survived to the modern times. The English translation of *Lun Yu*, "Selected Sayings", serves as the most accurate description of the masterpiece — basically it is a collection of sayings rather than a coherent text. The power of Confucian thought is as much a tribute to the discerning scholars who interpreted his sayings over the years as it is to Confucius' wisdom and understanding. Though many view his philosophy as lofty, Confucius addressed the practical aspects of day-to-day living almost exclusively. His great appeal today may stem from his being the most human of "Great Officials", and the Great Official of all humanists.

LAO TZU[5]: THE ULTIMATE DUALITY PARADOX

Many believe that Lao Tzu was an older contemporary of Confucius. The name "Lao Tzu" actually means "The Old Man". Some believe he was a man named Li, a historian in charge of the Zhou dynasty's archives, often called Tan the Historian. Others state that he was a man named Lao Lai Tzu, who was born in Ch'u, the same state as Tan the Historian, and was a contemporary of both Confucius and Tan. The historical biographies of both Confucius and Lao Tzu record a meeting between them in which Lao Tzu bested Confucius. The meeting occurred when Confucius visited Lao Tzu for instruction in the rites and, depending on whether the story is told by a supporter or a critic of Confucius, Confucius returns either showing respect for Lao Tzu's age and great wisdom (appropriate behavior as Lao Tzu was older), or admitting that Lao Tzu had an understanding far beyond his own (admission that he lost face to Lao Tzu).

Tradition has it that Lao Tzu had retired from public life and was beginning a contemplative life, when the Keeper of the Pass out of the Zhou Empire's Western realm asked him to write a book. Lao Tzu wrote the *Tao Te Ching*, in which he explains the meaning of the Way and virtuous behavior. Though he wrote it in 5,000 Chinese characters, the *Tao Te Ching* today consists of some 5,250 characters and has become the most translated book of Chinese literature and philosophy. Lao Tzu then passed through the gates to his life of meditation and into history as one of the world's greatest philosophers. Folklore has him living for at least 160 years, and some say for over 200 years.

Just as Lao Tzu would have intimated in one of his duality paradoxes, the harder historians try to establish his existence, the more evasive his physical essence becomes, and finally he disappears. Chinese historians record his meeting with Confucius taking place in 518 BC; yet, they also record his son as a general in the Principality of Wei's army in 273 BC. Also, many stories exist of meetings between Confucius and elder scholars who severely outclassed Confucius. Confucius' critics spread these stories over the years in order to undermine his philosophical credibility.

THE ESSENCE OF CHINESE PHILOSOPHY

This section surveys the building blocks of Chinese moral, social and legal philosophies and identifies reasons for the civilizational chasm with the West.

▲ Chinese moral philosophy

While Western moral philosophy is sprinkled with truisms such as "Thou shalt not kill" or "Thou shalt not steal", few truisms exist in Chinese moral philosophy. One Chinese maxim approximates the Commandment "Honor thy mother and thy father": *The Analects*[6] states, "Behave in such a way that your father and mother have no anxiety about you, except concerning your health." A second Chinese maxim seems like the Golden Rule: *The Analects*[7] reads, "Do not do to others what you would not like yourself." Finally, a third maxim urges following "the Way" (proper, righteous and upright behavior): "In the morning, hear the Way; in the evening, die content," *The Analects*[8] advises. Confucius and Lao Tzu proposed an applied philosophy of specific social behaviors for followers; they espoused a moral philosophy based on reason, circumstances and historical precedent, rather than the unchanging Word of God as in the West.[9]

In the West, the influential ancient Greek philosopher Aristotle attempted to collect, to study, to classify and to categorize everything in nature in order to understand the world. This approach to organizing knowledge and to understanding the world remains highly influential in the West. Simplified, quantitative models of specific aspects provide a greater understanding of the whole world. Much like Aristotle, Confucius and Lao Tzu also attempted to classify, to categorize and to understand their world, but they concentrated, rather, on human behaviors and human situations. Despite having few moral commandments, Chinese moral philosophy does not approximate situational ethics. Situational ethics generally imply flexible norms and morals that change conveniently with circumstances. Chinese morality and ethics, while situation-specific, have limited flexibility. Specific and binding moral duties and appropriate behaviors exist for every situation and derive from specific categorizations and groupings of situations and individuals in society. The following section delineates some organizing philosophies of Chinese society.

▲ Chinese social philosophy

Fei Xiaotong, China's most prominent sociologist, expounded on the differences between Western and Chinese society, arguing that the differences amounted to a civilizational divide.[10] Fei stated that Western society resembles a haystack that the Chinese use to build fires; several hay stems form a bundle, and several bundles form a haystack. In Fei's analogy, each hay stem represents a single individual that retains this individuality despite voluntarily joining a group. Voluntary groups in

Western societies incorporate social contracts that guarantee the individuals' minimal rights. Conversely, the individuals pledge loyalty to the groups, and to the overarching group, the haystack. Fei recognized that a hay stem can only belong to one bundle within the haystack, while a Western individual can join more than one social group.

FEI XIAOTONG[11]: CREATOR OF CHINESE SOCIOLOGY

Fei Xiaotong is one of China's most prominent, brilliant and complex scholars of the 20th century. He proposed that to understand China, one must use research and concepts originating in China. Prior to Fei's groundbreaking work, Chinese sociologists assumed that research done on Westerners, primarily Americans, would apply to the Chinese. Consequently, when Fei transferred to Yenching University as a junior, he found that the Sociology department taught the same courses as American universities: Fei studied the fundamentals of social-science field research with an American professor, Robert Park. Disillusioned with Sociology's irrelevance to China, in graduate school, Fei changed his major area to Anthropology, in which he could both teach and practice field-research methodology. He studied for his Master's degree in Anthropology at Qinghua University under another foreign professor, S. M. Shirokogoroff, a Russian Anthropologist with a passion for field research. Finally, Fei obtained his doctorate from the London School of Economics and Political Science as a student of Bronislaw Malinowski. In 1938, he returned to China to build a school of Sociology based on field research conducted in China on Chinese populations.

Fei attained prominence through his research. Through World War II and the post-war years his reputation, both in academic ranks and among China's educated urban dwellers, continued to grow. Then in 1949, the Chinese Communist Party seized control and outlawed the discipline of Sociology and Fei's research. Because Fei chose to stay in the People's Republic of China (PRC), the

Nationalist government in Taiwan also banned his research. Hong Kong, the last bastion of the British Empire in East Asia, also served as the last bastion of Fei's Chinese-based school of Sociology. In the PRC, Fei survived the hardships, the stifling censorship and the suppression of the Great Leap Forward and the Cultural Revolution to be officially reclaimed when reforms began under Deng Xiaoping in 1978.He returned to his academic life and founded the Chinese Sociological Association in 1979. Taking a more practical road, he joined the government and, over the years, served in several prominent positions including Vice-President of the Chinese People's Political Consultative Conference, Vice-Chairman of The Standing Committee of the National People's Congress and Vice-Chairman of the Drafting Committee for the Basic Law of the Hong Kong Special Administrative Region of the PRC.

Fei represented Chinese society as the circular waves that emanate from throwing a rock into the middle of a pond. The waves form a perfect circle around some central invisible point and, as they move further from that point, become weaker. Unlike Western society, Chinese society displays no distinct individualism (the hay stems have tangible form while the waves do not). Yet, Fei argued, in reality, Chinese society exhibits more egocentrism than Western society (the circular waves emanate from one central point, while the piled haystacks enclose relatively equal hay stems).[12]

Fei contended that Western society consists of individuals who volunteer their loyalty to groups they choose, with reciprocal guarantees that the groups recognize the individuals' inherent rights. In Chinese society, the individuals, forever at the center of their worlds, generate waves that begin with themselves and expand through a series of bipolar relationships into their families, lineages, localities, provinces and countries. Waves closer to the center elicit stronger relationships, and hence, greater loyalty.[13] Additionally, Fei indicated that relationships exist between people, not between people and abstract entities such as states.[14] The Chinese society's egocentric structure applies equally to all people within this society — to the peasant and merchant as well as to the duke and emperor. Networks, not states, comprise the most complex organizations. To enforce their will on society, emperors or other leaders do not employ the state's laws but, rather, use their networks to pressure the transgressing individuals' network to bring the individuals into line.

Chinese philosophers have always argued that society serves to extend the families and the families' preeminence has profoundly affected the evolution of Chinese society.[15] Families comprise a collection of very personal relationships that elicit specific duties and behaviors but that, generally, also tend to forgive transgressions. Hence, Chinese society transmits highly personal perspectives and interpretations of events. As many Western managers know, doing business in China requires developing strong personal relationships with Chinese business associates; indeed, personal relationships indicate business relationships which often appear as mutations of familial relationships.

For foreign companies, personal loyalties in Chinese business relationships have several implications. First, personal loyalties indicate difficulties in maintaining arms-length perspectives in many business decisions. Second, loyalties do not extend beyond the individuals; hence, companies cannot expect goodwill to extend beyond the tenure of the executives that earned it. Individuals hold the franchises on business relationships, not the companies. Third, Chinese individuals view much less harshly than Westerners transgressions and errors between equals in relationships, such as unintentional failures to meet contractual requirements while conducting business in good faith. Finally, strong business relationships have attendant important social obligations, commitments and expected behaviors as they extend familial relationships. The effects of this social philosophy on Chinese legal systems are examined in the following section.

▲ Chinese legal philosophy

In Western societies, states maintain social order and guarantee certain rights to members through laws that limit other rights and freedoms. In traditional Chinese society, social order is maintained through social pressures — through rites and customs — rather than through laws.[16] Family ties, especially between fathers and sons, comprise the strongest and most important relationships. Consequently, parental duties include ensuring the families' good behavior. If parents fail to maintain appropriate behavior within their families, then the duty passes to neighborhood and village elders and, finally, to provincial and central governments.

Importantly, birth, not choice, traditionally decided group membership in China. Second, the immediately superior social units, not police authorities, reined in the miscreants. Social units failing in their duties became miscreants too and the next hierarchical social units attempted a return to order. Thus, networks structured and controlled traditional Chinese society. Individuals' rights and freedom depended entirely on whether they could control their families, on whether familial networks could control neighborhood and village elders and so on, up to the emperors. The state neither guaranteed individuals' rights and freedoms nor limited individuals that could control the networks that comprise Chinese society. Thus, the Chinese never developed a rights-based legal system or cultural perspective.

Superficially, adherence to common-law or code-law systems appear to distinguish national legal systems. Yet, virtually all nations, and certainly those with extensive trade relations, have developed their own commercial codes. Consequently, codes form primary influences, if not the foundations for national commercial laws. A deeper distinction revolves around rights-based systems, as in the industrialized West, or public-law systems, as in China.[17] The US Declaration of Independence in 1776 heralded the first rights-based legal system by proclaiming: "We hold these truths to be self-evident: That all men are created equal; that they are endowed by their Creator with certain unalienable rights..."

Public-law systems do not endow their citizenry with rights independently of the authorities that grant them. These rights reside with the authorities, not in the "unalienable rights" of the nation's citizens; hence, the authorities can grant or withdraw rights at leisure.[18] With this perspective, China did not develop a legal system, or even written laws, until the 20th century.[19] The next section identifies differences between Chinese and Western cognitive styles that cement civilizational differences and affect managerial decisions and effectiveness.

EASTERN VS. WESTERN COGNITIVE STYLES

Societal concepts of relevant information, rationality and logic shape strategic environments and business decisions by affecting:
- environmental perceptions
- situational interpretations
- perceptual analysis
- feasibility analysis
- conflict resolution
- cognitive processes.

Unlike Fei Xiaotong, Western researchers have historically assumed that people from different cultures thought about different subjects yet processed this information in similar fashions.[20] Recent experimental studies have shown that Western researchers may have made erroneous assumptions about similarities between Asian and Western cognitive styles. In a series of studies, researchers found that East Asians and Americans of European descent did indeed emphasize different aspects of problems and think through problems differently.[21] They found that each civilization's members displayed different strengths and weaknesses in their approaches to information processing. Asians emphasized perceived contexts and relationships in their information processing to a greater extent than Westerners did. Asians also accepted the validity of weaker arguments, contradicting their own views, more than Westerners did. Additionally, whereas Asians favored experiential and empirical data and reasoning to explain their worlds, Westerners favored building models of explanatory rules and using formal logic to explain theirs. The four experiments outlined below shed additional light on these differences in cognitive styles.

▲ The fish-tank experiments

When presented with a fish tank, Asian subjects focused on the environment, the context in which the fish existed and how the fish related to their environment. Western subjects focused on the fish, first noting the prominent fish — the largest, fastest or brightest fish in the tank. When researchers moved the fish from one tank to another, Western subjects, more than Asian, could recognize the old fish in the new environment. The Westerners emphasized the particular; the Asians emphasized the contexts and relationships of problems or situations.

Richard Nisbett and his colleagues concluded that the following implications followed from their findings and those of other researchers such as David Meyer:[22]

- Easterners focus on wholes whereas Westerners focus on parts
- Easterners more often see the relationships among the different objects in given fields but
- Westerners can better differentiate between objects and the fields in which they lie and
- Westerners appear to believe that they exercise greater control over situations, affecting their behaviors and perceptions.

Many people who have lived and worked in both Asian and Western cultures have noted these differences between Asian holistic and Western particularistic cognitive styles;[23] however, Nisbett and his colleagues provided experimental proof of the phenomenon. In business situations, Asians appear to place greater emphasis on experiential knowledge than on formal logic; Westerners tend to focus on the particulars, to separate objects or problems from their contexts and to rely on formal logical analysis. This difference in cognitive styles has a tremendous effect on the decision models, information desired for strategic planning, and the strategic-planning processes in the respective business cultures developed by the two societies. In previous research, we observed that when making business investments, the Chinese develop holistic views of the business situations, invest relatively small sums, and fill in the blanks on the particulars as they manage and, if successful, expand their investments.[24] This business tendency seems to reflect the Asian tendency to focus on the environment of the tank as a whole, rather than on the particular fish in the tank. The results of this experiment also explain the Chinese managers' abilities to apply lessons learned from particular business environments to entirely different business environments encountered in the course of expansion — geographic or conglomerate.

▲ The essay experiments

Incheol Choi and Nisbett conducted another experiment that confirmed that Asians appear to be more prone to noticing the effects of situational pressures on people's behaviors.[25] In a controlled experiment, the researchers instructed Korean and American subjects to read essays that either supported or opposed France's atomic testing in the Pacific. Despite knowing that the essay writers followed specific instructions on the positions that they took, both Koreans and Americans judged that the writers believed in what they wrote. After researchers similarly assigned both groups to write essays according to instructions, the Koreans adjusted their estimates of the original essay writers' beliefs in their essays' positions; the Americans maintained their estimates of the original essay writers' beliefs in their essays' positions. This experiment emphasizes another important difference between Asians and Americans: Asians tend to view people as part of their environments, and as influenced by it; Americans tend to view people as independent of their environments and as removed from it. The experiment also re-affirms the emphasis Asians place on experiential learning as opposed to formal training: the Koreans responded to their experiences and adjusted their perceptions more than the Americans did.[26]

▲ The contradiction experiments

Marion Davis, Richard Nisbett, and Norbert Schwarz found that East Asians were more likely to accept contradictory statements than Westerners.[28] Researchers presented Western and Asian subjects with relatively weak arguments that contradicted the subjects' original positions on issues. The Westerners saw the weak, contradictory arguments as confirming their positions, which they then endorsed more strongly; Asians moderated their original positions. This tendency would encourage Western managers to take stronger positions in business circumstances, when relatively weak contradictory evidence exists, than would their Asian counterparts.

▲ The justification-effect experiments

Finally, Donnel Briley, Michael Morris and Itamar Simonson found evidence that justifying their decisions affected choices that Westerners made, but that this was not the case with choices that East Asians made.[29] The researchers presented Western and East Asian subjects with three choices, A, B, and C, that combined different levels of two dimensions, 1 and 2. Choice A was clearly superior in Dimension 1, Choice C in Dimension 2, and Choice B along both dimensions. Westerners and East Asians chose Choice B when they did not have to justify their decisions. But, when subjects had to justify their decisions, Westerners selected either Choice A or Choice C and employed simple decision rules to aid their decisions; East Asians did not.

DELINEATING THE CHASM: RUSSIA VS CHINA

That culture shapes the historical trajectories of nations is clearly evidenced by the different courses taken by the Soviet Union and China in their respective responses to Communist rule. Wee Ee Cheong, Deputy Chairman and President of United Overseas Bank, noted the difference between Chinese and Russian civilizations when he told us, "You look at China: the Chinese were destroyed by the Cultural Revolution. The Russians, they have also gone through the same Communist rule; why didn't the Russians produce the same kind of thing? I think ultimately it is cultural." Many are predicting a collapse of the Chinese Communist government in the same fashion as the Soviet government; yet Chinese history, philosophy and culture make this unlikely. Communism in Russia and Eastern Europe imposed foreign subsistence-based economic and philosophical systems on body politics oriented towards amassing wealth. The Communists used force of arms to impose their philosophy on the populations. Yet, in Russia, for example, the aristocrats were discarding these ruthless, autocratic and absolutist exercises of power that many Western societies had manifested throughout history, when the Communists seized control. Two merchant contemporaries, Grigori Ivanovich Shelekhov of Russia and Wu Ping Chien of China, present a prism to contrast the respective attitudes of the two civilizations towards success in commerce. Shelekhov, born a commoner, became one of Russia's most influential and honored citizens through his commercial success. Wu Ping-Chien, also born a commoner, became better known by the derogatory title given to him by China's Mandarins — *Howqua* or "Great Official".

SHELEKHOV AND WU: A TALE OF TWO MERCHANT PRINCES

One can glimpse Russia's and China's differing philosophies on private wealth by comparing their two greatest merchant princes and contemporaries, Grigori Ivanovich Shelekhov and Wu Ping Chien. Both started life as commoners, loved their countries passionately, attained unimaginable material success, and committed their lives and fortunes to their countries. Yet, their countries' ruling elites treated each differently.

Arguably one of Russia's greatest explorers, adventurers, imperialists and merchants, Shelekhov co-founded the Shelekhov-Golikov Fur Company in 1781 with Ivan Golikov. It is no exaggeration to say that Wu Ping Chien was one of China's greatest merchants and businessman. In the early 19th century, Wu obtained control of the bulk of China's external trade and became one of the wealthiest men in the world. Shelekhov's company evolved into the Russian-American Company and the primary tool for Russian imperial expansion in the Americas and the Pacific Rim. The Russians established the first permanent European settlements in Alaska, extended these as far south as Fort Ross in California, attempted to colonize the Sandwich Islands (present-day Hawaii), and tried to establish trade relations with China (the trade would have flowed through Wu), and with the Spanish colonial governments of California and Chile.

Wu gained control of most of China's trade through Canton. Prior to the Opium Wars with Great Britain, he personally funded improvements in China's Southern coastal defenses to stave off the British and to halt their opium shipments to China. Stopping the opium trade became Wu's lifelong crusade. After the Wars, he paid one-third of the reparations imposed on China out of his personal wealth.

Though not as wealthy as Wu, Shelekhov became Russia's wealthiest private citizen. The Russian aristocracy, including the Tsar and his family, openly sought his favor. He died a wealthy and honored citizen of Russia. Some of Russia's most illustrious, aristocratic bachelors courted his daughter, who finally married a Russian Count. Baron Nicolai Petrovich de Rezanov, a nobleman, succeeded him as the Russian-America Company's chief executive.

Meanwhile, China's mandarins actively campaigned against Wu. The mandarins ridiculed Wu by giving him the title of *Howqua* ("Great Official" in English, a prestigious honorific for a Chinese bureaucrat, but a term of ridicule for a private citizen). They imprisoned his only son on false charges of smuggling opium, a trade that Wu had long and valiantly opposed, much to the distress of the mandarins who were accepting British bribes. The mandarins hounded Wu until he died, penniless and heartbroken.

Unlike Imperial China, Czarist Russia had taken several substantial steps towards greater democracy and freedom. In 1861, Czar Alexander II freed the serfs and granted them small allotments of land. Similarly, in 1905, after Japan defeated Russia in the Russo-Japanese War, the autocratic Czar Nicholas II reluctantly accepted a constitution, the creation of an elected parliament and several other liberalizing measures. In China, Communism's absolutist rule has epitomized the citizenry's normal life for centuries. Chinese citizens could not challenge their autocratic rulers but could live with them when necessary, subverting them when possible; leave the rulers' domains and move to other parts of China — something Confucius did more than once; or, leave China altogether — something even Confucius considered.

As indicated earlier, Confucius argued that citizens cannot challenge rulers; but, unlike the Chinese Communist Party (CCP), he also contended that the rulers could not expect loyalty to the state or themselves through patriotism. Ancient Chinese philosophy and culture did not perceive loyalty as abstract patriotism but rather as personal loyalty.[30] The CCP has influenced Chinese culture and society, but despite concerted efforts, as in the Cultural Revolution, has not supplanted Confucianism in Chinese society.

Chinese civilization has never incorporated direct internal challenges to authority. Consequently, the Chinese Communist Party may eventually share power in China without the tumultuous overthrow that occurred in Russia. Challenges to power in China have occurred extremely rarely and only after long periods of political ossification. So far, the government of the PRC has shown flexibility and a willingness to change. A recent move by the previous president, Jiang Zemin, to encourage private entrepreneurs to join the Communist Party provides evidence of this flexibility.

CONCLUSION

Part 1 has mapped the civilizational chasm between ancient Chinese and Western philosophical and strategic assumptions and interpreted its relevance for modern-day businesses. Neither Easterners nor Westerners should assume that standard operating procedures they follow at home will lead to successes abroad. Indeed, managers should recognize that assumptions they have treasured through their careers will quite likely turn to dust under foreign suns. To maximize benefits to shareholders, Eastern and Western managers will have to adapt to their different environments, and to develop effective business systems that transcend both environments. This book provides ideas to aid these endeavors.

The new global planning systems that we propose stem from our experience, extensive research and numerous in-depth interviews with senior executives in the PRC, Hong Kong and Southeast Asia. As Appendix A reveals, we have interviewed some of the most successful PRC and Overseas Chinese entrepreneurs, together with the most senior executives of major European and US multinational companies' successful Asian subsidiaries and joint ventures.

Unlike other researchers, such as Geert Hofstede, we found many similarities between the philosophies and strategies of the Overseas Chinese and PRC's entrepreneurs.[31] Both, for example, recognize the importance of networks. Edward Zeng of

Sparkice, China's largest Internet-access provider, indicated that three networks controlled China's business environments: business networks, local familial networks and governmental networks. He concluded that "to be truly successful in China you must be able to work in all three network environments". Pan Shi Yi, Beijing's largest private developer, endorsed the importance of governmental networks when he said, "A developer must have a clear idea of what he wants to do, and then be able to convince the governments (municipal, provincial and federal) to let [him] do it." Similarly, both the Overseas Chinese and those from the PRC recognize a move towards greater professionalization. As Henry Yu, president of Beijing McMahan Investment Consultation Co., one of China's growing number of venture capitalists, concluded on traditional networking, "*Guanxi* is very important, but losing ground to competence."

Later chapters extend concepts and strategies we have introduced. Part 2 explores the ancestry of Chinese strategy, including its philosophical, economic, historical, technological and legal roots, and, importantly, the networks' roles. Part 3 distinguishes between Western and Chinese strategic planning, isolates their components and evaluates their strengths and weaknesses. Finally, Part 4 offers a convergence model for effective strategic planning that blends the two strategic styles and bridges the civilizational chasm.

PAN SHI YI[32]: CHINA'S MODERN-DAY ALGER HERO

In the late 19th century, the legendary American writer, Horatio Alger, penned stories about boys who rose from poverty to wealth and fame through hard work, virtue, cheerful perseverance and good luck – all the while keeping their home-spun values; Pan Shi Yi of Beijing, personifies an Alger hero. Unlike most of Beijing's leading citizens and businesspeople, Pan does not come from Beijing, nor did he study overseas at Western universities. He was born on a farm to poor parents who worked on a commune. Pan's mother became seriously ill and his father cut sources of income and benefits to take care of her. These circumstances forced the family to give up two of Pan's sisters for adoption to a wealthier neighbor.

Pan attended an engineering/technical school in Lanjon, where his performance earned him a scholarship to attend a local Chinese university where he graduated in Petroleum Engineering. After graduation, he worked for the state-owned petroleum industry until the early period of China's liberalization. In 1987, he started working as a developer in the real-estate industry in Shenzen and Hainan. He had gained familiarity with these provinces while working in the petroleum industry. He had also seen first-hand how early, government-sponsored, liberalization programs had enabled these remote areas to become two of China's wealthiest.

Pan's success grew along with the government's liberalization programs that expanded to cover all of China. He moved to Beijing's large market and continued to work in real-estate development. He is currently Beijing's largest private developer, now developing properties across from Beijing's World Trade Center, an area that the government envisions as China's equivalent of Wall Street.

Like Horatio Alger's heros, Pan has never abandoned his roots (among China's farmers and workers) or forgotten the traditional teachings on which he was raised. He fervently believes that to know China, one must know all of China, not just Beijing and Shanghai; must learn about China's 56 minority nationalities; and must visit Western China which, Pan told us, "still represents the mainstream of China where religious influences are strongest".

Pan sees China changing, though slowly in some respects. He told us that to succeed in China "*Guanxi* is important, but the most important relationship is the relationship with the workers, not with the government or anyone else". He believes that all philosophies originated from Taoism: — "The philosophies have become confused only in recent centuries with the intrusion of Western philosophies. The most important philosophy is that of Lao Tzu — you cannot go against nature, but have to work with it."

endnotes

1. Biers, D., "A Taste of China in Camden".
2. Ibid.
3. Lau, D. C., *Confucius: The Analects*, Book 8, verse 13.
4. Haley, G. T., C. T. Tan and U. C. V. Haley, *New Asian Emperors: The Overseas Chinese, their Strategies and Competitive Advantages.*
5. Ibid.
6. Lau, op.cit. Book 2, verse 6.
7. Ibid. Book 12, verse 2.
8. Ibid. Book 4, verse 8.
9. Haley et al, op.cit.
10. Fei, X., *From the Soil: The Foundation of Chinese Society.*
11. Hamilton, G. G., and Z. Wang, "Introduction" to Fei, op.cit.; and, the Chinese University of Hong Kong press release (1999).
12. Fei, op.cit.
13. Ibid.
14. Ibid.
15. Lau, D. C., *Mencius Says*; Lau, D. C., *Confucius: The Analects*; and Pan, C. C. H. (1984), "Confucian Philosophy: Implication to Management".
16. Fei, op.cit.
17. Carver, A., "Open and Secret Regulations in China and their Implications for Foreign Investment".
18. Ibid.
19. Fairbank, J. K., and M. Goldman, *China, a New History.*
20. Nisbett, R. A., K. Peng, I. Choi, and A. Norenzayan, "Culture and Systems of Thought: Holistic Versus Analytic Cognition".
21. Ibid; Davis, M., R. E. Nisbett and N. Schwarz, *Responses to Weak Argument on the Part of Asians and Americans*; Briley, D. A., M. Morris and I. Simonson, "Reasons as Carriers of Culture: Dynamic Versus Dispositional Models of Cultural Influence on Decision Making"; Peng, K., and R. E. Nisbett, "Culture, Dialectics and Reasoning About Contradiction".

22. For example, Nisbett et al, op.cit.; Meyer, D. E., "Adaptive Executive Control: Flexible Multi-Task Performance Without Pervasive Immutable Response-Selection Bottlenecks"; Meyer, D. E., and D. E. Keiras, "A Computational Theory of Executive Cognitive Processes and Multiple-Task Performance: I, Basic Mechanisms"; Meyer, D. E., and D. E. Keiras, "A Computational Theory of Executive Cognitive Processes and Multiple-Task Performance: II, Accounts of Psychological Refractory-Period Phenomena".

23. Haley et al, *New Asian Emperors*, op.cit.

24. Ibid; Haley, G. T., and C. T. Tan, "The Black Hole of Southeast Asia: Strategic Decision-Making in an Informational Void"; Haley, G. T., and U. C. V. Haley, "Boxing with Shadows: Competing Effectively with the Overseas Chinese and Overseas Indian Networks in the Asian Arena".

25. Choi, I., and R. E. Nisbett, "Situational Salience and Cultural Differences in the Correspondence Bias and in the Actor-Observer Bias".

26. Haley et al , *New Asian Emperors* op.cit.; Haley, and Haley, "Boxing with Shadows" op.cit.

27. Davis et al, op.cit.

28. Briley et al, op.cit.

29. Haley et al, *New Asian Emperors*, op.cit.

30. Hofstede, G., "Cultural Constraints in Management Theories", *International Review of Strategic Management*.

31. Taken from authors' interview with Pan Shi Yi.

Part II

THE ANCESTRY
OF CHINESE
STRATEGY

2

ECONOMIC AND ETHICAL ROOTS OF CHINESE STRATEGY

"Exterminate ingenuity, discard profit,
And there will be no more thieves and bandits."
Tao Te Ching

Book 1, Chapter 19, Stanza 43

"All originated from Taoism"

Pan Shi Yi,

Founder & CEO,
Redstone Development Co.,
People's Republic of China

INTRODUCTION

Chinese markets introduce a bundle of contradictions for Western managers. With a potential market of 1.3 billion consumers, China presents awesome untapped markets for Western companies. Indeed, automobiles and telecommunications may comprise two of the largest potential markets in the world. Yet, despite high sales and productivity, profits have eluded the bulk of Western companies operating in China, including those in automobiles and telecommunications. The lure of enormous markets, profits and growth, comes entangled with unseen problems that strike at the core of the Western companies' competencies. The economical and ethical realities of operating in China appear sobering. For example, Peter Humphrey, chief representative in China for Kroll Associates (Asia), the business-risk consulting firm, placed China in a league of its own as regards copyright violations. Similarly, Transparency International, a Berlin-based non-governmental organization that fights corruption worldwide, ranked China as the eighth-most corrupt country in the world.[1] Yet, an understanding of the economical and ethical roots of Chinese strategy can help Western managers steer through an apparent obstacle course pitted with mines.

Although Chinese economics and ethics appear replete with contradictions, they also converge like *Yin* and *Yang*, which literally mean a hill's "dark side" and "sunny side". The phrases appeared for the first time in *Hsi tz'u* or *Appended Explanations* an appendix to the *I Ching* (*Classic of Changes*, 4th century BC): "One time *Yin*, one time *Yang*, this is the *Tao*." Yin and Yang form two contradictory, interdependent principles or phrases, alternating in time and space, and evoking the harmonious interplay of opposites in the universe. As we noted in Chapter 1, Confucianism and Taoism constitute major sources for the development of Chinese philosophy from ancient to modern times. Rather than distinct philosophies, both appear as two sides of the same coin: while Confucianism analyzes power and organization from the rulers' viewpoint, Taoism does so from that of the subjects. Indeed, the neo-Taoism to which we refer in this book has coalesced with Confucianism, and Buddhism, to provide a uniquely comprehensive Chinese economic and ethical perspective which Western managers should understand if they wish to operate effectively, and harmoniously, in China without compromising their own standards and principles.

We first discuss the economic roots of Chinese strategy, including contradictory attitudes towards profits and the dominance of the family. Next, we elaborate on the ethical roots of Chinese strategy including the five relationships and uprightness. In the ensuing section, we analyze how economics and ethics fuse to form the Chinese network-based economy. Finally, we explore the continuance of Taoism through the Communist era in China.

MENCIUS VS. MO TZU VS. YANG CHU[2]: THE GREAT DEBATE

Chinese economics and ethics owe much in their evolution to debates among three renowned teachers: Mencius (Meng-tzu), Mo Tzu and Yang Chu. These three great Confucian interpreters and their followers competed for dominance among China's many princely and aristocratic courts and shaped Taoist philosophies.

Known in China as the Second Sage, Mencius, born in 372 BC, most strongly helped Taoism to evolve through his teachings into the mildly puritanical philosophy we know today.

The other two teachers presented very different interpretations. Mo Tzu's philosophy strongly resembled the West's peace and free-love movement of the 1960s and 1970s. Like Mencius, he propounded the inherent goodness of man. He preached that all men were brothers and should love each other as brothers. Mo Tzu argued that if all practiced his "Way", standing armies, national borders, princes and governments, would dissolve. As stated in the *Tao Te Ching* (Book 2, Chapter 46, Stanza 104, and Book 2, Chapter 60, Stanza 138): "When the Way prevails in the empire, fleet-footed horses are relegated to plowing the fields; when the Way does not prevail in the empire, war-horses breed on the border" and, "Governing a large state is like boiling a small fish" (as one can ruin a small fish just through handling it.)

The third teacher, Yang Chu preached extreme greed and egotism. He argued that individuals should single-mindedly aim at lives of comfort and selfish indulgence. He depicted charity and sacrifice as false virtues. Yang Chu argued that if all practiced his "Way" standing armies, national borders, princes and governments would dissolve too: No one would sacrifice comforts to support those institutions.

Mencius contended that both alternative philosophies could destroy society: the principle of universal love towards all men and the principle of supreme egotism diminished the father's and the family's primacies in Chinese society. As governments and society extended the family, chaos would overtake the societies and governments that did not maintain the primacy of this institution.

THE ECONOMIC ROOTS OF CHINESE STRATEGY

The dualities and contradictions of *Yin* and *Yang* appear prominently in ancient Chinese economics. The ruling Chinese elites' understanding of economic principles over the centuries appear highly insightful. From ancient times through the Renaissance and into the early years of the West's Industrial Age, wealth vaulted China into the ranks of the richest countries in the world. More impressively, the Chinese elites showed they could maintain and augment that wealth over centuries. While China remained among the richest countries in the world, countless other empires including those of Egypt, Persia, Alexander's Macedonia, Rome, Carthage, Byzantium, the Celts, France, Spain, the Arabs, the Toltecs, Maya, Incas, and Aztecs, rose to great power and wealth, and fell. Different ruling dynasties, with varying degrees of effectiveness, also rose and fell in China over these thousands of years, and some external invaders conquered China. Yet, except for short transitional periods, such as the Warring States Era, a wealthy, recognizable Chinese state existed. Table 2.1 presents rationales from the ancient philosophies that promoted economic development.

TABLE 2.1: CONFUCIAN ELEMENTS PROMOTING ECONOMIC DEVELOPMENT IN CHINA[3]

✔ Confucianism maintained Chinese unity.

✔ Confucian peasantry had more freedom and independence than did the European peasantry.

✔ Confucianism provided an orderly and secure society.

✔ Confucianism championed the agricultural peasantry and required the government to allocate lands to it, thereby letting the producers control the land.

✔ Confucianism emphasized education and provided an intelligent, well-trained workforce.

✔ Confucianism's call to wealth creation had a spiritual dimension.

✔ Confucianism emphasized cautious, conscientious and diligent labor.

✔ Confucianism emphasized sincerity, honesty and trust, and created an environment in which economic activities could prosper.

Conversely, other rationales from the ancient philosophies hindered economic development and maintained poverty among large segments of the Chinese populations. Several rationales that hindered development appear as the opposite sides of those that promoted development. Table 2.2 presents rationales from the ancient philosophies that hindered economic development.

TABLE 2.2: CONFUCIAN ELEMENTS HINDERING ECONOMIC DEVELOPMENT IN CHINA[4]

✗　Confucianism maintained a feudal society.

✗　Confucianism promoted a bias against profits.

✗　Confucianism persecuted the merchant classes.

✗　Confucianism glorified the agricultural peasant over commerce.

✗　Confucianism demonstrated a bias against using knowledge to promote the economy.

✗　Confucianism emphasized gaining feelings of prosperity through the Taoist proposition of "not to value goods which are hard to come by".

THE CONTRADICTION OF PROFITS

We have argued that Confucianism promoted subsistence-based economic systems that discourage amassing great wealth.[5] This evaluation appears to contradict another posited in Table 2.1 that Confucianism viewed wealth creation as an ambition of "the highest moral order". Yet, China's princes, emperors, mandarins and sages historically interpreted Confucian and Taoist economics so that no conflict emerged. Confucianism always frowned upon profits, and always viewed the merchant classes as the lowest in society. The ruling Chinese elites viewed wealth creation as desirable only to the extent that the individuals could care, feed, house and educate their families, and honor properly their familial ancestors. The elites viewed any substantial amounts of wealth over these levels as immoral and infringements upon the emperor's rightful dues. Confucius stated, "A gentleman takes as much trouble to discover what is right as lesser men take to discover what will pay."[6]

In this fashion, ancient Chinese philosophy sought to prevent individuals from seeking profits and wealth that challenged the princes and emperors. Chinese laws manifested these philosophies by requiring merchants to dress in the coarsest clothing in public and to walk alongside their wagons and carriages, rather than to ride in them. Thereby, the rulers exhibited control by showing publicly that merchants, despite their wealth, had the same social standing as the poorest farmers who did not own horses or carts.

THE PRIMACY OF THE FAMILY

In traditional Chinese society, Mencius and the First Sage, Confucius, in their teachings emphatically emphasized the primacy of the family, living and ancestral, and of one's parents, especially one's father.[7] In modern-day Chinese society, the family continues to be the institution that most influences the conduct of business.[8] Describing the role of the family, Shi Zhonglian said, "In the Confucian tradition, the family is not only an elementary social unit of production and life, but also a social being with which alone the life of mankind can exist and reproduce."[9]

Chinese philosophers throughout history have contended that society serves as an extension of the family. The family provides the "foundation of the management of the state."[10] This interpretation has profoundly affected the evolution of traditional Chinese economics, business and behavior with all their apparent contradictions. Taoism furnishes the cultural ethos to explain Chinese industriousness and productivity, as well as poverty, over the centuries. Taoism merges the secular and spiritual worlds, thereby making the act of building wealth not just a worldly goal but also a spiritual mission to honor familial ancestors; it extols wealth creation to sustain one's family and ancestors as the highest moral ambition. Yet, Taoism also frowns on the quest for profits and limits the creation of wealth that could threaten the emperors. The next section explores some of the important ethical manifestations of the emphasis on the primacy of the family.

THE ETHICAL ROOTS OF CHINESE STRATEGY

This section explores the contextual system in which ethics functions in Chinese society. It delineates the limits of ethics, as well as concepts of trust and uprightness that permeate Chinese business.

GAUTAMA BUDDHA:[11] BUDDHISM AND TAOISM

The Buddha was born around 566 BC, as Siddhartha, into a princely Hindu family that ruled from its capital city, Kapilavastu, in present-day India. He died around 483 BC. He enjoyed a traditional upbringing but, at 29 years of age, he abandoned his princely rank, home and family and embarked upon the life of a wandering ascetic. He tried the traditional Indian ascetics' activities of penances, austerity and self-denial, and failed to attain enlightenment. He then turned to meditation. For seven weeks, he meditated under a Bo tree. He attained enlightenment and came away with his philosophy firmly developed. He concluded that the true path to *Nirvana*, or salvation, lay in mastering and conquering desires. He taught that as one progressed through rebirths, the soul reached *Nirvana* through the Noble Eightfold Path: Right Aspirations, Right Conduct, Right Effort, Right Livelihood, Right Meditation, Right Mindfulness, Right Speech, and Right Views. As Siddhartha preached his philosophy, the people called him the Buddha, or the Enlightened One. The Mauryan Emperor, Ashoka, became one of the new philosophy's most ardent supporters, sending missionaries to spread Buddhism to China and Southeast Asia.

Buddhism became popular in China during the Han dynasty and a virtual symbiosis occurred between Buddhism and Taoism. Early Chinese translations of Buddhist texts used Taoist vocabulary to communicate the Buddhist principles of breath control and mystical concentration. The Buddhist principles of charity, compassion and suppression of desires approximated Taoist principles of benevolence, charity and self-restraint. Both traditions emphasized knowledge and learning. Many Chinese, including the Han Emperors, believed that Lao-Tzu, the founder of Taoism, had reincarnated in India as the Buddha.

The golden age of Buddhism in China occurred during the T'ang dynasty. The T'ang emperors expanded the number of Buddhist monasteries and their lands. Many Chinese scholars made pilgrimages to India that greatly enriched Chinese Buddhism. However, in 845 AD, the emperor Wu-tsung, fearing the growing influence of Buddhism and the growing wealth of Buddhist monasteries, began a major persecution of Buddhism, destroying 4,600 Buddhist temples and 40,000 shrines and de-frocking 260,500 monks.

Buddhism in China, though hurt by persecution, continued to play a major role in Chinese ethics. It retained its identity and generated new forms such as the *yü lu* or famous teachers' recorded sayings, *Journey to the West* (16th century) and *Dream of the Red Chamber* (18th century). Buddhism also coalesced with Confucian and Taoist traditions to form a complex, multi-religious ethos that comfortably encompassed all three traditions. During the Cultural Revolution (1966–69), the government and its followers again severely repressed Buddhists in China. Since 1976, the Chinese government appears to be following a more tolerant policy.

THE LIMITS OF ETHICS

The ancient Chinese philosophies elucidated specifically on duties in contextual systems; these contextual systems sketch the boundaries of ethical behavior in modern-day Chinese societies.

Confucius originally listed five relationships of unequal, bi-polar contexts that defined Chinese society.[12] These relation-ships included rulers and subjects and covered:
- ruler–minister
- father–son
- husband–wife
- elder–younger (or elder brother–younger brother)
- friendship.

Neo-Taoists extended Confucian arguments to identify six more-restrictive relationships that limited ethical behavior. While Confucians had merely enumerated the number of bi-polar relationships that existed in Chinese society, the neo-Taoists propounded that any two individuals in a relationship owed different and bi-directional duties.[13] These restrictive relationships included only the family and explicitly excluded rulers and subjects per se. The Taoist relationships covered:

❖ Father ←→ son

❖ Older brother ←→ younger brother

❖ Husband ←→ wife

Taoism limits all ethical relationships to the family. Superiors (fathers, older brothers and husbands) owe weaker ethical duties to the inferiors (sons, younger brothers and wives) than the inferiors owe their superiors. In this fashion, Chinese ethical duties, though very strict, vary by the relational contexts in which they occur. No ethical duties exist outside these relationships other than the duty to maintain social harmony.

Situational contexts also affect ethical duties. While the sons owe absolute and uncompromising duties to their fathers, duties in other relationships frequently vary by situations at particular points in time. For instance, the duties that younger brothers owe to older brothers can change if they conflict with duties they owe to their fathers. Relationships and ethics in Chinese business networks vary by the participants in the particular businesses.[14] For example, the Chinese may consider a person as part of the network in one business deal, but exclude him or her from the network in another, because the person has no relationship with a third party who is part of the second deal but not the first. This contextual nature of ethical duties in relationships leads to fluid boundaries in Chinese networks, as opposed to the more fixed boundaries in other network systems, such as the Mexican *grupos*. As noted in Chapter One, Edward Zeng of Sparkice indicated that in today's China, dealing with the ubiquitous networks had attained Byzantine complexity. Successful managers had to manage effectively three separate sets of networks; the traditional familial networks, the growing private-business networks, and the government networks from the Communist era.

Taoist ethics, with their familial perspectives, have extensive and very profound effects on Chinese business practice and relationships. First, the level and degree of ethical duties depend on the extent to which personal relationships exist between two parties. Second, the relationships must exist between two or more people as Taoism does not recognize loyalties to institutions or organizations other than to society as a whole. Without personal relationships, commercial partners can expect no ethical behaviors.

Stories abound of business associates and governments in Asia behaving in ways that Westerners generally consider unethical. For example, in November 2000, Proctor & Gamble (P&G) cancelled contracts with two of its biggest suppliers in China, Dalian Dafu Plastic and Colour Printing Co., and Zhongshan Dafu Plastic Packaging, after it discovered that counterfeit shampoos and detergents bearing the P&G name were using Dafu-manufactured packaging. Counterfeiting poses P&G's biggest problem in China, and conservatively some 15—20% of all products on the shelves purporting to be from P&G are fakes. For all the time and energy P&G spends chasing counterfeiters, however, it has had little success. Additionally, on the rare occasions when counterfeiting cases get court dates in China, government officials, law-enforcement agencies and even local courts have often protected counterfeiters. In some cases, local government departments control wholesale markets that trade in counterfeit goods. P&G has won just two criminal cases that have gone to court and the counterfeiters received paltry jail terms of between two and three years apiece.[15]

Conversely, stories also abound of Asian managers' extraordinary generosity towards their business associates and employees with whom they enjoy established, long-standing relationships approximating familial relationships. The holding company, Wuthelam Group of Singapore, presents one such example. Wuthelam operates as a traditional Overseas Chinese company, and has had great success using traditional Chinese management and decision-making techniques. Wuthelam's successes include making Nippon Paints the largest-selling paint in Asia; Nippon constitutes Wuthelam's primary manufacturing unit and a brand name it owns in Asia outside Japan. Nevertheless, in the 1990s, Wuthelam's top managers decided that they needed to make management procedures and processes more professional and standardized. They discovered, however, that many valued and loyal employees and business associates were unable to make the transition to the new regime. Rather than outplacing their employees, or pushing them into early retirement as many Western companies have, Wuthelam founded a subsidiary that would retain the employees and use the more traditional business practices to which they were accustomed. This subsidiary would keep the old ways of doing business, while Wuthelam continued to mutate for the fast-moving global economy. Subsequent tracking of the traditional subsidiary revealed, surprisingly, that it had become one of Wuthelam's most profitable subsidiaries. Goh Hup Jin, the son of Wuthelam's founder, explained to us that Wuthelam felt compelled to act not to attain high profit levels, but because "you do not abandon your elders simply because they no longer feel comfortable in the modern company. Without them you would not have prospered in the first place." The next sub-section elaborates on Chinese ethical concepts of trust and appropriate behaviors.

TRUST AND UPRIGHTNESS

An old Western adage identifies that "A person's word is his/ her bond"; that is, people trust those who keep their word. In Chinese business societies, keeping one's word constitutes a necessary but not sufficient condition to generate trust; one must also strive for "uprightness". Uprightness involves displaying the appropriate behaviors in any situation based upon the respective positions held by the individuals involved.

Uprightness in Chinese business can assume complex proportions: uprightness tests the quality of a manager's ability to obtain information within the networks and to interpret the informational clues that he or she receives. In Chinese business networks, especially at the lower and middle levels, an individual's position within a network hinges on his or her last business deal or performance rating. A well-connected member of a network would have the contacts to obtain this information quickly. Additionally, an upright individual can correctly interpret the latest information about people's positions within the networks and the influence on relative positions within the network. The bi-directional and dyadic duties and behavioral norms within Chinese society make interpreting information on relationships a crucial managerial skill. An individual may hold an inferior position to another within the network on one day; on another day, because of business losses or gains, the relationship could reverse. Though many Asian managers do not expect Westerners to maintain uprightness, understanding uprightness helps to decipher business environments in Chinese societies. The next section begins to unravel Chinese network-based economies drawing on traditional economic and ethical philosophies.

NETWORK-BASED ECONOMIES: FUSING ECONOMICS AND ETHICS

While, Western economies have companies as their primary economic units, traditional Chinese economies have networks. Network-based economies depend upon the performance of the networks or related companies for their economic progress and well being, not upon the performance of individual companies. The networks also dominate their economies more than any group of companies in modern, Western economies. Other than Southeast Asia and China, networks control the economies of South Korea (through the *chaebol*), Japan (through the *keiretsu*), and Hispanic countries, such as Mexico (through the *grupos*). The US economy also displayed some networks in the pre-Depression days. For example, the Sloans (of General Motors) and the DuPonts (of the Delaware-based conglomerate) had family connections and worked together to create dominant positions for their companies in their respective industries.

OTHER NETWORK-BASED ECONOMIES: JAPAN AND MEXICO

In Asia, Japan presents an example of another network-based economy. Japan's six traditional *keiretsu* dominate every major industry and about 60% of all companies traded on the Tokyo Stock Exchange. Traditional *keiretsu* generally formed around major banks. As a result of the severe financial crises of the past decade, however, the government has partially broken this *keiretsu* foundation by forcing mergers of major banks such as that between the healthy Mitsubishi Bank (Mitsubishi *keiretsu*) and the larger, devastated Sumitomo Bank (Sumitomo *keiretsu*). Some of Japan's best-known companies, such as Toyota and Honda, exemplify vertical *keiretsu*. Companies and vertical *keiretsu* sometimes have affiliations with horizontal *keiretsu*. For example, Toyota has affiliations with the Mitsui *keiretsu*; and the financially-strapped trading company Nissho Iwai has affiliations with both the DKB and Sanwa *keiretsu*.

Non-Asian economies also exhibit network bases. Mexico's *grupos* consist of family-controlled holding companies centered on dominant companies. A *grupo* presents a galaxy of companies rotating around core companies or groups of companies. Associates of the central familial clans almost always own affiliated companies, some of which may have public listings. A super-cluster, the Monterrey Group, based in Monterrey, comprises Mexico's best-known *grupo*. It includes Grupo Vitro (Mexico's largest company), Grupo Visa (controlling Mexico's second-largest brewer and largest soft drink company), Grupo Alfa (controlling Mexico's largest steel company), Grupo Cydsa, Grupo Cemex (Mexico's largest and the world's third-largest cement company), and Grupo IMSA. A set of related families control all these *grupos*. With about 3% of Mexico's population, Monterrey produces about 10—15% of its industrial output.

Some analysts and researchers have equated the Asian economies' network bases with "crony capitalism", arguing that networks forge fundamental flaws that prevent their economies from attaining extended prosperity.[16] However, all economies, Communist or Capitalist, network or company-based, have the potential for corruption and cronyism. These weaknesses emerge more from human nature than from the systems and tools that humans use. In the USA, the recent Enron and Arthur-Andersen cases provide vivid examples of cronyism, corruption and economic wrongdoings in a company-based economy. Similarly, the Federal Reserve Bank's New York branch arranged the bailout of Connecticut-based Long-Term Capital Management, an international hedge fund, which would otherwise have collapsed. The company had been controlled by US financial luminaries such as John Meriwether, Salomon Brothers' former star bond trader; Myron Scholes and Robert Merton, the 1997 co-winners of the Nobel Prize in Economics; and James McEntee, formerly of Carroll-McEntee, the US government's principal bond trader. The Federal Reserve used the same rationale as an institution in a network-based economy — the need to maintain confidence in a fundamentally sound financial system that showed no danger of collapsing!

The 1997 Asian financial crisis and the decade-long Japanese recession provide examples of the setbacks that network-based economies can suffer; but company-based economies, such as the USA, similarly experience down periods, as the stagflation of the 1970s and 1980s demonstrated. Both systems have tremendous strengths and efficiencies as well as weaknesses. Despite their weaknesses, the Asian and Latin American network-based economies have exhibited amazing growth over the past 40 years, surpassing the global average. As we will elaborate in later chapters, aggressive and well-managed Western companies can exploit both systems' strengths to achieve the greatest possible success. The next section highlights the influence of Taoism on Communism and its continuity through the ages.

COMMUNISM AND TAOISM: HARMONY IN DISHARMONY

Many falsely assume that because Chairman Mao Zedong campaigned so viciously against Confucianism and Taoism, both he and Chinese Communism opposed the ancient philosophies and garnered nothing from them. Indeed, despite some dissimilarities, several similarities exist between Taoist and Chinese Communist beliefs that contributed to the Communists' hold on Chinese society.

▲ Political harmony and disharmony

The neo-Taoist philosophies espoused authoritarianism. As we indicated earlier, Confucius argued that subjects could never challenge their emperors or princes. Mencius softened this position, but the neo-Taoists still advocated that unhappy subjects leave their countries rather than challenge their rulers. Mao Zedong and the Taoists also agreed on political participation. According to Mao, only members of the government and the ruling CCP could comment upon government policies; ordinary citizens could not. Confucius maintained similar views: "The Master said, 'He who holds no rank in a state does not discuss its policies.'"[17]

Unlike Chinese Communism, Taoism never proposed or envisioned either an end to private ownership as the means of production, or an end to the peasantry's ownership of their farms. Additionally, neo-Taoists argued against nationalism and patriotism:

> "The Duke of She addressed Master K'ung saying, 'In my country there was a man called Upright Kung. His father appropriated a sheep, and Kung bore witness against him.' Master K'ung said, 'In my country the upright men are of quite another sort. A father will screen a son and a son his father — which incidentally does involve a sort of uprightness.'"[18]

Mao disagreed vehemently with the traditional Taoist views on patriotism and nationalism. For Mao, the CCP commanded more loyalty than other institutions, including the family.

▲ Economic harmony and disharmony

Mao's Communist economic philosophies can be tracked to their neo-Taoist roots. Zhang Qingxiong traced Chinese economic philosophy's modern evolution from the first stirrings of economic and political reform in the mid 19th century through to Mao's Communist era.[19] Zhang noted that both Nationalist and Communist leaders agreed on the importance of traditional Confucian thought, with the Nationalists considering it the "sharp weapon against Communism".

Mao recognized that Communist ideology would have difficulty replacing Confucianism and Taoism. Much like his Nationalist opponents, he considered Communism an outside, transplanted ideology for China. During his childhood, Mao had received a very traditional village education in the Chinese classics. He feared that Communism would mutate into a Taoist version of the original, just as other foreign philosophies, including Buddhism, had. Buddhism, Mao argued, entered China from India and had tremendous initial influence for a couple of centuries; over time, it coalesced with traditional Chinese philosophy and altered from its original Indian form. Consequently, to preserve Communism, Mao aimed to eradicate Confucianism and Taoism from China. He knew the power of these ancient philosophies.

However, neo-Taoism continued to exercise an enormous influence over other Chinese economic reformers. Table 2.3 identifies some of the most influential Chinese reformers over the last 150 years. All of these reformers championed socialistic policies and, unlike Mao, acknowledged that their philosophies owed much to *The Analects*, and other great Confucian, Mencian and Taoist treatises, especially the *Evolution of Rites*.

TABLE 2.3: CHINA'S GREAT MODERN REFORMERS[20]

Hong Xiuquan:	Leader of the Taiping Revolution (1850–1864)
Kang Youwei:	Leader of the Reform Movement of 1898
Chen Duxiu:	Chief Editor of New Youth (a reform publication championing socialist ideals) and founder of the Chinese Communist Party
Dr Sun Yat-sen:	Leader of the Revolution of 1911
Mao Zedong:	Leader of the Communist Movement

Zhang traced Mao's economic philosophies back to Kang Youwei, a long-time critic of Chinese society.[21] In the 1880s, Kang composed two influential treatises, the *Grand Commonality* (also translated as the *Book of Great Harmony*) and *Confucius as Reformer*. After China's defeat by Japan in the Sino-Japanese War of 1894–95, many elements within Chinese society recognized the need to reform and to modernize society, government and bureaucracy. In 1898, the reformers finally had their chance. Supported by the Emperor Guanxu, Kang led a reform admin- istration in 1898 to modernize China, but to retain the Manchu Dynasty.[22] The Dowager Empress Cixi exploited the military's resistance to these reforms. One hundred days after the reform administration began, she seized power in a palace coup, im- prisoned the Emperor and executed most of the reformers. Kang escaped and continued to raise funds and support for reforms in China through Overseas Chinese communities worldwide.

Unlike Mao, Kang argued that Confucius was a great re- former. Kang concluded that, had Confucius lived in the late 19th century, he would have fought to develop systemic inno- vations that reflected modern requirements, reformed China and helped it to succeed. Kang accepted the Confucian view of history as comprising three eras that hold sway in evolutionary succession through societies: the Period of Disorder, the Period of Approaching Peace, and the Period of Universal Peace. Kang associated these eras with those he compiled. Most importantly, he associated the Confucian Period of Approaching Peace with his Society of Small Tranquility; and the Confucian Period of Universal Peace with his Society of Great Harmony. He also maintained the Confucian distaste for profits and excessive wealth. He argued for land reforms that would give all Chinese equal portions of land, including allotments for women and children. Like Confucius, Kang advocated an ideal society in which people had sufficient, but not excessive, wealth and property, and private ownership of the means of production.

When Mao developed his own proposals, he substituted state for private ownership, but viewed the Communist system of government ownership as a method for achieving an end. Mao openly stated that Kang's Society of Great Harmony provided the ideal goal, but that Kang failed to identify the appropriate means to achieve this goal. Mao specified that Communism and his Great Leap Forward provided the means to achieve Kang's goal. Though Mao sought to eradicate the memory of Confucianism and Taoism from Chinese society, his goals included creating an ideal neo-Taoist society, via Kang Youwei.

Because of the harmonies between the ideal Confucian society that China strove historically to achieve, and Mao's ideal society that China strove towards more recently, we argue that the CCP and Chinese government will survive. Indeed, today, we are probably seeing in China's new reform movements the Confucianization of Communist China that Mao so dreaded. The next chapter highlights the historical roots of Chinese strategy.

endnotes

1. Haley, U. C. V., "Here There be Dragons: Opportunities and Risks for Foreign Multinational Corporations in China".

2. Chan, W. T., *Chinese Philosophy*; De Bary, W. T. and I. Bloom, *Sources of Chinese Tradition, From Earliest Times to 1600*, 2nd edition.3.	Shi, Z., "The Dual Economic Function of Confucianism", p. 19.

4. Ibid.

5. Haley, G. T., C. T. Tan and U. C. V. Haley, *New Asian Emperors: The Overseas Chinese, their Strategies and Competitive Advantages.*

6. Lau, D. C., *Confucius: The Analects.*

7. Chan, W. T., op.cit; De Bary and Bloom, op.cit.; Legge, J., *The Works of Mencius.*

8. Haley et al, op.cit.; Redding, S. G., "Overseas Chinese Networks: Understanding the Enigma".

9. Shi, op.cit.

10. Ibid.

11. Haley et al, op.cit; *Encyclopedia Britannica*, "Buddhism, Historical Development, Central Asia and China".

12. Lau op.cit.

13. Lau, D. C. (1963), *Lao Tzu: Tao Te Ching.*

14. Haley et al, op.cit.

15. Haley, U. C. V., op.cit.

16. Backman, M., *Asian Eclipse: Exposing the Dark Side of Business in Asia.*

17. Lau op.cit.

18. Ibid.

19. Zhang, Q., "Marxism and Traditional Chinese Philosophy".

20. Ibid.

21. Ibid.

22. Ibid; Becker, J., *The Chinese.*

3

THE HISTORICAL ROOTS OF CHINESE STRATEGY

"Hold fast to the way of antiquity
In order to keep in control the realm of today.
The ability to know the beginning of antiquity
Is called the thread running through the Way."
Tao Te Ching
Book 1, Chapter 14, Stanza 34

"The more things change, the more they remain the same."
Alphonse Karr
Les Guêpes, 1849

INTRODUCTION

Persistence and change characterize Chinese history and strategy. On 1st October, 1949, Mao Zedong declared the founding of the People's Republic of China from the Gate of Heavenly Peace, the main entrance to the Ming and Qing Emperors' Forbidden City. "We the 475 million Chinese people have now stood up and the future of our nation is infinitely bright," he said. Mao made the old imperial capital of Beijing the seat of Communist power.[1]

Despite his Communist beliefs and titles, Mao viewed himself as a modern-day successor to the ancient Chinese emperors, a sentiment echoed by former President Jiang Zemin. Both leaders drew on imperial trappings, symbols and tools to establish social control. The emperors had their Forbidden City; the Chinese Communist rulers have their leadership compound in central Beijing, Zhongnanhai. The Imperial court had its bureaucracy to control the masses; and the Communist government has its even-larger CCP hierarchy. When central control became too difficult, the Imperial court decentralized by passing the control of localities to their scholarly class, "the gentry";[2] the Communist government, encountering similar difficulties, decentralized by passing their localities to the CCP's cadres.

This chapter elaborates on persistence and change in Chinese strategy. First, we discuss the historical Chinese attitude towards commerce. Next, we trace the evolution of Chinese bureaucracy and its impact on modern-day China. In the ensuing section, we analyze how Communism inherited and continued to implement Confucian and neo-Taoist philosophies despite its radical stance. Finally, we explore some of the implications of 2,000 years of history and philosophy for business in China today.

THE EMPERORS AND THE MERCHANTS

A failed strategic move may have determined the historical destiny of China's merchants. In 498 BC, the Duke of Lu tried unsuccessfully to break the power of Lu's three great merchant families, and failed. The Duke had acted on the advice of Confucius, then the Duke's Police Commissioner. Confucius' first notable failure destroyed his successful bureaucratic career. The following year, Confucius left Lu and began life as an itinerant bureaucrat seeking service in successive foreign states. He never again attained the success he had achieved in his home state of Lu. When Confucius finally returned to Lu in 484 BC, after an undistinguished foreign career, the state's government hired him as a counselor at the lowest level. He died five years later, in 479 BC, at the age of 68 or 69.[3]

Despite his incomparable influence on the evolution of Chinese history and culture, Confucius died as a relatively unsuccessful nonentity. We may never know how much he attributed his tribulations to his failed strategic move against Lu's merchants. Did his failure lead to the extreme authoritarianism and anti-commerce bias reflected in his philosophy? Again, we cannot answer this question centuries after his lifetime. However, to understand Chinese strategy and business today, it is necessary to comprehend the effects of Confucianism on the development of Chinese commerce.

Chinese business strategies and practices developed during the long Imperial era, under the influence of neo-Taoist social philosophies. As discussed in Chapter 2, the emperors viewed the merchants as the lowest class in Chinese society. While they exalted the virtues of agricultural peasants, the emperors did not elevate their social class. Wealthy, propertied landowners occupied a higher social class than peasants, and the scholars occupied the highest social class in Chinese society.

Despite this rigid social stratification, ancient Chinese society possessed social mobility. Merchants could elevate their social class by buying large tracts of agricultural land to lease to farmers, thereby becoming wealthy landowners. By training to pass government-sponsored exams, anyone could become a scholar, qualify for the gentry or even higher levels within the scholarly class.

Scholars could also become merchants, thereby lowering their social class but enhancing their ability to accumulate wealth; and indeed, many scholars did. Successful merchants had to obtain the sponsorship and protection of government mandarins at municipal, provincial or central governmental levels; these mandarins came from the scholarly class. Hence, over time, scholars could cultivate support among the mandarins, and use this network to start businesses and build fortunes. Once wealthy, the former scholars would refrain from commerce, seek bureaucratic employment again, and return to the mandarin ranks. Their newly acquired fortune could enhance their political position and those of the mandarins that assisted them when they worked as lowly merchants. Their uprightness, or the appropriate behaviors they displayed for each role they played, whether merchant or scholar, would build and maintain their supportive networks. On at least one occasion, a lowly, landless peasant worked his way up the social classes to become emperor through wealth, political power and uprightness.

THE EVOLUTION OF CHINESE BUREAUCRACY

The civil-service administration gave the Chinese empire stability and bureaucracy for more than 2,000 years and provided one of the major outlets for social mobility. It later served as a model for the civil-service systems and bureaucracies that developed in other Asian and Western countries.

THE CHINESE CIVIL SERVICE[4]: 2,000 YEARS OF CONFUCIAN BUREAUCRACY

The Qin dynasty (221–206 BC) established the first centralized Chinese bureaucratic empire and national administrative system. The Qin bureaucracy recruited through the recommendations of local officials. The succeeding Han dynasty (206 BC–AD 220) adopted this system. In 124 BC, the Han emperor Wu-ti founded an imperial university to train and to test officials in the techniques of Confucian government.

The Sui dynasty (581–618) adopted the Han tests. The central government, rather than local aristocrats, appointed the prefectures' officials; and local militia obeyed central governmental authorities. The T'ang dynasty (618–907) created a system of local schools where scholars could pursue their studies. Those desiring to enter the upper levels of the bureaucracy competed for the *chin-shih* exams that tested knowledge of the Confucian Classics. By the end of the T'ang dynasty the scholar-gentry who staffed the bureaucracy had displaced the old aristocrats. The West named these non-hereditary elites, the "mandarins", from the Portuguese *mandarim* and the Sanskrit *man* ("to think").

The Sung dynasty (960–1279) established national public schools to help the talented but indigent, barred business contacts among officials related by blood or marriage, barred members of the imperial family from holding high positions, and established a merit system in which a person who nominated another for advancement held complete responsibility for that person's conduct and uprightness.

The civil service reached its final form under the Ming dynasty (1368–1644). The succeeding Qing dynasty (1644–1912) kept the Ming system virtually intact. No man could serve in his home district, and the administration rotated officials every three years. The administration took elaborate precautions to prevent cheating and established quotas to prevent any district from dominating the national bureaucracy.

The *Nine Classics of Confucius* comprised the entire tested material and the eight-legged essay (*pa-ku wen-cheng*) provided the set form with eight main headings and no more than 700 characters. The exam had no relation to the candidates' abilities to govern and critics alleged that it rewarded command of style over thought.

The Qing dynasty finally abolished the examination system in 1905 in the midst of modernization attempts. In 1912, Sun Yat Sen's government overthrew the dynasty and abolished the civil-service administration, but its legacy and influence continue.

The ancient Chinese also outsourced their bureaucracy to generate extraordinary efficiencies and also, unfortunately, abuses. The Chinese bureaucracy grew from approximately 18,000 positions during the T'ang dynasty to 20,000 positions during the Qing dynasty, or by roughly 2,000 positions over a thousand years.[5] By comparison, Texas Governor William Clements, an anti big-government Republican who campaigned on the promise of limiting bureaucratic growth, saw the Texas state bureaucracy grow by about 25,000 positions over his second four-year term, from 1987-1991 despite instituting a state-government hiring freeze. Table 3.1 presents the Chinese bureaucracy's increasing efficiency. However, the bureaucracy's efficiency did not always translate to good governance or fair dealings with the Chinese populace or even with the emperors.

TABLE 3.1: GROWTH AND EFFICIENCY OF THE IMPERIAL CHINESE CIVIL SERVICE[6]

Dynasty	Year	No. Sub-prefectures	Approximate Population (in millions)	Approximate Population/ Magistrate
Later Han	80	1180	60	51,000
T'ang	875	1235	80	65,000
Southern Sung	1190	1130	110	97,000
Ming	1585	1385	200	144,000
Qing	1850	1360	425	313,000

The central government assigned each sub-prefecture a magistrate to conduct the government's business. The magistrates commanded the local military forces, held court to judge malefactors, collected taxes, forwarded the taxes to the central government, and supervised the sub-prefectures in the emperor's name. The sub-prefectures attained considerable autonomy, which has lasted until today.

Over time, fraudulent practices seeped into the civil service, including the selling of positions in the scholar-gentry. The civil service became highly corrupt, inefficient and self-serving. The magistrates and scholar-gentry imposed confiscatory taxes, the peasantry became impoverished, merchants could not maintain profitable operations, and all classes began subverting the civil service to survive. Many reformers, such as Kang Youwei, attempted to change the civil service with support from influential bureaucrats, such as Emperor Guanxu. However, conservative, entrenched elements, such as the Dowager Empress Cixi, defeated the reformers every time.

▲ The hills are high and the Emperor is far away

As indicated previously, Chinese society resembled the waves that emanate from a stone thrown into a pond; each successive wave represented a level of relationship for any individual. Using this analogy, the emperors had larger and more powerful waves than common individuals. However, the waves became fainter — that is, their influence receded — as they moved further from the emperors. In the civil service's infancy, the magistrates and their aides conducted the emperor's business in the prefectures. However, as demonstrated in Table 3.1, tremendous expansion occurred in the scope of control. As the population grew, the magistrates outsourced day-to-day operations to the scholar-gentry. For the most part, Chinese bureaucracy developed along regional lines with strong regional loyalties that survive today.

Anyone in ancient China who wanted to progress in life could undertake a series of government-sponsored national exams. Passing the first exam gave anyone automatic entry to the scholar-gentry and the opportunity to contract to mediate between citizens and the government. These individuals obtained their compensation by retaining a percentage of the take, a system that still seems alive among Chinese bureaucracies today. The magistrates would assess taxes that the scholar-gentry collected within specific geographic regions; these taxes included the required emperor's taxes plus additional taxes to cover the magistrates' needs. The scholar-gentry responsible for specific regions would then assess taxes to cover the magistrates' assessments and additional monies for themselves. The central authorities did not control the amounts the scholar-gentry and the magistrates collected for their own expenses and income. Consequently, final tax assessments on individuals varied by district and sub-prefecture, and could devastate despite low government levies. Besides the ability to collect taxes and to set effective tax rates within the regions, scholar-gentry lived under more benign laws than those applying to the lower classes. The scholars who passed the highest level of examinations could eventually advise key administrators, including the emperors, on policy.

The civil service also granted major traders, such as Howqua (see Chapter 1), rights to manage imperial trade relationships for certain ports, commodities or trading partners. Though the traders acted under government licenses and for the government, the civil service had no particular affection for them. For most of his career, Howqua, alone among Cantonese merchants, avoided bankruptcy caused by excessive tax assessments. Near the end of his career, even Howqua succumbed to the government's excessive taxation and harassment and lost his great fortune.

Because of outsourcing, regional differences and vast distances, Chinese bureaucracy, despite very authoritarian central governments, developed along regional lines. Out of necessity, Imperial China utilized regional planning, with regions enjoying operational and financial autonomy. The Communists maintained this ancient cellular economic system, rather than the Soviet-style centrally planned system where individual ministries governed all activities in specific sectors, across provincial borders. Drawing on the ancient civil service, the Communist government divided the country's tax base and responsibility for financial management by administrative zones rather than by industries. Sub-national governments (provinces, prefectures, counties, towns and villages) run state-owned enterprises (SOEs) in China today. As in ancient China, political units, not economic ones, own and control the means of production and markets. The higher an SOE's level of government supervision, the more easily it secures capital and foreign exchange. For example, provincial SOEs enjoy more privileges and benefits than counties' SOEs. Private companies without bureaucratic affiliations or contacts have little access to capital necessary to expand. The central government allows private companies to function only in labor-intensive, non-strategic industries such as the garment industry. Many of the private, competitive, export-oriented companies have to sell equity to foreigners to secure the working capital they need. The next section elaborates on the Communist influence on Chinese strategy.

THE COMMUNIST SOJOURN

Kong Fanyin, a descendent of Confucius, stated, "No one likes Confucius before they come to power. Once they do, they begin to see his good side." In 1949, the CCP under Mao Zedong seized control of China and Mao saw the practicality of Confucian and Taoist philosophies.

▲ Persistence and change

As discussed in Chapter 1, the Chinese transition to Communism did not mirror the transition from the Russian aristocracy to the Soviet era. Mao Zedong may have lambasted Confucianism, but he used the ancient philosophies to implement his changes. Table 3.2 depicts how, in his efforts to create a bureaucracy that did not directly oppress the rural peasantry, Mao created one that mimicked the Imperial bureaucracy. Additionally, the differences in per-capita income (Imperial Russia's was roughly four times greater than Imperial China's), in the level of economic development (Imperial Russia comprised the world's largest producer of steel, concrete and armaments), and in the ratio of natural resources to population hindered the effectiveness of Soviet-style policies in China.

Like the Chinese emperors before him, Mao built a public-law and network-based society, not one with constitutionally guaranteed rights. Since the CCP seized control in 1949, the five Chinese constitutions have approximated mission statements more than constitutions.[4] Mao also cemented his network system through the same measures as the emperors — personal loyalty and dependence. The central government appointed the local cadres that the CCP's loyalists recommended, thereby increasing the appointees' dependence on the central authorities, not the peasantry.

TABLE 3.2: A COMPARISON OF THE IMPERIAL AND MAOIST BUREAUCRACIES[7]

The Imperial bureaucracy	The Maoist bureaucracy
Small policy-making core in capital	Small policy-making core in capital
Decentralized implementation by trained/semi-trained local elite — the scholar-gentry class	Decentralized implementation by trained/semi-trained local elite — the local Communist cadres
Local bureaucracies beholden to the rulers, not to the ruled —	Local bureaucracies beholden to the rulers, not to the ruled —
Imperial rulings must be attained or surpassed	Central government's rulings must be attained or surpassed
Strong provincial governments following the center's lead — tended to go their own way when center was weak	Strong provincial governments following the center's lead — tended to go their own way when center was weak

Minimum standards of taxation contributed to center & set by center; local gentry set actual taxes collected from populace	Minimum standards of taxation collected for center & set by center; local cadres set actual taxes forwarded to center in names of cadres
EFFECT: Excessive taxes collected to amass personal wealth for local elites and enhance social standing and power	**EFFECT:** Excessive payments made to central government to impress superiors with performance and enhance political position and power

Mao used network systems throughout his era to surmount opposition. In 1959, when Marshall Peng tried to professionalize the military, Mao promoted General Lin to subvert Peng's efforts. Lin sabotaged Peng by building networks of officers who supported the politicization of the military. The CCP's leaders, including Deng Xiaoping and Liu Shaoqi, objected to Mao's policies. Mao responded by using his army-based networks, through Lin, to build the student Red Guard organization and to attack the CCP's leaders through the Cultural Revolution. Whenever challenges arose, Mao responded as an ancient emperor trained in Confucian philosophy would, brooking no opposition or debate. When he built organizations to administer China, Mao chose network systems, just as any ancient emperor might have done. Mao never questioned the importance of networks within the government — only the individuals to whom those networks expressed loyalty. Consequently, while Mao ruled, the only major changes he instituted in Chinese bureaucracy included the central government's nationalization of the means of production and its promotion of Chinese nationalism.

▲ Botched policies

While Mao wanted rapid industrialization and a centrally-planned economy, he despised the bureaucratic and professional elites that emerged to sustain these goals. In 1949, the CCP did not have enough trained personnel to run the government, so it left most of the Nationalist government's bureaucrats in place to administer the new policies. Initial policies included educating the local elites — educational, agrarian and capitalist — together with government personnel in Communist philosophy and converting them to the CCP's cause. Unfortunately, Mao viewed bureaucrats as converted only when they accepted orders unquestioningly and never criticized the government, an exaggeration of the neo-Taoist philosophy of self-effacement and obedience to superiors. His irreconcilable ambitions led to the concept of "permanent revolution" and then "continuous revolution". These theoretical notions resulted in the excesses that epitomized his rule: the Hundred Flowers Campaign, the ensuing Anti-Rightist Campaign, the Great Leap Forward and the Great Proletarian Cultural Revolution.

In 1956–57 the government announced its Hundred Flowers Campaign where intellectuals could criticize the government and its policies. The Campaign mimicked an Imperial policy that periodically opened the government to criticism to promote improvement. To Mao's chagrin, criticism actually appeared; and he responded not with improvement, but with the Anti-Rightist Campaign. The central government labeled between 300,000 and 700,000 intellectuals, academics and government bureaucrats as rightist traitors, and hounded them from their jobs and social positions.[8] This Campaign removed virtually every trained economist, social scientist and bureaucrat, as well as many trained engineers, from government and academic service.

Mao's Great Leap Forward derived from an accurate assessment of China's economic situation. The first Soviet-style five-year plan had ended in a disaster that even the inflated numbers produced by Mao's CCP cadres could not camouflage. However, rather than change the goals of China's industrialization, from producing heavy industrial goods such as steel, Mao changed the methods of accomplishing the goals. Rather than building large, centralized Soviet-style plants, he chose to move production to small, backyard production units, with disastrous results. For example, the backyard smelters may have achieved government quotas, but produced steel of unusable quality. Concurrently, the government aggressively pushed the full-scale collectivization of agriculture. In both instances, the central government passed control to new, untrained and poorly educated cadres that staffed the bureaucracy after the Anti-Rightist Campaign.

The new small-scale industrialization, and emphasis on collectivization, demanded enormous time and effort from farmers. Under the new programs, Chinese farmers could no longer grow their own, small, family-plot crops. Mao had created a recipe for catastrophe. Between 20 and 30 million Chinese died from starvation and severe malnutrition.[9] In an effort to curry favor with central government authorities, local CCP cadres forwarded reports that inflated production of industrial goods and foodstuffs and failed to report any negative consequences arising from the new policies. To some extent, this problem continues to plague China today.

By making untrained and under-educated cadres his local tools, Mao once again introduced intermediaries between the government and the governed. Just as in the Imperial era, the intermediary groups owed their jobs to the bureaucrats that appointed them, not to the governed. Perhaps unsurprisingly, they presented Mao with reports indicating the success of his policies. Some senior officials, such as Liu Shaoqi and Deng Xiaoping, questioned the cadres' reports and obtained their own, more-accurate reports, providing evidence of the building disaster. Mao ignored their arguments and marked the officials for future purging during the Cultural Revolution when he proclaimed them as "Capitalist Roaders".

GENERAL LIN BIAO[10]: COMMUNIST STRAW DOG

As in the Confucian and neo-Taoist traditions, General Lin Biao played straw dog for Chairman Mao Zedong. Lin served as an army commander during the revolution, and many consider him to be the most brilliant tactician of the People's Liberation Army (PLA). He also proved a brilliant political tactician in the CCP's infighting after it gained control of China. In the PRC's early days, leaders resolved their differences through debate and compromise. However, as the CCP consolidated its control, these debates irritated Mao. He first turned against the PLA's head, Marshall Peng Dehuai, who wanted to build the army into a professional fighting force on the Soviet model. Mao preferred to retain the army as a political tool rather than as a fighting force. Mao used Lin against Peng. Lin moved to politicize the army, evicting Peng's supporters, and developing the CCP's greatest and best-known propaganda tool, Mao's Little Red Book, *Quotations of Chairman Mao*. Lin continued his unflinching support for Mao in all the subsequent infighting.

In 1969, to reward his loyalty and success in squashing threats to Mao's authority, Mao appointed Lin as Vice Chairman and identified him as "Comrade Mao Zedong's close comrade-in-arms and successor". Simultaneously, Mao also moved to undermine Lin. Lin's efforts on Mao's behalf had put Mao in an impregnable position. Though he never defied the Chairman, Mao no longer needed him.

Mao appointed one of Lin's opponents as his second in command. Premier Zhou Enlai, number three in the CCP's hierarchy, and two senior, old-guard generals who had supported Peng, escorted Lin's opponent to military headquarters, signaling official attitudes. Mao toured the provinces making negative remarks about Lin in speeches before the troops. At official functions, Lin no longer stood beside Mao but behind him.

Lin recognized the warning signs and began to organize his defense. His son, a planner in the army's high command, started garnering support for a coup against Mao. Mao uncovered the plot.

The Chinese government announced that Lin died in a plane crash in Northern Mongolia as he fled towards the Soviet Union. The announcement of his death came a year after it happened. Lin had lived and died as a straw dog with no recognition of his passing.

In 1966, Mao launched the bizarre Cultural Revolution, an attempt to destroy Chinese tradition, customs, habits, culture and thinking. Millions of youths roamed the country, slashing at the sacred; state-sponsored terrorism destroyed temples and universities. The PLA finally restored order after clashing with youthful Red Guards. By 1969, the government had declared the campaign over, though revisionist history extended it to 1976 when the government captured the infamous Gang of Four, including Mao's wife. Though unnamed and defaced, Confucianism and neo-Taoism survived, enshrined in Mao's own institutions and policies. China's economy, shattered by the Cultural Revolution emerged from an era of struggle and began the arduous task of rebuilding.

IMPLICATIONS FOR BUSINESS IN CHINA

History has had an enormous influence on business operations and environments in China today. In this section, we explore its implications for business-government relations, markets and information.

▲ Laws, leaders and the led

Chinese bureaucracy and attitudes, both ancient and recent, delayed the reforms necessary to encourage foreign direct investment (FDI) until after Mao's death. Mao was pragmatic in his analysis of issues and implementation of solutions. For example, he immediately and accurately read the disastrous results of China's first, Soviet-style, five-year plan; and he used the Nationalist government's bureaucrats after the CCP seized power. But, Mao frequently devised anachronistic solutions including the Anti-Rightist Campaign, the Great Leap Forward and the Cultural Revolution. While deriding neo-Taoist philosophies and attitudes, he nevertheless appeared unable to discard them.

Such rhetorical challenges to, and practical reaffirmation of, neo-Taoist philosophies have greatly influenced Chinese business practices. For example, as Lu Qun, Director of Product

Engineering for Beijing Jeep Corp. (the first US-Chinese joint venture) noted, "*Guanxi* [the art of relationship building] is very important in China, and also in the US. The difference is that in the US, companies put more effort into relationships with the value-chain members, and some effort into relationships with the government. In China, you must make a better effort to develop relationships with the government."

The economic reforms that Deng Xiaoping initiated, and Jiang Zemin continued, have contributed to some change in business environments. As noted by Yan Lan, chief litigator for the French law firm Gide Loyrette Nouel in Beijing, a major issue concerns "whether China will be ruled by rulers or ruled by law". "Historically," she argues, "China has been ruled by rulers. Under the present government, however, the argument has been getting resolved on the side of law. In five years, Chinese business law will fully conform with WTO [World Trade Organization] standards... Each administrative unit has been given a list of improvements necessary to conform with WTO standards in its area, but it is a long march."

The central government is implementing several of the changes that Yan mentioned to us. However, as she noted, "a long march" lies ahead. Most analysts agree that the central government will probably fail to implement many of the planned administrative changes within the next five years, especially as it maintains a decentralized administration. Implementation of administrative changes will fall to provincial governments and the CCP's institutions on the historical principle that, as a result of variations in Chinese economic development, economic environments and cultures, regional institutions will respond better to local needs. As we argue below, regional independence carries considerable costs.

▲ One nation, thirty-one markets

The 31 provinces still retain considerable independence from the center in China. For example, FDI of less than US$30 million does not need approval from Beijing's central government, but only from the provincial governments that oversee the regions of the investments. This independence provides some opportunities for foreign companies, but also confounds business operations and policy implementation.

Rivalries permeate the provinces. For example, China exports 90% of the world's silk, but Shanghai has to buy raw silk from abroad, despite having the largest producers, Zhejiang and Jiangsu, as next-door neighbors. Most Chinese provinces do not sell their raw materials or finished goods to one another. Indeed, each of China's 31 provinces erects barriers to protect local SOEs from those in other provinces. In recent years, inter-provincial trade has trended down even as China's external trade has trended up.

Provincial governments impose fines for buying goods from other provinces, confiscate profits earned on such goods and subsidize the buying of local goods. Some Hubei counties even issue their own currencies to prevent residents from shopping in neighboring Hunan province!

Without an integrated market where goods, services and capital can move freely between provinces, the price of raw materials, capital and products varies widely across China. For example, steel costs anywhere from 1,857 yuan to 2,435 yuan, depending on the province. Provinces compete for FDI, creating enormous excess capacity in manufacturing. For example, in 1995, China's 122 assembly lines made 1.45 million vehicles or 12,000 units per line. The minimum production for efficient automobile manufacturing the world over approximates 250,000 units of one basic model per plant. China's automobile industry appears highly inefficient — but 20 provinces plan to build their own automobile-manufacturing plants from scratch. The next sub-section explores historical problems with information for strategic decision-making.

▲ The trouble with numbers

We noted that during Mao's era, the CCP's lower and middle-level cadres misreported and exaggerated performance reports to curry favor with superiors, thereby confounding policy implementation and analysis. This problem plagues the current government. Many experts have questioned the economic statistics reported by the government (see the PBS, Wideangle debate between Usha Haley and Mark Clifford at http://www.pbs.org/wnet/wideangle/shows/china/debate.html).

The exaggerated economic data can have significant effects on perceived performance and projected performance of FDI in China. As Elmar Stachels, managing director of Bayer China Company, Ltd., told us "You manage by objectives — objectives that must be clearly stated — then determine what kind of tools you can use to determine if you achieved them, but stick with your objectives. However, if it comes to financial figures, it will be challenging. What good will numbers be if the base rates used for comparison of performance are not reliable?"

Unreliability of data is a serious problem. For example, in February 2002, the Chinese government said that China's GDP had grown by 7.3% in 2001, making it the world's fastest-growing economy. But growth rates reported by individual provinces told another story. Only one, Yunnan, said its product had grown slower than the national rate. Taken together, the provincial figures produced a national growth rate nearly two points higher than the official rate! The National Statistics Bureau (NSB) conducts sample surveys and uses these to estimate the country's GDP and growth rate. The results have invariably been at odds with provincial figures. In 1995, the GDP growth rate suggested by provincial data averaged three percentage points higher than the figure of 10.5% produced by sample surveys. Opinions vary as regards the accuracy of the central government's estimates. However, in China, few scholars publicly attempt any detailed justification of alternative figures because of political sensitivity.

Thomas Rawski, a US economist, has stated that China's NSB lacks the capacity to collect data outside normal information channels and lower-level officials interfere with its surveys. As in Imperial and Maoist days, the numbers generated by provincial governments remain an important criterion in evaluating the performance of local officials, creating an incentive to falsify statistics. In the first 10 months of 2001, Beijing authorities uncovered more than 62,000 offenses against the country's statistics laws. In March 2002, the *Guangzhou Daily* reported that a township official in Hunan province had fudged GDP and profit figures — and was promoted to chief of a county statistics bureau. The pressure to exaggerate statistics grew in the late 1990s as Chinese officials sought to pump up the economy to stave off the effects of the Asian economic slump. Beijing declared that the country had to grow at least 7% a year to create jobs and to forestall social unrest. Not surprisingly, reported growth rates have not dipped below that level since.

Researchers estimate that officials may also routinely underreport other sensitive data such as debt numbers, unemployment or even FDI to avoid tax payments and governmental scrutiny.[11] The methods used by the central government to ascertain the validity of data, a process it calls *yasuo shuifen* or "squeezing the water", involves sample surveys, price-index adjustments and plenty of guesswork. Rawski has argued that the NSB's statisticians "are not the cause of the unreliability of Chinese numbers... [Just among] the prominent victims."[12] The next chapter explores the legal roots of Chinese strategy.

endnotes

1. Chang, G. G., *The Coming Collapse of China*.

2. Fairbank, J. K. and M. Goldman, *China, a New History*.

3. Lau, D. C., *Confucius: The Analects*.

4. Fairbank and Goldman, op.cit.

5. Ibid.

6. Ibid.

7. Compiled from materials in Fairbank and Goldman, op.cit.; Starr, J. B., *Understanding China: A Guide to China's Economy, History, and Political Structure*; and Shi, Z., "The Dual Economic Function of Confucianism".

8. Fairbank and Goldman, op.cit.; Starr, op.cit.

9. Fairbank and Goldman, op.cit.

10. Ibid.

11. Chang, op.cit.; Liu, M., and P. Mooney, "Why China Cooks the Books: The Reputation of the People's Republic as an Economic Powerhouse is Based in Part on Pure Bunk"; *The Economist*, "How Cooked are the Books?".

12. Liu and Mooney, op.cit. .

4

THE LEGAL ROOTS OF CHINESE STRATEGY

"The fish must not be allowed
to leave the deep;
The instruments of power in a state
must not be revealed to anyone."
Tao Te Ching

Book 1, Chapter 36, Stanza 80

INTRODUCTION

In its 2002 white paper on China, the American Chamber of Commerce identified greater transparency in the legislative processes and regulatory environment, and better law enforcement, as top issues of concern for US companies in China. Around 170 US companies responded to the survey, expressing apprehension about China's implementation of its WTO commitments. Some 35% believed that China would not meet its commitments or that protectionism could increase, and 25% reported that their business plans synchronized closely with China's implementation schedule.[1]

Initial statistics from the Supreme People's Court indicate that between 1979 and October 2001, courts in China had dealt with 23,340 civil and commercial cases involving foreign parties. The actual statistics could be much higher. Grass-roots and intermediate courts can hear commercial cases involving foreign parties under current practices. However, the traditional overlapping of administrative and judicial divisions has contributed to protectionism in local Chinese courts, and hindered the fair handling of cases. Aware of concerns, China's central government has taken dramatic steps to improve the situation by announcing that as of 1st March, 2002, only approved courts can handle cases involving foreign interests. Such courts include the high courts; intermediate courts in municipalities, capital cities of provinces and autonomous regions, special economic zones and cities directly under State planning; and some courts in the cities' economic and technological development areas. In conjunction with this, listed companies and large companies in China have to hire chief legal advisers. However, the new practices do not apply to cases of border trade, real estate and intellectual property-right violations involving foreign parties, the primary concerns of foreign companies.[2]

Historical developments can explain many of the contradictions in China's legal system, including the central government's commitment to initiate reform and the obdurate problems of implementing this reform. The Chinese economist Chen

Yun described the Chinese economy as a "bird in a cage". The owners must let the bird fly — that is, the central government must introduce market forces and some measures of decentralization — but only within the confines of the cage — the central plan — lest the bird escape.[3] Both the imperialist legacy and the Maoist overlay failed to differentiate between the functions of law and administration; both placed the judicial system at the same level as the state's bureaucracies in the political hierarchy. Thereby, both the emperors and the Communists failed to give authority to the courts over administration and limited the powers of judicial interpretation. Despite its burgeoning market economy, law in China still serves more as an instrument of control than as a framework to facilitate private transactions or to protect rights. This chapter explores China's complex legal system, the traditional roots that obfuscate it today and how Western companies can overcome some of these problems.

First, we discuss the historical influences on China's legal system. Next, we highlight some characteristics of Chinese commercial law, including the emphasis on negotiation. We then discuss counterfeiting, a major legal problem facing Western companies in China. Finally, we discuss how China protects intellectual-property rights, and the limits of that protection.

HISTORICAL INFLUENCES ON CHINA'S LEGAL SYSTEM

Westerners generally differentiate between common-law and code-law systems; the former dominate Anglo/American cultures, and the latter other Western cultures. Yet both legal systems converge, especially on issues of commercial law. By guaranteeing their citizens basic minimum rights, both constitute rights-based legal systems. Additionally, common-law countries have adopted commercial codes to apply in business situations. Superficially, China's legal system appears similar to code-law systems; yet, substantial differences exist.

China enjoys a public-law rather than a rights-based system. Public-law systems do not guarantee individuals' rights;

rather, individuals' rights exist at the rulers' behest, and the rulers can withdraw the rights at whim.[4] To ensure that the emperors could enforce their will without legal challenges, the imperial Chinese courts desired that commoners had no knowledge of the law.[5] A poem of the Western Zhou era, *Bei Shan*, eloquently communicates this Chinese perspective:

"Everywhere under Heaven
Is no land that is not the king's
To the borders of all those lands
None but is the king's slave."[6]

Sir Henry Maine[7] identified three stages of historical development in Western legal systems:

1.) royal applications of divinely inspired laws;
2.) applications of customary or unwritten laws by oligarchical privileged groups; and
3.) code-based laws.

China's public-law system seemingly froze in the era of customary laws till the 20th century. For instance, China's last imperial dynasty, the Qing, enacted its first Civil and Commercial codes in 1908 (just three years prior to the dynasty's collapse in 1911), terminating thousands of years of public law, but not its influence.

China's first imperial dynasty, the Qin, instituted the "Law of the Five Punishments", the first known legal system in China. The five punishments ranged from various forms of physical disfigurement and amputation to death. The rulers could apply any punishment to any perceived crime, regardless of severity.[8] In subsequent dynasties, the less-severe punishments evolved into enforced labor and canings, while the ultimate punishment remained death by execution. The emperors, their representatives, or clan and family heads could decree and enforce the punishments. This legal authority of clan and family heads emphasizes the importance of family in Chinese culture, and serves to differentiate further between Chinese and Western laws.

The imperial courts developed separate sets of detailed laws, rituals and more-lenient punishments, *li*, for the scholar-gentry and aristocracy. *Li* specified appropriate rituals and behaviors for these social classes and, according to Confucius, its mastery constituted a key element on the path of "the Way".[9] *Li* varied depending on individuals' social stations, activities and stations vis-à-vis others, and thereby provided an important precursor to both *guanxi* and uprightness in Chinese business today.

The Communist government has made several attempts to move towards a code-based legal system, including drafting five constitutions; however, until recently it has failed in practice. The CCP's overwhelming power, together with a lack of legal precedents and poor legal training, have directed the country towards what is in practice a public-law system.[10] The Chinese judicial branch has no independence from the executive branch. On issues that the national or provincial CCP hierarchies consider strategically important, the courts follow the government's directives. This characteristic can be a significant concern in some industries. For instance, because of national security concerns, the Chinese government has always been suspicious of foreign software and foreign-owned intellectual property in the Information Technology (IT) sector, and has sometimes even encouraged the cracking of computer codes. In 2000, some Chinese IT experts affiliated with the government warned that secret holes in Microsoft's computer code might leave Chinese networks vulnerable to US government access and enable it to shut those networks down. To the extent that the government listens to these experts, the courts will rule accordingly.

Unlike that of the USA, the Chinese legal system also places much greater emphasis on mediation rather than litigation,[11] reflecting the Chinese culture's historical tendency to seek social harmony through compromise. The Chinese tend to view disputes that result in blatant conflicts, such as a court case, as systemic failures, not as efforts to seek justice or equitable settlements. Also, as indicated earlier, until the early 20th century

Chinese law did not incorporate the concept of commercial law, much less practice it. In the Communist era, no commercial laws dealt with domestic business until Deng Xiaoping promulgated his reforms, and adopted the General Principles of Civil Law (GPCL) and the Bankruptcy Law in 1986. Laws dealing with FDI first appeared in 1979. China's evolving Law for Foreign Business now comprises a nine-volume set available in Chinese and English. For Western companies in modern China, however, mediation produces compromises in commercial complaints more than victory for the aggrieved parties.

The late development of commercial law in China contributes to the theft of intellectual-property rights, an issue of primary concern to Western companies. Throughout China's imperial and pre-reform Communist eras, the government had exclusive ownership of technology and restricted access to strategically important technologies. In ancient China's public-law system, private individuals could not hold intellectual-property rights for technological or artistic achievement, unless the emperors specifically granted these rights. The emperors never granted ownership, as by doing so they would have acknowledged that individuals could usurp their rights. Much the same held true under the pre-reform Communist regime. Consequently, both neo-Taoist philosophy and political systems stunted the concept and understanding of intellectual property in China. Since Deng's economic reforms, the central government has made a Herculean effort to align Chinese commercial laws, legal structures and procedures with those of other industrial powers, unfortunately with mixed results.[12]

CHARACTERISTICS OF CHINESE COMMERCIAL LAW

As noted earlier, the Chinese government has enacted commercial laws approximating those in Western democracies; yet these laws continue to operate within the constraints of Chinese society and culture. Compromise and negotiation remain at the crux of the legal structure.

Foreign companies can settle commercial disputes through

conciliation, arbitration and litigation. Conciliation and arbitration comprise negotiated settlements. The Chinese government encourages conciliation by providing the parties with greater flexibility to reach agreement, by extracting lower fees, and by promoting conciliation during arbitration or litigation procedures.

▲ Conciliation vs. arbitration

Conciliation and arbitration differ in practice and effect. Conciliation comprises a consensus-based dispute-resolution process in which the parties to a dispute meet with a third party to discuss mutually acceptable options for the resolution of the dispute.[13] The contending parties choose mutually agreeable individuals as conciliators. The conciliators strive not to establish fault, but to help the parties attain compromise. Conciliation carries less cost and has more informality than arbitration. Table 4.1 details the respective characteristics of the two approaches.

Government-approved centers conduct both conciliation and arbitration: 35 government-sanctioned centers engage in conciliation; and over 400 government-licensed arbitrators, about 25% of whom come from foreign countries, perform arbitration. In conciliation, the parties may negotiate any mutually acceptable settlement. In arbitration, the arbitrator must also consider the fairness of any settlement. For disputing joint-venture (JV) partners, fairness includes the partners' relative capital contributions limiting the settlements. Chinese law enforces arbitration, but not conciliation without arbitration or litigation, thereby giving this more costly alternative a decided advantage for foreign companies. Both conciliation and arbitration have substantial procedural advantages over litigation, as they utilize more developed infrastructures.

▲ Business-government influences on litigation

True litigation is a relative newcomer to China and many Chinese managers consider recourse to litigation as a failure. Additionally, especially when the litigants operate in strategic industries, the Chinese government (central, provincial and municipal) and CCP intervene openly in courts. Consequently, the litigants must consider the strategic interests of provincial and municipal governments, as well as those of the central government. Finally, as sketched in earlier chapters, the central government has little effective control over provincial governments. To succeed in China, and to ensure smooth operations, companies must build strong relationships with the many levels of government authority. Chen Jiulin, managing director of China Aviation Oil (Singapore) Corp, Ltd., underscored the need for strong business relations with provincial governments when he said, "A foreign dragon cannot compete with the local snake."[15] The "foreign dragon" he referred to here is Beijing's central government, and the "local snake", a provincial government.

TABLE 4.1: CONCILIATION VS. ARBITRATION[14]

CHARACTERISTICS	Conciliation	Arbitration
Conciliator	Anyone	Board-certified arbitrator
Meetings	Informal & anywhere	Formal
Resolution Limitation	None	Must be considered as fair by the arbitrator to be accepted
Relative Cost	1.75–2.5%	4%
Enforceability	Not enforceable*	Enforceable

*Conciliation agreements reached under the auspices of a litigation court or an arbitration institution are enforceable

Kenneth DeWoskin, a partner in PricewaterhouseCoopers, China, also highlighted the importance of aligning companies' interests with local interests to facilitate the building of sustainable and profitable businesses in China. He advised against excessive dependence on legal instruments and advocated a thorough understanding of regulations and actual practices. Foreign companies should, he emphasized, embark upon expansive and systematic identification and selection of local partners to obviate litigation. Finally, he recommended that foreign companies should invest in due diligence to assess the real-revenue potentials of investments in China and again sidestep time-consuming and often futile litigation.[16]

COUNTERFEITING IN CHINA

Even a casual observer will notice that bogus goods seep through China. Some Western pharmaceutical manufacturers based in the PRC put the counterfeit rate for certain branded drugs at 10% or more. The Chinese government estimates the value of fake goods produced domestically at about 130 billion yuan annually (about US$15.7 billion), resulting in direct losses of 25 billion yuan (about US$3.01 billion) in taxation revenues. However, according to the China Anti-Counterfeiting Coalition, a lobby group of 49 multinationals, including Nike, Bayer, Gillette, Philip Morris, Kodak and Heineken, counterfeiters cost the Chinese government much more — upwards of hundreds of billions of yuan in lost taxes each year. Under current laws, victims of counterfeiting can press criminal charges only if administrative officers have caught and fined a counterfeiter three times. The low fines typically encourage counterfeiters to resume business within a day of apprehension.[17]

Earlier, we spotlighted Proctor and Gamble's (P&G) problems with counterfeiters. So far, counterfeiting has not stopped P&G from investing in China, but it could become a deciding factor in the future, according to William Dobson, P&G's Guangzhou-based vice-president of external relations. "If the problem continues to escalate, I can guarantee it will become the determining factor on whether we invest or not. We might decide to put a plant in another place where we would have more control over the whole supply chain: raw materials, production and packaging." The counterfeiting problem has also influenced P&G's ability to raise the prices of its products, ranging from shampoos and soaps to Pampers-brand diapers. Counterfeiters can undercut on price, sometimes by as much as 50—90%. "It's a factor in pricing," admitted Dobson. "Any time you increase the margin of the price differential between you and a counterfeiter, you're giving them an opportunity to make more money."[18]

In the automobile industry, a lack of severe punishment together with local government protection of makers of counterfeit parts has resulted in resounding losses for foreign companies, including top-selling Shanghai Volkswagen. In 2000, Shanghai Volkswagen, maker of the popular Santana model in China, reported it spent 1.4 billion yuan (about US$170 million) to repair parts annually for the Santanas. However, Volkswagen sold only a third of the replacement parts for the 1.5 million Santanas driven in China and makers of counterfeit, unauthorized parts claimed the other two-thirds. A fake Santana headlight sold for 90% less than a legitimate one, also hindering Volkswagen from recouping resounding losses by raising prices. The Chinese government has demolished 770 factories producing illegal goods and confiscated 90 million yuan-worth (about US$10.9 million) of Santana parts since 2000, but these efforts have touched just the tip of the iceberg. Similarly, copycats have taken at least 20% of Bosch Trading (Shanghai)'s potential 40-million yuan (about $4.83 million) market. Bosch, a German company, has found a counterfeit version for almost every one of its components on the Chinese market.[19]

In computer software, a report by Deutsche Messe AG found that software piracy cost China US$9.5 billion in 2001, making it the second-largest software-piracy market in the world. Sales of genuine software generated about US$4 billion in 2001.[20] Business Software Alliance released a report in early 2002 confirming this high rate of piracy: China's usage rate of unlicensed software runs at about 92%. For example, although Microsoft Windows constitutes the best-selling software in China, pirated copies comprise an estimated 90% of those sales.[21] Like many other foreign companies, Microsoft is not making profits in China.

Software makers in China are taking steps to curb piracy. In August 2001, more than 200 software developers and 3,000 software retailers initiated a campaign to encourage the use of low-cost licensed software. By selling their products at greatly reduced prices, between 60¢ and $1.21 per package, the companies hoped to increase licensed software's market share from 10% of total sales to about 40%.

Efforts by the central government to crack down on these counterfeiting activities have proven futile because local governments protect counterfeiters as a way to keep jobs and tax revenues in their jurisdictions. The enormous profits and windfall tax income have allowed counterfeiters to become pillar industries in provinces such as Zhejiang and Jiangsu. Ineffective prosecutions of criminals, and light penalties, have also curbed efforts to stem counterfeiting. Foreign companies hope for more legal transparency and enforceability through China's WTO membership; yet they simultaneously fear that smaller exporters from the PRC may flood global markets with counterfeits. As a corollary, in early 2001, the Chinese government announced that it would loosen restrictions on private companies seeking foreign-trade licenses.[22]

TOSHIBA IN CHINA: A FREE LUNCH?[23]

The Japanese company Toshiba is one of the leading producers of notebook computers in the world and is striving for a major share of the Chinese market for computers and components.

Surprisingly, in 2002, Toshiba reported that it had garnered 11.5% of the notebook-battery market in China, even though it sells no batteries in the country. How could this transpire? Obviously, someone is using Toshiba's copyrighted name to increase the desirability of a counterfeit product. When Kenneth DeWoskin of PricewaterhouseCoopers, China, related this story in mid 2002,

Toshiba still could not ascertain the phantom batteries' quality or impact. The Japanese company was struggling to regain control over its name and image, and over perceptions of quality that customers will come to associate with the Toshiba brand in China, before this becomes a prohibitively expensive free lunch.

INTELLECTUAL-PROPERTY RIGHTS IN CHINA

The preservation of intellectual-property rights provides one of the most difficult legal issues facing China. As outlined earlier, historically emperors and governments, not individuals, possessed these rights. Additionally, China's neo-Taoist philosophy, enshrined in the emperors and mandarins, encouraged the diffusion of societal innovations through copying, fostering a benign attitude towards piracy.[24] Today, because successful piracy provides economic payoffs, individuals have continuing incentives to violate intellectual-property rights. Finally, as the saying goes, the hills remain high and the emperors far away. Beijing has passed some of the most stringent anti-intellectual piracy laws in the world and invested heavily in enforcing them. Yet the central government cannot overcome the piracy of intellectual-property rights without the support of the provincial governments, which remains hard to obtain.

China's government has recognized the difficulty of moving the country from traditional legal roots to modern practices in an intertwined global economy. Besides passing laws to initiate change, the government has supported several semi-governmental agencies such as the Hong Kong Ethics Development Centre (HKEDC) and the Independent Commission Against Corruption (ICAC). Rita Liaw, executive director of the HKEDC told us that the center focused on educating Chinese businessmen in the new legal standards but, more importantly, on the economic advantages of following international standards of ethical practice. The center underlined the point that failure to synchronize with international ethical standards caused economic damage to Chinese companies and Chinese society. Liaw accentuated the government's recognition of the difficulties caused by traditional Chinese practices, and its determination to bring traditional practices into accord with international standards.

▲ Patents

Although China has enacted comprehensive and stringent laws governing intellectual-property rights, there are significant differences between Chinese and US laws. Chinese laws follow European models and adopt a "first-to-file", rather than a "first-to-invent" system. In the US, individuals who can prove they invented the technologies first own the intellectual-property rights. In Europe and China, the first individuals or companies that file for the patents own the intellectual-property rights; these first filers may or may not have invented the technologies. Consequently, companies that originate from countries that do not recognize Chinese patents, or have not signed the Paris Convention, should patent their technologies in China as soon as possible to protect their intellectual property.

To seek a Chinese patent, a foreign company or individual must appoint a patent agency designated by the China Patent Office. China's present patent laws derive from the Patent Law of the PRC passed in 1984, and a subsequent amendment, the Implementing Regulations of the Patent Law of the PRC, passed in 1992.[25] Together, these satisfy any legal requirements that most investors in China could desire. The difficulties lie in implementing the laws. Since Mao, the central government's power over the provinces has been continuously eroded. Also, as we have noted, patent violations provide major avenues of economic development in provinces such as Zhejiang and Jiangsu, further weakening the Beijing government's abilities to enforce the laws.

APEX AND DVDS²⁶: CHANGING RULES FOR A CHANGING CHINA

Advocates argued that WTO membership would get China to play by internationally accepted rules of trade, benefiting foreign companies that had long suffered unfair treatment. Indeed, since December 2001, some foreign companies have seen benefits to China's changing legal environments, as a Chinese DVD manufacturer's woes demonstrate.

China has quickly become a major exporter of DVD players, selling more than 10 million players in 2001. Apex Digital, founded in 1998 by two Chinese-American businessmen, sells more DVD players in the US than any other company. Revenues in 2001 reached US$1 billion. Apex's manufacturing base is in Zhejiang province, but it maintains corporate headquarters in Ontario, California. Though not competing with Sony and Panasonic on brand name, the company's low prices (some Apex DVD players sell for less than US$70) have contributed to its dominant market share in the US.

Foreign competitors claim that high-profile Apex, and about 100 smaller, Chinese DVD manufacturers, have grown so quickly because they openly flout intellectual-property rights. Apex has denied any wrongdoing. In early April 2002, a frustrated Sony filed suit in New York against Apex. Within days, the Japanese electronic giant dropped the suit; Apex agreed to pay royalties to Sony as well as to Philips and Pioneer.

Tian Yujing, a senior engineer at the China Electronic Video and Audio Industry Research Institute, said the whole dispute stemmed from a big misunderstanding. The Chinese were not cheating the foreigners, but were simply confused. Two years ago, when the foreign companies first demanded royalties, the Chinese refused to pay. "We just buy their parts, not the technology," said Tian. "All of us believed that you pay 'tuition' when you learn the technology." And, logically, since the Chinese had not learned the technology, they did not need to make tuition payments.

Apex spokesman Colton Manley argued that the foreign companies had not registered their patents in China and so royalties were something of a gray zone. However, Apex CEO and co-founder David Ji clarified that the Chinese don't pay royalties because "they don't want to". To reap the benefits of patented technology, Toshiba and five other companies, including Hitachi and AOL Time Warner, wanted US$4 or 4% royalties, whichever was higher, of a Chinese DVD's selling price. With the thin margins that many Chinese manufacturers experience, this cost increase would expunge their profits.

▲ Copyrights and trademarks

Copyright protections in China derive from two laws passed in 1990; the Copyright Law of the PRC and the Implementing Rules for the Copyright Law of the PRC. Both laws, though strong, importantly fail to recognize that copyrights protect computer software. In its continuing efforts to align Chinese laws with international standards, Beijing signed the Berne Convention in October 1992, giving precedence to the Convention's rules in the event of conflict.[27] Patches of this type help the Chinese to move from a neo-Taoist and Communist legal philosophy, to one compatible with international standards. However, the patches have also added to the confusion in implementing the laws. In China, owners of literary copyrights hold these rights through their lifetimes and for 50 years after their deaths; but, owners of other artistic copyrights, such as films, video and photographs, hold these rights for only 50 years.[28] China recognizes copyrights filed in countries that recognize Chinese copyrights or that have signed the Berne Convention; nevertheless, companies from these countries should re-file for Chinese copyrights, especially for software. In addition, copyright protection for software in China does not include the thoughts, concepts, discoveries, principles, algorithms, processing procedures or operational methods used by the developers of the software. [29]

Chinese trademark laws derive from the Trademark Law of the PRC, passed in 1982; the Detailed Rules for the Implementation of the Trademark Law of the PRC, passed in 1988; and additional major amendments to the Trademark Law passed in 1993. These laws follow international practice. However, foreign holders of trademarks need to hire officially sanctioned Trademark Agents in China to file for the trademarks in the foreign applicants' names and to deal with other matters for the trademarks' protection. The next chapter introduces the networks and their traditional influences on Chinese strategy.

THE HEROIC SAGA OF BEIJING JEEP[30]

Lu Qun, director of Product Engineering and head of Product Development for Beijing Jeep Corporation, Ltd, introduced us to the unusual saga of the Heroic, a reversal of the norm in intellectual property disputes in China. In the late 1990s, Chrysler's engineers in Beijing were poring over an exciting sports utility vehicle (SUV) design, the Heroic, generated by their Chinese JV partner, Beijing Jeep (BJ). The US engineers had at first expressed doubt about the potential of the new design. When BJ first mentioned the Heroic to Chrysler, US engineers argued that the new SUV would prove an unmitigated disaster. After all, BJ had only 100 automotive engineers while Chrysler had over 7,000. Each Chinese engineer would have to put in colossal man-hours to complete the design, they said. Yet the resulting design surprised the US engineers. The Heroic was smaller than the Grand Cherokee but larger than most of the small SUVs on the market. The Chinese Jeep seemed just the kind of vehicle Chrysler needed. The engineers packed their bags, and left Beijing for Detroit.

BJ, the oldest US-Chinese JV, also appeared the most effective. No other automotive JV in China was designing its own vehicles. The Chinese JV had developed a highly competitive design with a skeletal engineering staff to provide the first Chinese-designed vehicle. BJ requested the licensing of some newer, more-advanced technology to make the Heroic truly world class. Chrysler's engineers vowed to support BJ's request upon their return to the US. However, circumstances prevented the US engineers from fulfilling their promises. Not much later, Daimler engineered its takeover of Chrysler and problems of meshing the two corporate operations engulfed everyone. Chrysler lost BJ's request to license new technology.

BJ never received any additional feedback from Chrysler or, later, from Daimler-Chrysler on the Heroic. Soon after the new millennium, Daimler-Chrysler's hot new Jeep Liberty hit the market, to rave reviews. A little while later, Daimler-Chrysler's US unit, Chrysler, started to turn around; and, now, Daimler-Chrysler's engineers have rediscovered the BJ-2 (Heroic) project. Foreign engineers have started to see the same potential and express the same interest in Chinese design that Chrysler's engineers had several years earlier.

The Heroic never made it to market, but had progeny. The Jeep Liberty, though a success in the US market, generated one complaint: it had substantially greater ground clearance than the Grand Cherokee and, with its narrower profile, rolled over on US highways. However, the higher ground clearance made the Liberty a great off-road performer. The greater ground clearance also would have made it an appropriate vehicle for the poorer road conditions generally found in developing economies — the conditions that the Chinese engineers saw for the Heroic. The Heroic obviously influenced the Liberty.

chapter 4

endnotes

1. *China Business Review*, "Amcham survey highlights issues for US business in China".
2. Shao, Z., "New Practice to Better Protect Investors".
3. Lubman, S. P., *Bird in a Cage: Legal Reform in China after Mao.*
4. Carver, A., "Open and Secret Regulations in China and their Implications for Foreign Investment."
5. Wang K. H., *Chinese Commercial Law.*
6. Quote taken from Chang, .K-c, *Shang Civilization*, p.158.
7. Maine, H., *Ancient Law.*
8. Liu Y., *Origins of Chinese Law: Penal and Administrative Law in its Early Development.*
9. Ibid.
10. Wang, op.cit.
11. Ibid.
12. Ibid and authors' interviews with Yan Lan and Austin C. T. Hu.
13. Wang, op.cit.
14. Compiled from material in Wang, op.cit.
15. Taken from panel discussion at the Joint Wharton-Singapore Management University Conference, Singapore, 2002.
16. Ibid.
17. Haley, U. C. V., "Here There be Dragons: Opportunities and Risks for Foreign Multinational Corporations in China".
18. Ibid.
19. Ibid.
20. Nicholas, K., "High Prices Encourage Software Piracy".
21. China Business Information Network, Business Daily Update — China, September 11.
22. Haley, op.cit.
23. Kenneth DeWoskin in panel discussion at the Joint Wharton-Singapore Management University Conference, Singapore, 2002.
24. See Lubman, op.cit., and Liu, op.cit., for a more complete discussion of pre-Communist China's legal traditions and their effects on modern-day China.
25. Wang, op.cit.
26. Einhorn, B, "Learning to Play Fair in China".

27. Wang, op.cit.
28. Ibid.
29. Ibid.
30. Taken from authors' interview with Lu Qun of Beijing Jeep. Photos taken from Beijing Jeep and Daimler-Chrysler promotional materials.

5

THE ROOTS OF THE NETWORKS

"The way begets one;
one begets two;
two begets three;
three begets the myriad creatures."
Tao Te Ching
Book 2, Chapter 42, Stanza 93

INTRODUCTION

The opening quote from the *Tao* indicates the traditional power of the networks in China, a concept that many foreign companies recognize. China is the second-largest recipient of FDI after the USA, with contracted FDI rising about 15% year-on-year to US$53.5 billion in 2003.[1] Indeed, when China opened its markets to foreign companies, many saw JVs with local partners not just as a regulatory requirement, but also as a short cut to garnering the support of influential networks in China. For most foreign companies, this strategy yielded bitter results.

Foreign companies have invested through three types of enterprises:

- Sino-foreign equity joint ventures (EquityJVs); limited-liability corporations, incorporated in China, with both foreign and Chinese investors holding equity and operating the enterprises
- Sino-foreign cooperative joint ventures (CoopJVs); limited-liability corporations or business partnerships registered in China and with foreign-capital contributions. Unlike in EquityJVs, labor resources and management services form part of the partners' contributions but partners need not assign monetary values to these. Contracts, not proportions of investments, delineate divisions of profits, risks and assets between partners
- Wholly foreign-owned enterprises (WFOEs); limited-liability corporations wholly-owned and operated by foreign investors who receive all profits and bear all risks. WFOEs must meet more stringent investment requirements, including introducing advanced technology, providing technical or managerial training or promoting exports.

As Figure 5.1 shows, EquityJVs were the dominant mode of FDI until 1998, but have steadily lost their appeal. WFOEs, on the other hand, have gained popularity and since 1999 have become the preferred mode of FDI. No short cuts exist to acquiring networks.

FIGURE 5.1: UTILIZED FDI IN CHINA BY ENTERPRISE TYPE[2]

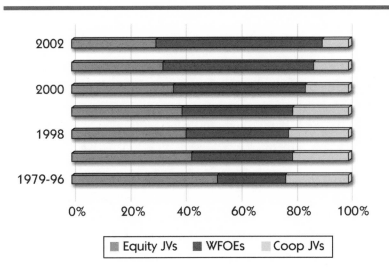

This chapter explores the power and limitations of networks in Chinese business. First, we indicate the economic circumstances that spawned and maintain Chinese networks. Next, we describe some general characteristics of Chinese networks and distinguish them from other Asian networks. We also differentiate the Overseas Chinese networks from those in the PRC. Finally, we discuss the boundaries that limit the networks' strategic influences.

ECONOMIC ROOTS OF THE NETWORKS

Outside of the family, networks probably form the most pervasive form of organization in human society. Historically, some networks sought to dominate or to replace others for political supremacy. Our survey of China's history revealed that though the mandarins and emperors sought to persecute China's merchants and their networks, the central and provincial governments maintained rule and order through their own webs of bureaucratic, military and political networks. Networks in China continue to have both an economic and cultural imperative.

HISTORY'S MOST PERVASIVE MANAGEMENT STRUCTURE: A PAN-CULTURAL LOOK AT NETWORKS[3]

Networks have existed throughout history and in all societies. We present here some past and present-day networks,

❖ **The Greek *phylae* and *phratry***: In antiquity, Greek society consisted of *phylae* — familial clan groups, and their component parts — and *phratry* — groups of allied clans. In 508-507 BC, as the population of Athens grew, the city state expanded and reorganized its four original *phylae* to 10.

❖ **The Roman *clientela***: A vast *clientela* ruled the West's most centrally controlled ancient empire, Rome. In the *clientela* system, clients allied themselves to patrons in pyramids of patronage with influential senatorial families at their apex. The clients pledged their support for their patrons' political and military ambitions, in return for favors. At the height of the Roman Empire, these networks extended throughout Europe, Asia Minor and North Africa.

❖ **The Islamic clans**: Early Arabian Islamic empires with capitals in Damascus, Baghdad and Cordoba, consisted of clan-based networks. The clans owed loyalty to increasingly fewer and more influential clans and individuals, culminating with the royal families and the *caliphs*.

❖ **The feudal system**: Europe's feudal system operated through mutual pledges between powerful families from the nobility. The nobility pledged to maintain the peace locally, to forward tax collections and to provide troops to the ruling family. The ruling family, in turn, recognized the titles, rights and prerogatives of the nobility who had pledged their loyalty. This system maintained and enhanced European civilization through difficult periods when uncertainty and danger threatened. For instance, it prevented the total collapse of European society and its replacement by more cohesive and unified competitors, such as Islam.

❖ **The Overseas Chinese networks:** Immigrants from China in the late 19th and early 20th centuries control substantial portions of the Southeast Asian economies. These Overseas Chinese demonstrate a distinct style of business relying on speed in strategic decision-making, *guanxi* and insider knowledge of their industries and markets.[3] Their business systems consist of networks deriving from clan, dialect, locality, guild and, most importantly, trust.

❖ **The Overseas Indian networks**: The Overseas Indian networks form a growing force in Southeast Asia and elsewhere. They show many of the same managerial traits as the Overseas Chinese, with a slightly greater tendency to depend on family members and friends as the source of their network partners. Indian networks also tend to have less-diversified investments than the Overseas Chinese.

❖ **The Hispanic *grupos***: The Hispanic *grupos* are competent and fierce competitors. They develop through family and friendship ties. The *grupo* usually centers on a major enterprise. Growth appears diversified, but generally follows backward or forward expansion up or down value chains. Once the *grupo* builds two or more companies of substantial size, the companies may spin off. The famous Monterrey Group of companies in Mexico represents such a pattern among its component *grupos*.

❖ **"The old school tie"**: School-tie networks have played a tremendous role in the economic and business development in the UK and the USA. There, the premier universities have always offered more than just good education. The universities offered meeting grounds for the young elites to build bonds of friendship and trust with peers, to receive education and training, and to build mutuality of interests that advance the nation's economy without endangering the class-based *status quo*.

❖ **Japanese inter- and intra-firm networks**: The well-known Japanese *keiretsu* are inter-firm networks. Many major Japanese companies also facilitate class-based networks within their managerial groups ("class-based" here refers to the year of hiring rather than social status). At lower levels of corporate hierarchies, companies consolidate the networks by simultaneously promoting entire classes and providing individuals with substantial incentives to cooperate.

❖ **The Korean *chaebol***: The *chaebol*, family controlled giant corporate conglomerates, and their networks continue to dominate the Korean economy despite restructuring efforts. The Korean *chaebol* epitomize trust-based relationships. Unlike the *keiretsu* or *grupos*, the *chaebol*'s heads almost never hold legal positions within the *chaebol* or their component companies.

❖ **Criminal networks**: Criminal networks based on ethnic or linguistic groups, or other factors, exist in all societies and countries. They have irretrievably negative effects and represent a substantial tax on legitimate businesses.

❖ **Secret societies**: Secret societies are networks that exist in all societies and countries. The Masonic Order (generally Protestant) and Opus Dei (Roman Catholic) are two particularly influential secret societies in Western countries. Many have claimed that the USA originated in Masonic meetings where the founding fathers formulated plans, and expounded upon the philosophy of governance on which they later built the nation. Many have also accused the Opus Dei of engineering the overthrow of the Marxist President Allende regime in Chile in 1973, and replacing it with General Pinochet's regime.

Earlier, we outlined the argument that China has a relation-based rather than a rule-based system of governance. Both rule-based and relation-based systems incur expenses. Both encounter fixed costs to keep the systems running, such as training and paying judges, regulators and auditors; and incremental costs such as the effort and expense of signing additional contracts, and sealing additional transactions. The Mandarin term *guanxi*, loosely translated to mean "trust", "connections" or "relationships", often describes the system of relationships that evolves into Chinese networks.

Li Shuhe and Li Shaomin have provided an economic rationale for the continuance of networks in China.[4] Developed Western, economies have rule-based systems that incur enormous fixed, but negligible incremental costs. The fixed costs cover a huge number of transactions and business relationships and reduce the average costs of single deals. By contrast, developing Asian countries, including China, cannot afford the high fixed costs of such a system and have therefore accepted the large incremental costs of a relation-based, or network system.

The Chinese network system derives from relationships rather than rules. Business transactions emerge from personal agreements, not contracts. Companies and individuals engage in purely private transactions that they cannot enforce in the public sphere. To avoid deception, parties to transactions check each other's backgrounds, status and assets thoroughly. Governance becomes a heavy-handed tit-for-tat affair: if someone cheats you, you know how to seize his assets, blackmail him or even kidnap him.

Rule-based systems need high and costly levels of public order. Relation-based systems need only minimum public order. Yet, finding, screening and monitoring potential partners contribute to very high marginal costs. Consequently, participants cannot delegate relationships, but have to manage them personally. Given the high marginal costs of cultivating new relationships, individuals do business first with close family;

then neighbors from their home towns; then former classmates; and finally, reluctantly, with strangers.

According to Li Shuhe and Li Shaomin, as long as the numbers of transactions and business relationships remained comparatively small, the Chinese network system could bear the average costs of transactions.[5] But as the economy grows and continues to become more complex, the average cost of doing business exceeds that in rule-based systems. As outsiders see new rules that protect investment, insiders see a state of flux created by changing relations among market participants. Outsiders see opportunities to invest and insiders to loot. This may explain why so many JVs fail.

Goh Hup Jin, chairman of Nipsea Holdings and son of the founder of the Wuthelam Group, provided some support for the economic rationale behind networks. As he told us:

> "There is a reason why the so-called *guanxi* or relationship begins in many business dealings. In a lot of cases, it is not because I like your face or because your sister is my brother's wife; sometimes it is like that, but not usually. If I have a choice of dealing with any one of 10 people, and I know one, I will choose the one I know, assuming I like what I know about him. At least I know something about his background — he didn't steal, he didn't kill anyone, and so on. Somehow, you feel there is less of a communication gap. That's where *guanxi* starts and it's not wrong at all... In fact the so-called professional management depends exactly on the same thing. You don't do a deal with somebody you don't know. But many times, people start a relationship and it progresses very fast because he came from Citibank — he should be OK because he is a Citibank banker and Citibank has a reputation. So if you are from Citibank, I place you in a certain category. I know that you belong to a certain background; I know how to deal with you; I don't have to know your brother and sister; and so on."

Instead of promoting reforms that expand social networks for an open and inclusive society, recent periods of modernization have invigorated economic networks of a different sort. China's reforms from 1978 boosted *guanxi* centered on local governments, while contributing to nationwide networks of corruption linked to a lack of political modernization. Sometimes, networks have battled for dominance in modern China, as Amway's history reveals.

THE BATTLE OF THE NETWORKS: AMWAY IN CHINA[6]

The Chinese travails of Amway, the US multi-level marketing (MLM) and direct-sales giant provide some insights into network rivalry and economic competition. Despite its reassurances to ease restrictions on services after its WTO entry, the Chinese government has continuously obstructed companies that use direct sales to customers, rather than retail outlets. One Western manager suggested that this attitude reflects the Chinese government's fears of large-scale, uncontrollable, nationwide organizations that could burgeon into competing networks.

Amway has always followed a straightforward business model. Its massive manufacturing facility in Ada, Michigan, churns out 400 products that its direct-sales network sells in more than 80 countries. But in the early 1980s, the Chinese government clearly communicated that Amway had to change its business model for China. In order to sell in China, Amway had to manufacture in China. In 1992, despite huge capacities in the US, Amway (China) began construction of a $100-million manufacturing plant in the Guangzhou Economic Technological Development Zone (GZETDZ) — its only manufacturing facility outside the US and Korea. In 2002, seven years after beginning operations, Amway's Chinese plant provided less than 40% of its product line. The company also had to import and to pay duty on more than 65% of its raw materials.

Despite these setbacks, by 1997 Amway's annual China sales had reached US$181 million. Then, in April 1998, Beijing dealt a crushing blow to Amway's huge investment. Worried about the proliferation of pyramid-selling schemes, the State Council banned all forms of direct selling. Amway's sales plummeted 80% year on year in 1998 to US$36 million and its full-time workforce fell from 1,800 to 900. After revamping its manufacturing strategy to enter China, Amway had to overhaul its trademark sales strategy as well. In July 1998, the company reached a compromise whereby it could continue direct sales if it established a nationwide network of retail outlets. It invested about US$5 million to open 58 retail outlets. Each of the company's 130,000 direct sellers registered with specific outlets, whose territorial limits they had to respect. Amway operates such a retail network nowhere else.

Amway adjusted and its sales rebounded to US$290 million in 2000 and about US$480 million in 2001. But, on 1st April, 2002, the government outlawed the system of multi-layer commissions that the company uses around the world. Only individuals making sales could collect commissions, further altering Amway's traditional business model. In every other country, Amway markets products through agents who receive commissions for their own sales and sales made by others they have introduced and trained. The money that other companies spend on shops, marketing and advertising, Amway spends on its staff. But agents in China can no longer hold training meetings; only Amway can organize meetings and must inform government authorities in advance. The new government rules specifically emphasize that Amway, and other companies engaging in direct sales, cannot organize their direct-sales force into networks under the names of divisions, teams or groups. The companies also cannot challenge other established networks by hiring civil servants, active service men and women, full-time students and others.

Amway is currently considering how to attract, reward and retain senior managers in its network. The company emphasizes its legitimacy by indicating that it has paid US$278 million in taxes, has made US$4 million-worth of charitable contributions, and that 13% of its direct-sales force had no previous employment. In August

2002, Amway sponsored 57 senior Chinese provincial and city officials for a month's study of ethics and business at Harvard University's Kennedy School of Government. The battle of the networks continues.

WHAT IS A CHINESE NETWORK?

Xiaotong Fei identified five distinctive general characteristics of Chinese networks.[7] The networks:

- are discontinuous.
- have hierarchical and dyadic ties.
- emphasize uprightness.
- view morality as contextual.
- have flexible boundaries that change with circumstances.

▲ Discontinuity

Edward Zeng, CEO of Sparkice, most eloquently sketched for us the traditional family, government and modern business networks that successful managers in China have to navigate. "To be truly successful today," he said, "you must be able to build and call on all three networks."

Traditional Chinese family networks have the bases of clan, dialect, location and guild.[8] The Communist regime tried to destroy traditional, property-based networks after it came to power in 1949. But, since the central government relaxed its grip on rural economies, traditional networks based on kinship are returning, especially in southern provinces such as Guangdong, Jiangxi and Hunan. Without property, the traditional networks act as chambers of commerce, sharing among their members vital information and *guanxi* to facilitate deals and to help business. The government networks emanate from membership in the CCP as well as key posts that members occupy. The CCP is the most powerful force in China today and its tentacles reach everywhere. All government departments, state-run factories and enterprises, including JVs with foreign partners, have party committees. In 2002, the CCP's leadership, under President Jiang, invited entrepreneurs to join the Party. This invitation highlights both the CCP's flexibility and its determination to retain control of society. Business networks can draw on clan and guild membership, as well as networking through formal venues such as the World Economic Forum, but trust forms the cement that binds them.

Chinese businesspeople participate in more than one network and membership in one does not guarantee membership in another.[9] For example, influential members of traditional clan-based and locality-based networks may fail to gain membership to crucial, government-based networks in strategic industries, thereby hampering the members' effectiveness. Individuals enjoy unique duties, responsibilities and authorities within networks and across networks, empowering them differently on behalf of their businesses or associates. In business or government networks, individuals with similar titles may exercise drastically different levels of authority and responsibility — and their stature may vary across networks, affecting their overall power.

Consequently, when doing business in China, foreign companies seeking partners can choose from several different networks — though they must do so with care. Allies in particular networks may oppose projects or business partners in other networks, as well as incur opposition in third networks as interests clash. Generally, though, Chinese businesspeople try to sidestep enemies or opposition and work to create support for their projects and interests through providing benefits rather than friction. Indeed, as Pan Shi Yi said when discussing the property development industry, "It is necessary to know the appropriate government representatives, to discover their hopes and aspirations for a particular property, and know how to provide them with their desires in a profitable manner."

DISCONTINUOUS NETWORKS: YAHOO CHINA[10]

Yahoo launched its Chinese website from Beijing and Shanghai in 1999 as a JV with Founder, a Chinese software firm. On 31st August, 2002, the Chinese government blocked access to popular search engines Google and AltaVista for a few weeks, but spared Internet portal Yahoo. Before major public events, such as the CCP Congress, the Beijing government routinely blocks Internet portals and chat rooms that it considers independent. Yahoo has escaped scrutiny by voluntarily agreeing to purge its Chinese website of subjects that the Beijing government considers taboo. The agreement, called the "Public Pledge on Self-Discipline for the Chinese Internet Industry", requires Yahoo to remove sensitive material about dissident groups and human-rights organizations, among others. Yahoo is the only US company to have signed this agreement. Google and Altavista have continued to provide links to millions of websites, including some that the Chinese government considers politically sensitive.

In 2002, Yahoo released a statement reiterating that "Yahoo China along with 140 media outlets in China has signed voluntary trade industry guidelines which govern the Internet space in China. Yahoo China is committed to adhering to all local laws and customs in the 23 countries in which we conduct business." Yahoo's website in China carries no critical mention of the CCP and does not offer working links to information on banned religious groups such as the Falun Gong.

Because it has voluntarily accepted constraints that the Beijing government considers appropriate, Yahoo has suffered very few problems in China. Although it has cultivated *guanxi* with Chinese government networks, it has encountered criticism and disdain for its actions among human-rights and free-press advocates, such as the Electronic Frontier Foundation. These critics have acknowledged that Yahoo was in a sticky situation in China, as were so many others in the media. Yet, they argue, Yahoo could have waited till the Chinese government instructed it to remove material, thereby acting on general principles concerning free media, rather than taking a path that smacks of opportunism and a lack of principles.

▲ Hierarchical and dyadic ties

Even today, despite Communist rule, relationships within Chinese networks approximate the dyadic and directional relations that existed within Confucian families, wherein the relationships are defined by their senior members. Individuals of higher status within the dyads have the upper hand within relationships. Respect within networks derives from the individuals's abilities to move seamlessly between the different dominant and subordinate roles, and between the different networks. Success in business dealings then stems from individuals' relative positions in key business and social activities, and on their choosing networks that provide effective support in business situations. The positions occupied by individuals within networks and the types of networks in which they operate, affect expectations of duties, responsibilities and behavior.

Positions in networks can vary according to recent performance, especially among younger, untried members, as well as changes within government factions (government positioning) and government policy. The Mandarin term, *li*, loosely translated to incorporate respect for age, hierarchy and authority, shapes bureaucracies and networks. For example, older members generally retain rank and prestige through age and seniority, unless significant changes in government positioning and policy destabilize them.

Foreign managers doing business in China should garner as much information as possible on the individuals they deal with. They should also give special consideration to how changes in government positioning and policy will affect the networks to which those individuals belong and to their effectiveness. Foreign managers should remember that older members of Chinese government and business organizations often enjoy significantly greater power and influence than their official titles may indicate.

▲ Uprightness

As we identified in Chapter 3, uprightness involves the ability and willingness to behave appropriately, in accordance with expectations. Trust develops in the West when people gain a reputation for keeping their word. In traditional Chinese society, trust has two elements: the first, as in the West, includes keeping one's word; the second includes uprightness. Uprightness is an important behavioral ideal; without it, complete trust in the Chinese sense cannot exist.

Uprightness has suffered in those Chinese societies that frequently interact and do business with Westerners: the Chinese recognize that Westerners do not understand the subtleties of Chinese behavior and modify their expectations. However, in large swathes of China (for example, the West, North and far Northeast) and parts of Asia with Overseas Chinese populations (for example, Cambodia, Laos, Myanmar, parts of Indonesia, and Vietnam) people rarely interact with Westerners, and may still expect traditional uprightness in business situations. Western managers, unfamiliar with uprightness but acting in good faith, may see business relationships disintegrate despite sincere efforts. Good intermediaries may aid in preserving upright behavior until the Western managers have gained appropriate experience, goodwill and a local reputation. Because of the emphasis on personal relationships, however, any local reputation will probably not extend beyond the Western manager's tenure in Asia when dealing with more traditional Chinese businesspeople.

▲ Contextual morality

As outlined in Chapter 3, contextual morality does not synchronize with Western concepts of situational ethics, which imply flexible ethical standards. Chinese ethical and moral standards are generally inflexible, but can vary according to the context. For example, ethical standards in business vary with business relationships: longer, better-established relationships with equals or superiors entail higher standards than shorter, fleeting relationships with inferiors.

Western companies should also remember the personal nature of relationships among the Chinese. Western companies tend to rotate managers through Asian subsidiaries and offices. However, incoming managers do not automatically inherit the goodwill and strong relationships of their predecessors; nor do they necessarily inherit their opponents. As Goh Hup Jin, chairman of Nipsea Holdings, indicated, managers of major companies such as IBM, Citibank or Nokia may benefit from company-generated halo effects. Yet, most companies have comparable competitors: IBM has Dell, Citibank has HSBC, Nokia has Motorola, and even Coke has Pepsi. In Chinese societies, generally it is individuals, not organizations or companies, who own the franchises of trust and uprightness.

▲ Flexible boundaries

The boundaries of Chinese networks are flexible and vary with circumstances much more than do Western networks. They exhibit very personal, though relatively low-strength, ties of loyalty. Among the Chinese, individuals' personal networks expand and contract with their relative successes just as Westerners' personal contacts do; however, in China individuals' networks for business projects also vary with partners, locality and the nature of the projects. A plethora of circumstantial factors affect the precise make-up of any individual's business network in any one instance or point in time.

The worst mistakes made by Western companies in China involve the choice of wrong, untrustworthy partners. In the PRC, such wrong partners may include government-linked companies (GLCs) or SOEs, both of which can exhibit great variation in management quality. At the high end, the Chinese home-appliance manufacturer Haier, though a GLC, appears indistinguishable from a private company on most management issues. It strives for high quality, bases its decisions on market trends and projected profitability, and has entered Western markets with its products. However, some of the problems that can occur when companies choose partners poorly are illustrated by Pepsi's experiences, outlined below.

THE NOOSE OF NETWORKING: PEPSI IN CHINA[11]

Pepsi started its Sichuan JV in 1994, when the Chinese government provided partners for projects. Pepsi teamed up with an unlikely partner, the Sichuan Administration of Radio, Film and Television Department (SARFTD), and ploughed US$20 million into the venture. Pepsi's investment included advertising expenditures as well as interest-free loans and free equipment. Alleging that its Chinese partner breached the contract in numerous ways, in 2002 Pepsi took the dispute before an international arbitration panel in Stockholm, Sweden, seeking to terminate the contract and be reimbursed for its investment.

The alleged breaches of contract include the JV's failure to provide standard financial disclosure and to allow PepsiCo's accountants to conduct internal audits. The Chinese government also transferred the ownership of the JV from SARFTD to a new company, Sichuan Yunlu, without Pepsi's prior permission. Pepsi alleges that the JV skimmed money through inflated advertising fees for promotional campaigns. The local management secured low-cost home loans and Mercedes cars from the JV without the board's approval. The JV allegedly breached Pepsi's intellectual copyrights by passing patented designs to non-approved plastic-bottle suppliers. The JV's management also pushed to produce locally formulated drinks at the plant without Pepsi's approval.

Sichuan Pepsi's vice-president, Qu Zhidi, reacted angrily to Pepsi's charges, claiming that Pepsi sabotaged the JV by unilaterally raising the price of soft drinks. He said the contract specifically allowed for proposals to develop local-drink formulas. He has stated that the JV had no financial problems, that PepsiCo's auditors behaved unprofessionally, and that the Chinese government had noted no problems.

To avoid taking disputes with local governments to local courts, international arbitration — usually in neutral Stockholm — has become a standard clause in foreign JV contracts. But, even if foreign companies obtain favorable judgments in six to 12 months, their enforcement is generally given extremely low priority by local judicial agencies. Meanwhile, the Chinese partners can apply government pressure through their networks. For example, PepsiCo has noted that the State Administration of Taxation, Customs and other government departments have started making regular visits to PepsiCo's other Chinese JVs and have termed these operations as suspicious.

The Sichuan JV comprises one of 14 in China to bottle Pepsi, and one of 40 JVs between the US beverage giant and Chinese partners. Pepsi has invested US$500 million in China over the last 20 years and has yet to make a profit. The company has optimistically indicated that it hopes to break even in China over the next few years.

DISTINGUISHING CULTURAL TRAITS OF ASIAN NETWORKS

Researchers have firmly established the influences of culture and personality — and combinations of the two — on strategic decision-making.[12] Table 5.1 summarizes some significant cultural differences between the Chinese, Indians and Japanese that influence the concepts of loyalty, decision-making, expectations, ethics and the bases for commercial trust in business dealings.

TABLE 5.1[13]: CULTURAL CHARACTERISTICS OF THE CHINESE, INDIANS AND JAPANESE

Attributes	Chinese	Indian	Japanese
Company-related			
Merchants	Reviled	Specialized	Exalted
Primogeniture	None	Very strong	Strong
Company Lifespan	Short	Medium	Long
Loyalty-related			
Family Definition	Blood	Blood	Role
Focus	Individual	Group	Institution
Intensity	Low	High	High
Filial Piety vs. Patriotism	Opposed	No relationship	Equivalent
Commercial Trust-related			
Ethical Foundation	5 relationships & social harmony	Dharma	Mutual self-interest
Ethical Focus	The "Way"	Family	Service to father figure
Expectations of Benefits	Immediate & up-front	Immediate & up-front	Long-term & delayed

▲ Company-related attributes

Merchants: Attitudes towards merchants in the Japanese, Chinese and Indian cultures vary greatly. Historically, the Japanese incorporated an economic philosophy of growth that exalts the business and merchant classes. The neo-Taoist Chinese culture exalted the peasantry and reviled merchants; Confucian philosophers frowned upon excessive concern with profits rather than the "Way".[14] Imperial courts also saw merchants as mobile, and thus as unreliable supporters of rulers.

India's Hindu culture encouraged and provided specialized places for their merchant classes. The Vaisya or Jain merchant castes conducted business within the broad Hindu system. Other merchant classes originated from small, highly-prosperous, niche, non-Hindu communities, such as the Parsis, which local rulers, Hindu and Muslim, protected and encouraged.[15]

Primogeniture and company lifespan: Attitudes to primogeniture, with its emphasis on a single heir — traditionally, the eldest son — are different in Chinese, Japanese and Indian cultures. The neo-Taoist culture emphasizes large families and bans primogeniture; hence, the ancient Chinese saying "No fortune survives the third generation". Japanese culture promotes primogeniture; however, the son regarded as the most competent, not necessarily the oldest, becomes the heir. Japanese companies have thus concentrated and continued wealth over long periods of time. Large Japanese companies such as Mitsubishi have survived in some form for centuries. Some of Japan's major companies began hundreds of years ago as family companies that eventually evolved into the Japanese *keiretsu* conglomerates.

In India, primogeniture was culturally endorsed to an even greater degree than in Japan. Many large Indian companies have evolved from traditional, small, family businesses into third- or fourth-generation family-controlled conglomerates.[16] However, oldest sons often succeed their fathers as heads of family companies regardless of competence or aptitude, thereby debilitating top-management cadres and increasing the need for professionalization. Consequently, just as for family-owned companies in the West, succession forms a major concern for Indian companies.[17] In this fashion, primogeniture in the three cultures has had a great influence on company lifespans.

▲ Loyalty-related attributes

Family, focus and intensity: Highly intense loyalty exists in Japan, but even within the family it has functional bases: family members owe filial loyalty to the breadwinners, not to the actual fathers. Conversely, in both China and India, family members owe filial loyalty to the fathers, regardless of the bread-winners; members of these two network-based cultures share highly personalized, as opposed to functional, bases for loyalty. In India, within extended families and their businesses, some groups may command individual loyalties. However, historically, in China, loyalties accrued only to individuals; members rarely transferred loyalties to friends or employers and hence employees' loyalties rarely survived individual managers. More recently, education and other acculturation have modified this characteristic to one more akin to Indian notions of loyalty.

Patriotism: Significant differences in attitudes to patriotism affect the ways in which the networks contribute to their adopted and native countries. A Japanese adage posits that "To be a good patriot is to be a good son". The equivalent Chinese adage argues that "One cannot be both a good patriot and a good son". In Indian cultures, no relationship exists between patriotism and filial piety. Hence, a Japanese company perforce must contribute to the nation to which it belongs; but Chinese and Indian companies may likely limit their contributions to their owners' home communities.

▲ Trust-related attributes

Ethical foundations: Concepts of ethics also differ profoundly between the three cultures, affecting the bases of commercial trust.[18] The Japanese view contractual duties as binding; familial and friendship ties as helpful; but ties of personal and corporate self-interest assume paramount importance. Trust in commercial relationships derives from perceived, mutual self-interest. Hence, Japanese business negotiations include numerous social gatherings in which potential business associates seek out similarities in outlooks, perspectives and values. Without these similarities, the Japanese do not attain trust.

Neo-Taoist ethics spotlights the five relationships. If relationships fall outside these boundaries, then Confucianism and

Taoism require that individuals maintain social harmony. Consequently, unlike Western ethics, Chinese ethics have contextual rather than normative standards. Without familial or established friendship ties, trust rarely exists in Chinese commercial relationships. For instance, applicants for business loans in Chinese societies have found that in certain cases bank officials have had no compunction about passing on this personal information to other, related, companies which, in turn, used this information for their own ends. Yet in such cases, the bank officials have acted in accordance with neo-Taoist ethics![19]

For many Indian communities, *Dharma*, loosely translated from Sanskrit to mean "Natural Law", and incorporating duty, is central. *Dharma* covers duties to families, to business partners and to societies and requires that Indians, especially first-born sons, view succeeding financially as a familial duty.[20] This association with familial duty transforms success into a religious obligation. As virtue brings rewards, success is transformed into religious blessing, and in India, financial rewards from business success are linked with personal virtue. Thus, *Dharma* provides a special intensity to individual endeavor, drive and work ethics.

Ethical focus: The respective ethics of these three broadly defined cultures demonstrate different normative focal points. For the Chinese, individuals should behave in a manner appropriate to their station in life within the framework of the five relationships. Neo-Taoist philosophers referred to these appropriate behaviors collectively as "the Way". For the Japanese, individuals should serve their superiors (their father figures) and, through their superiors, their emperors. But, for Indians, families should provide the central concern: codes of *Dharma* regulate the duties of individuals to their families.

Expectations of benefits: The Indians and Chinese differ from the Japanese in their expectations of benefits from contractual relationships. The Indians and the Chinese generally enter into contractual relationships insisting on at least obtaining specific, minimal benefits and expecting to make immediate profits. The Japanese generally exhibit patience and willingness to postpone benefits as well as to accept low margins to build market share. The Chinese and Indians will invest time, money and effort into a business, but they expect to see tangible benefits up front.[21]

Although familial and friendship ties oil commercial relationships in Indian cultures, most view contractual duties in commercial relationships as ethically binding, as Westerners do.[22] Thus, commercial partners with signed contracts can have some confidence that the Indians will follow contractual terms. However, with the Chinese, signed contracts may often begin, rather than end, negotiations. Significant changes in business situations historically provided justification for renegotiating contracts; consequently, commercial partners should expect periodic quibbling over contractual terms.[23]

DIFFERENTIATING THE OVERSEAS CHINESE NETWORKS

Despite cultural and ethnic similarities, significant differences exist between East and Southeast Asia's Overseas Chinese business networks and business networks from Eastern and Southern China's industrialized areas. Among the Overseas Chinese, especially in Hong Kong and Taiwan, many first-generation entrepreneurs started as merchants and traders. These entrepreneurs left China as factors and representatives of prosperous traders, usually blood relations from their home districts. Other Overseas Chinese, especially those in Southeast Asia, left China in hardship or under indentured contracts to work for Chinese and European traders, plantation owners, and other interests. They worked hard, lived extremely frugally and saved money until they could strike out on their own.[24] Once they had built initial investments, they often moved into property-related businesses, and then into any business deemed profitable.

The founders of Overseas Chinese companies, though highly intelligent, generally had little formal education and even less formal, Western-style, business education. This does not hold true among the PRC's entrepreneurs currently founding and building their commercial empires. Generally, the patriarchs of Overseas Chinese companies resembled generations of Western businesspeople before the founding of business schools. However, their heirs have often attended top local schools and major Western universities. Similarly, many entrepreneurs of the modern-day PRC have received formal higher education, though not always at Western universities.

The Malaysian-Chinese tycoon, Robert Kuok recalled that, "as children we learned about moral values — mainly Confucian".[25] Business education for the founders of many major Overseas Chinese companies began in Confucian village schools. The expansion of their businesses followed the dictates of their education, their culture and their experiences and continued their education in business management and strategy. Their education and culture emphasized the family, and provided the neo-Taoist perspective on social relations as extensions of, yet subordinate to, familial relationships.

Similar influences exist for the PRC's entrepreneurs. Mao's vision of Chinese Communism dominated China for only one generation, from the Communists' assumption of power in 1949 to a little after Mao's death in 1976. Mao's extremely significant achievements in China included replacing the emperors and local warlords with the CCP as the source of political power and influence. Currently, no discernable challenge to the CCP has appeared at the national level, yet increasing challenges have occurred at provincial and municipal levels.

Because of their experiences, the patriarchs of Overseas Chinese companies reinforced their Confucian reliance on families and select networks. The Imperial era created a people fiercely loyal to their families and network partners; and dependent on one another rather than on governing authorities towards whom they harbored suspicion. In modern times, the PRC's government has relied on organizational networks, such as the CCP, to implement strategies such as family planning in the rapidly developing urban areas of the East and Southeast.

The Overseas Chinese also displayed pronounced preferences for maintaining significant proportions of their wealth in liquid, physically dispersed, forms rather than in large, concentrated, fixed investments. Liquid assets afforded convenience when the Overseas Chinese had to flee persecution; physically dispersed investments provided geographical diversity to hedge risks against government seizures of assets and anti-Chinese attacks. Physically dispersed fixed assets also reinforced the use of networks among Overseas Chinese businesses. The Overseas Chinese only trusted close associates. Local on-site managers had to display extensive, independent authority to make decisions in eras when technology limited communications and political circumstances created peril. Increasing diversification and growing physical dispersion of assets, together with sputtering communication, hindered constant surveillance and guidance from family heads. Consequently, purely trust-based relations emerged as a potent force in the networks.

Additionally, most Overseas Chinese protected their wealth through collections of relatively small, independent companies, thereby ensuring that confiscating or destroying single companies would not seriously affect a business's overall financial position. This also enabled the patriarch's heirs to dissolve and to distribute more easily collections of smaller companies than single large companies. Consequently, Overseas Chinese companies have historically failed to achieve the necessary scale or scope to compete internationally; those that did achieve large size often crashed after their founders' deaths. Increasingly, however, Overseas Chinese entrepreneurs are practicing primogeniture so that single sons, usually the eldest, inherit the greater parts of their estates.

As discussed earlier, today's CCP, contravening historical precedence, has adopted a more accepting and conciliatory stance, inviting entrepreneurs to join the Party. These incipient policies, however, may not survive the CCP's present leadership. The present government has also encouraged Chinese companies to grow large enough to challenge foreign companies. To this effect, the government has been forcing companies in strategic, though fragmented, industries, such as automobile manufacturing, to merge and to achieve economies of scale and international competitiveness.

Among the Overseas Chinese, neo-Taoist emphases on personal rather than institutional relations, and historical lack of government support, reinforced business networks. These factors also ensured that, for Overseas Chinese merchants, families and businesses fused. Many Overseas Chinese companies appear to be legal corporations with weak familial control; yet families sustain control through interlocking directorates with their networks' business associates and partners.

Overseas Chinese companies have often displayed extreme diversification. Other business networks in developing countries, such as the Korean *chaebol*, Overseas Indian networks and Latin American *grupos*, similarly display unrelated conglomerate diversification as methods to move external markets towards internal control.[26] Prior to the Great Depression, many American companies also engaged in unrelated diversification.[27] As the next chapter elaborates, the PRC's companies — though much younger than their Overseas Chinese counterparts and with studies based on a smaller, less-representative sample — also appear to engage in unrelated diversification.

Unlike their PRC counterparts, Overseas Chinese networks often viewed themselves as rebels and outsiders. They rebelled against the harsh economic realities at home. Rather than cultural teachings that endorsed husbandry and government service as methods of acquiring wealth, they drew on their own business experiences. Their culture viewed profits with suspicion and their governments advocated accepting their inferior lot in life. Yet the Overseas Chinese rejected cultural arguments and government restrictions and fought for their families' livelihoods through actively pursuing mercantile profits. Their uniquely neo-Taoist rebellion consisted of the groups' refusal to conform, rather than any one individual's. Within their structures, the Overseas Chinese groups continued to maintain the same conservative conformity as traditional Chinese society. The next section highlights the limits of networks for effective strategic management.

THE WORLD CHINESE BUSINESS NETWORK: TRIBAL NETWORK FOR THE INFORMATION AGE[28]

In 1995, the Singapore Chinese Chamber of Commerce and Industry (SCCCI) formally launched on the Internet what it called a new tribal network — The World Chinese Business Network (WCBN). With connections to Chinese chambers of commerce worldwide, the WCBN provides a computer network to link ethnic Chinese executives all over the world and a massive database containing information on businesses run by the Overseas Chinese. The SCCCI said, "The WCBN "is aimed at strengthening the networking of Chinese businessmen throughout the world It is designed to help Chinese businessmen worldwide in establishing contacts and exchanging information with one another in a speedy and systematic manner." The Singaporean Minister for Information and the Arts, Brigadier General (BG) George Yeo, predicted that "a lot of business will be done over these networks".

WCBN, a brainchild of Senior Minister Lee Kuan Yew, is the first on-line link among Chinese traders world wide. In 1993, at the Second World Chinese Entrepreneurs Convention, Senior Minister Lee proposed that the networking of the Overseas Chinese be made efficient by providing relevant data on the Internet. With the technical assistance of the Institute of Systems Science and Netcenter (Singapore) and a financial grant of S100,000 from Singapore's National Science and Technology Board, the SCCCI then undertook the S$500,000 project. The WCBN provides detailed corporate information on over 15,000 Overseas Chinese companies from over 15 countries, covering subsidiaries, products, marketing and distribution operations. Managers can access information in both English and Chinese by punching in key words. However, BG Yeo pointed out that such business networks could only provide "public domains" for the transfer of information: companies would have to move into the "private domain" to strike deals. "In the corporate world, those who can make more money are those who have more information than others. We all know that while some information can be made freely available, some must be kept confidential," he said.

In September 2001, in an effort to enrich the WCBN's content, the SCCCI entered into a strategic partnership with Alibaba.com to provide worldwide trade links to the WCBN. Hong Kong-run Alibaba.com provides the WCBN with up to 3,000 news updates on more than 200 countries. Access to the WCBN is free of charge on www.cbn.com.sg.

THE LIMITS OF NETWORKS

Business relationships that involve politics are invariably volatile and government networks may experience fluctuations that mar their effectiveness — as our earlier example involving Beijing Jeep Corporation clearly demonstrates.

BJ is the first joint venture between a Chinese and a US company. Its survival today may depend on the success of the Jeep Grand Cherokee, a luxury sports utility vehicle (SUV) that first rolled off the production lines in October 2001.[29] Flat sales in recent years are hurtling BJ towards bankruptcy.

BJ continues to demonstrate its capabilities: no other Chinese automaker can build luxury SUVs such as the Grand Cherokee; nor design vehicles such as the Heroic, which we highlighted earlier. Hu Hu, a company sales manager, confirmed that the Grand Cherokee is selling well. By early 2002, BJ had sold over 500 Grand Cherokees, with individuals accounting for 45% of sales. The SUV should be priced at 700,000 yuan (US$84,643) but actually sells for 520,000 yuan (US$62,878) because of price competition.The Grand Cherokee's low price may not garner BJ a profit.[30]

BJ failed to reach its sales goal of 12,000 units in 2001. The company sold 3,111 automobiles from January to August that year, about 25% fewer than it sold in the same period in 2000.

The JV's production in 2001 was between 4,000 and 5,000 units and it captured only 0.64% of the market. By contrast, in 1995, the JV produced more than 80,000 units, garnering 5.75 billion yuan (US$695.28 million) in sales, 350 million yuan (US$42.32 million) in profits, and 605,000 yuan (US$73,155.99) in output per worker.

Yet BJ has *guanxi*. In December 2001, the company was visited by Beijing's mayor and vice-mayor, the Municipal Government Secretary General, the Municipal Development Planning Commission Director and the Municipal Economic and Trade Commission Director. During the visit, the mayor assured the company that the municipal government would continue to support firmly the JV's development. This support, however, appears to be insufficient.

BJ's biggest problem appears to be a lack of funding. The company signed a memorandum of understanding regarding corporate restructuring at a special board meeting in August/ September 2000. According to the memorandum, Chinese and foreign shareholders agreed to inject US$226 million into the automaker to produce new products. Not all of this money materialized. Daimler-Chrysler contributed its share of the funds, but the huge outlay proved an embarrassment for the controlling shareholder, Beijing Automotive Industry Group and the Beijing municipal government, both of which have other commitments, including investments in the forthcoming Olympics. The lack of funding hurt the Grand Cherokee's roll-out as BJ could not spend enough on advertising and marketing.

As advocated earlier, having more than one carefully chosen government network can improve a company's chances of sustained success. A Chinese adage best describes this approach: "A cunning rabbit keeps three grottoes" — that is, choose wisely, choose networks that do not clash, and choose networks with different interests. In the next section, we will discuss the diverse strategic-planning environments, procedures and tools that have evolved in Asia and the West, together with their relative competitive strengths and weaknesses.

endnotes

1. MOFTEC, People's Republic of China.

2. *China Business Review* (2000), Data for 2001 are from January–November; Data for 2002 are from January–July.

3. Haley, G. T., C. T. Tan and U. C. V. Haley, *New Asian Emperors: The Overseas Chinese, their Strategies and Competitive Advantages,* and several others.

4. *The Economist*, "Tangled Web," and "The Greatest Leap Forward."

5. Ibid.

6. *South China Morning Post*, "Fresh Curbs on Direct Selling Might Carry Political Slant", and "Amway Learns Key Lessons on Direct-Sales Obstacle Course"; *China Online*, "China — Ban on Cross-Regional Direct Marketing Explained".

7. Fei, X., *From the Soil: The Foundation of Chinese Society.*

8. Haley et al, op.cit.

9. Ibid.

10. Kopytoff, V., "Search Engines in China Face Balancing Act".

11. *Asian Wall Street Journal*, "China Attracts more Investments from Foreigners"; *World Markets*, "China: Pepsico Troubles Highlight Worst-Case Scenario for Joint-Venture Enterprises"; *Wall Street Journal*, "Soda and Suckers in China".

12. Haley, U. C. V., "The Myers-Briggs Type Indicator and Decision-Making Styles: Identifying and Managing Cognitive Trails in Strategic Decision Making"; Haley, U. C. V., and S. A. Stumpf, "Cognitive Trails in Strategic Decision-Making: Linking Theories of Personalities and Cognitions"; Hofstede, G., "Cultural Constraints in Management Theories".

13. Ibid.

14. Lau, D. C., *Mencius Says*; Lau, D. C., *Confucius: The Analects*; Haley, G. T., and C. T. Tan, "East versus West: Strategic Marketing Management Meets the Asian Networks"; Haley et al, op.cit.

15. Haley, G. T., and U. C. V. Haley, "Boxing with Shadows: Competing Effectively with the Overseas Chinese and Overseas Indian Networks in the Asian Arena."

16. *Business Today*, "India's Business Families: Can they Survive?"

119

THE ROOTS OF THE NETWORKS

17. Gidoomal, R., and D. Porter, *The UK Maharajahs: Inside the South Asian Success Story*.
18. Haley and Haley, op.cit.; Haley et al, op.cit.
19. Haley et al, op.cit.
20. Haley and Haley, op.cit.
21. Haley et al, op.cit., p.21.
22. Haley and Haley, op.cit.
23. Haley et al, op.cit.
24. Chan, K. B. and C. Chiang, *Stepping Out, The Making of Chinese Entrepreneurs*.
25. Haley et al, op.cit, p.29.
26. Haley and Haley, "op.cit.
27. Heilbroner, R. L., and A. Singer, *The Economic Transformation of America: 1600 to the Present*, 2nd edition.
28. Haley et al, op.cit.; *Straits Times* (of Singapore), "Singapore Portal gets World Links".
29. *Zhonghua Gongshang Shibao* (2002).
30. *China Online* (2002a), "China — Grand Cherokee could be Beijing Jeep's Last Great Hope".

Part III

EASTERN VS. WESTERN STRATEGIC PLANNING

6

THE COMPONENTS OF CHINESE STRATEGY

"A man is supple and weak when living,
but hard and stiff when dead.
Grass and trees are pliant and fragile when living,
but dried and shriveled when dead.
Thus the hard and the strong
are the comrades of death;
the supple and the weak
are the comrades of life."

Tao Te Ching

Book 2, Chapter 76, Stanza 182

INTRODUCTION

Golf provides some insights into behavior and Li Ka-shing is an avid golfer. Indeed, his days begin with the game which he sees as crystallizing some aspects of management:

> "At six something [in the morning] I play golf... for an hour and a half. This period of time belongs to me alone. It takes a cool head to do business, as does playing golf. Even if you've teed off badly, as long as you keep your composure, stick to your plan, you may not lose the hole. Like living and doing business, there are ups and down. In adversity, you need to concentrate on dealing with problems."

His golfing partner, Raymond Chow, saw other similarities between Li's game and his strategic style:

> "I think he plays golf in the same fashion as he lives — very practical. He is a good, practical player. He may not have the best form, but his skills are practical and he hits awesome shots. I am just the opposite. Having had a coach at the start, I've got good form but I always lose to him."

Li adapts his game to the course, the circumstances and the players. When not playing golf, Li dominates Hong Kong's economy, where he runs most of the world's biggest port, has the monopoly on supplying electricity to the main island, ranks among the top landlords and retailers, and owns the biggest mobile-phone operator. He regularly makes his power felt around the world and influences the future of entire industries.

In previous sections, we have argued that neo-Taoist values permeate and uniquely shape Chinese networks and business strategies. Table 6.1 highlights the influence of Taoist values on the Communist regime and present-day business in China. Yet the statement from the *Tao* at the head of this chapter encapsulates the practicality of adapting and this chapter explores how Chinese strategic management has adapted to its environment, circumstances and players. First, we discuss available information and information-search in Chinese strategy. Next, we highlight characteristic decision-making styles among successful Chinese managers. Finally, we delineate some managerial functions in present-day China, including setting goals and enforcing contracts.

TABLE 6.1[1]: TAOIST VALUES, THE COMMUNIST REGIME AND PRESENT-DAY CHINESE BUSINESSES

Taoist Values	Implementation by Communist Regime	Implementation by Present-day Businesses
Respect for authorities (*li*)	Central planning; monopoly, state control	Centralized decision-making; vertical communication with authorities
Collectivism; group-oriented behavior; harmonious relations between individuals	Collective leadership; political incentives and disincentives	Companies as family-like multiple functional units; economic, political and social obligations for companies
Personal relations; trust; family kinship (*guanxi*)	Negotiated orders along government hierarchies	Power dynamics between managers and other personnel; bargaining power
Saving face (*mianzi*)	Presenting one's good side	Presenting one's good side; informal behaviors and communications; formal regulations and procedures

INFORMATION SEARCH IN CHINESE STRATEGY

Kazuo Wada, Yaohan's Japanese head, opened his mammoth NextAge department store in Shanghai's Pudong New Area in December 1995 to heavy operating losses. Yet, six months later, he brought forward from 2010 to 2005 his target date for opening 1,000 Chinese supermarkets, declaring, "It is now harvesting time." A year later, Yaohan Japan was filing for court protection ruined by Wada's expansion. Wada had amassed the biggest retailing debt in Japanese post-war history, ¥161 billion (US$1.3 billion), to that date. "We had failed to get returns on investments and loans," he explained. "We made overly optimistic projections of markets." Yaohan started only 27 of its planned Chinese supermarkets before it folded. The European retail giant Royal Dutch Ahold bought these supermarkets but, after posting perennial losses, left China by the end of 2000. Yaohan's Chinese partners took control of its Shanghai department store, the biggest in Asia.[2]

Yaohan's story is by no means unique. Poor information on markets and their potential contributes significantly to corporate mis-projections and has affected industries as diverse as automobiles, aircraft, insurance and beer.[3] Following, we highlight government statistics and market research that affect companies' performance and then spotlight how Chinese companies have adapted to their environments.

▲ Government statistics

In Chapter 3, we discussed how historical circumstances and political manipulation have detrimentally affected the quality of governmental data that can aid companies' strategic decision-making. Technical difficulties, such as staff reductions among statistical analysts, have aggravated errors in data. In January 2002, Hong Kong brokerage house CLSA declared that "the data that show China has the fastest-growing economy in the world are not worth the paper they are written on". The company refused to forecast China's 2002 and 2003 GDP growth.[4] There are no comprehensive measures for gauging the size of the fast-growing private-business and service sectors or even for what constitutes FDI. Indeed, for many years, the US Embassy in Beijing has sought in vain for an explanation of how China's Ministry of Foreign Trade and Economic Co-operation (MOFTEC) calculates FDI. As a result, many foreign companies fail to take account of competitors, local and foreign, entering their markets, or for the subsequent excess capacity, fierce price-cutting and government protection for local companies.

The Chinese government exercises strict control over economic data, even going so far as to classify some as state secrets. Consequently, independent economists have had to resort to detective work to ascertain China's macro-economic and industrial data. Thomas Rawski has estimated that Beijing's tendency to overvalue the stocks of unsold goods of the state-owned enterprises, and to underestimate inflation, reduces China's official growth rate of 7.3% in 2001, the highest in the world. Other Chinese statistics may provide clues to the real growth rate. Between 1997 and 2000, for example, China's GDP officially grew by 24.7%, yet energy consumption dropped by 12.8%. Rawski has argued that more efficient energy consumption, or the growth of industries requiring less energy, cannot explain this discrepancy. Periods of rapid growth in other Asian countries, as well as in China itself a decade ago, coincided with increased energy use, high employment and rising consumer prices. Conversely, in China, between 1997 and 2001, employment hardly grew at all, while prices fell by more than 2%.[5]

Another clue to China's growth rates comes from the civil-aviation industry. Chinese airline passengers belong to the most affluent parts of the population; their incomes are rising faster than the average. Passenger traffic should therefore grow faster than disposable income, a main component when calculating GDP based on national income. But Rawski noted that despite plunging ticket prices in 1998, passenger miles rose by only 2.2% on domestic routes between 1997 and 1998. In those years, the Beijing government officially stated that the economy grew by 8.8% and 7.8%, respectively. Rawski estimated actual growth in China at about 3—4% less than the official figure — about half the official growth rates.[6]

Other factors may push the GDP growth up. For example, Zhegiang province in Eastern China may have underreported growth to conceal the rapid development of private companies in its economy. Affluent provinces, such as Guangdong in Southern China, may also have underreported growth to avoid paying more taxes to the central government.[7] However, without more systematic data, economists cannot state definitively that these factors pushed up growth or that growth even occurred.

Unlike GDP growth, unemployment figures are downplayed by government officials to mask the suffering that economic reforms and restructuring have caused. The official unemployment rate of 3.6% in 2001 excluded *xiagang* workers (laborers receiving small, monthly stipends from former companies and not counted as unemployed) that economists estimate to number about 10 million. The official rate also excluded farmers who left their fields to work in cities, a floating population of around 150 million unemployed migrants. Using international standards, Hu Angang found that China's unemployment rate in 2001 was approximately 7.6% percent in rural areas and more than 8.5% in the cities, well above Beijing's red-flagged figure that would indicate inevitable social turmoil.[8]

Most disturbingly, the central government's debt numbers look highly erroneous. The Central Bank's governor, Dai Xianlong, confessed to parliament in April 2002 that national domestic debt appeared much higher than the official numbers (16% of GDP) suggested. Dai said the figure appeared closer to 60% of GDP if unfunded state-pension liabilities, local government debts, and nonperforming loans (NPLs) of the major banks were taken into consideration. Dai's unusual candor may mask more bad news. Independent economists have discovered that Dai's statistics drew on China's yearbook GDP growth statistics. Rawski estimated that debt more realistically appears closer to 100% or even 125% of GDP. The Bank of China has reported two different figures for its NPLs in 1999. One used Chinese accounting standards; the other used Western standards, which were 2.6 times greater. Moody's has openly called the books of China's "Big Four" banks, "meaningless".[9]

FISHY STATISTICS: CATCHING FISH IN CHINA[10]

Each year since 1988, Chinese officials have reported an annual increase in the number of fish caught off China's shores, even as fish stocks almost everywhere else have declined. In 2000, according to the official newspaper *China Daily*, fishermen caught a record 41 million tons of fish, for an average annual rate of 330,000 tons since 1988. According to the United Nations' Food and Agriculture Organization (FAO), in recent years, China's rising catch has outstripped the combined decline of every other country in the world.

But now, scientists have discovered gross errors in China's statistics. Reg Watson and Daniel Pauly found that China's fish stocks have actually fallen by 360,000 tons annually. They arrived at their estimates by building a statistical database that includes the FAO's historical data along with detailed information excluded from overall fishing numbers. They used the database to predict catch sizes of fish in different regions of the world, taking into account such information as ocean depth and coral reefs. Their predictions proved accurate against fresh reports from most all countries but China.

Antiquated Communist data-collection methods spawned the inflated numbers in China. Each year, local officials in China report their catches to Beijing, knowing that their promotions depend on good news. Local officials passed inflated numbers to Beijing's officials, who totaled them without validation, and sent them to the United Nations. Over time, social unrest increased in fishing ports because of decreasing fish stocks and, thus, employment. Beijing suspected that the statistics appeared too rosy. In 1999, the central government declared a temporary zero-growth policy on fishing statistics. For three consecutive years, Beijing has reported the same tonnage of catches to the United Nations.

Publicly, Chinese officials denied that they inflated their statistics. The Fisheries Bureau's director general, Yang Jian, argued that the country's statistics were "basically correct" and conformed to China's "statistics laws". But another fisheries official, who insisted on anonymity, acknowledged that "we don't have enough of a budget to do surveys. We don't have enough evidence to tell what the real situation is." Local fishermen may not view accurate reporting as important and may report their catches based on "feelings". "We often call local or provincial agencies and ask them if the numbers are real," the official said. "They say, 'Yes they are real.' But we have no proof."

▲ Market research

In China, many markets have reached saturation, increasing the necessity for accurate market estimates. Purchasing power appears very concentrated. Despite its 1.3 billion people, the average Chinese still makes less than US$1,000 per year. Since 1998, Beijing has issued US$43 billion in Treasury bonds, pumping the proceeds into public works and higher official salaries. This government spending has sustained the spending of the middle classes but has also resulted in monstrously high government debt, and may not continue. Currently, the purchases of 80 million middle-class consumers account for nearly half of China's GDP. Concurrently, more than 800 million rural residents earn less than a third of their urban counterparts, about US$270 a year. While most urban consumers have bought their color televisions, cellular phones, air conditioners and refrigerators, most rural residents cannot afford these items.

Also, the market potential for most sectors appears inflated: high increases in market growth from a low base look deceptively large when inexperienced investors make decisions. For example, prior to 1979, only the most senior government officials owned cars. Despite a year-on-year increase of 20%, China's car market enjoyed sales of 675,000 units in 2000, less than the combined sum of Europe's two small car markets — the

Netherlands and Belgium. China has agreed to cut import tariffs in this sector from the current 80—100%, to 25% within six
years of its WTO entry in December 2001. Changes in government regulation should increase competition, but may not increase companies' profits. By 2010, the Economist Group's
Graeme Maxton has predicted, car sales in China will increase
three fold, to around two million units, but China will still have
a smaller car market than France.[11] Also, recent trends indicate
that provincial governments have erected indirect barriers to
replace the tariffs. Some municipalities have given tax breaks
to local producers and others have raised taxes on the locally
made products of foreign companies, increasing operating costs.

The dangers of overestimating market size and underesti-
mating costs, are illustrated quite dramatically by the beer industry. Foreign brewers arrived after statistics showed China
had the world's second-largest beer market (after the USA), and
one that had grown 20% a year for over a decade. By the mid
1990s, foreign brewers had opened 60 breweries in China and
operated an additional 30 under licensing agreements. They
made huge investments. For example, Fosters, the world's
fourth-largest brewer, invested US$150 million for three brew-
eries and planned a mega-brewery in Shanghai's Pudong New
Area; Bass, Britain's largest brewer, invested US$40 million; and
Jack Perkowski, the Wall Street investment banker, invested
more than US$80 million with the US brewer Miller to acquire
two breweries. But the foreign brewers had not researched their
market adequately.[12]

The premium segment on which these brewers depended
turned out smaller than one-tenth of the total. Most of China's
beer consists of low-grade, low-cost alcohol retailing for less
than bottled water. Foreign brewers, despite huge advertising
expenditures, could not convince the Chinese to pay five times
more for their brands. Fosters cut prices below costs to build
market share. But when the company increased prices by $1/2$¢
per bottle, it lost half its market share in six months and never
regained it.[13]

After losing US$17 million in the first year, US$19 million in the second and US$20 million in the third, Fosters wrote off its entire investment and left China. Bass also sold its Chinese operations, writing off almost all its investment. Perkowski sold his two breweries to Tsingtao, China's biggest brewer, for US$22.5 million in mid 2000, US$60 million less than he had paid for them five years earlier. Of the 90 breweries, only one — South African Breweries has announced that it is making profits in China .[14]

▲ Information-gathering strategies for China

Chinese companies have adapted their information-gathering strategies to their information-scarce business environments. This adaptation incorporates traditional neo-Taoist concepts of trust and contextual ethics that relate to the efficient functioning of society.

Francis Fukuyama argued that commercial trust provides a necessary ingredient for economic prosperity.[15] Without trust, economic dealings will require very costly investments in screening and verifying commercial transactions and impede economic prosperity. Western cultures often perceive their own ethical norms as being universally applicable, and deception as evil. To gauge market sizes, Western companies often query consumers or suppliers in markets directly, and expect accurate responses regarding demand or supply. However, neo-Taoist societies such as China view ethical duties as contextual; deception may prove virtuous depending upon the deceivers' motives and the existing relationships. Without pre-existing relationships, consumers or suppliers have little social pressure to respond accurately to Western market-research techniques; indeed, Chinese consumers and suppliers may have considerable social pressure to deceive market researchers. Neo-Taoist ethics imply that Chinese respondents who deceive solely to harm researchers act evilly; however, respondents who deceive to promote employers' or friends' interests, act honorably. Chin-Ning Chu explained the rationale behind this: "While Westerners are practicing deception, they pretend they are not, whereas Asians accept the reality of deception as a necessary element in their daily lives."[16]

As we have indicated, available secondary data in China lack both quantity and quality. Wai Kwok Lo, managing director of Artesyn Technologies, Asia-Pacific, Ltd., told us how Artesyn collects information for its successful operations: "Basically, we use the same techniques as elsewhere in Asia, but we do not have the same structured information as we have in the US. We have less information, and hence market projections are much more influenced by our own judgment and the collective judgment of our sales force."

As Western-style market research becomes problematic, successful managers in China search for and collect information differently from their counterparts in the West. They rely heavily on their own experiences in the businesses and on those of smaller, subjectively selected groups of individuals with whom the managers have pre-existing relationships — their networks. Experience and networks inform the managers of realities as well as of the reliability of available, secondary data. Accordingly, Henry Yu, president of Beijing McMahan Investment Consultation Co., suggested that Chinese or non-Chinese companies entering Chinese markets with no prior experience should "use partners with skills in the area. Look for larger and fast-growing markets to help cover early mistakes caused by lack of knowledge and experience. Get good partners with good experience and good reputations, partners that provide synergistic benefits. Trust personal experience — market research cannot be trusted."

Once managers have gained experience and knowledge of Chinese markets and business practices, however, advice for success differs. To continue to get high-quality information, especially in untried markets, foreign managers may have to discard local partners. Austin Hu, deputy chief of mission, World Bank-Beijing, pointed out that one of the reasons Motorola is very successful in China ...is that they are wholly owned; they are not a JV. By doing that, they can make all the decisions top-down." Even with a JV, he said, "the question is, how do [you] get the real commitment from the local partner? Again I think that the most difficult part here is that, even with enterprise[s], we still have the party system." Hu had noted that often Chinese partners, and indeed the institutional environments in which foreign companies operate in China, appear very slow to abandon neo-Taoist ways. Resistance to processing new information may emerge, as was the case with product development at Audio & Electric Switchgear. The company's bank refused to fund its efforts to develop video equipment: Audio & Electric had a government license for audio equipment but did not have one to operate in business-to-business video markets, something that was unnecessary in the post-reform era. [17]

NAVIGATING INFORMATION LANDMINES: CERESTAR IN CHINA [18]

Cerestar's experiences display some of the difficulties of information search in China. A subsidiary of the Paris-based Eridania Beghin-Say agro-industrial group, Cerestar is one of the largest foreign companies in China, with a $230 million investment. When its initial JV partner, the Jifa Group, ran out of money in 1996, Cerestar searched for and obtained a new partner, the Jilin-based trader Jiliang Group. This development delayed construction of the plant by one year. The plant finally opened in January 2002 to produce high-grade starch, as well as the corn sweeteners dextrose, glucose syrup and dried glucose, and a bulking agent, maltodextrin — all aimed primarily at the Chinese market.

Tintin Delphin, who arrived in 1999 as vice-president of the JV's commercial department, discovered that demand for the product did not match expectations: the Chinese used native starch differently from Westerners. In the West, starch serves as a thickener in food and pharmaceuticals. In China, 40% of starch produces the flavor-enhancer monosodium glutamate. Consequently, in China, the price of starch assumes more importance than its quality. Cerestar had planned to charge a premium for the high quality of its starch, and had to revise downwards its financial projections as well as its estimates of market size. Delphin also learned that the dextrose market in China differed from that in the West: Chinese manufacturers use dextrose in pharmaceuticals but rarely in food. Similarly, Delphin found the market for dried glucose "very limited, because [the Chinese] don't know how to use it".

To estimate market size, Cerestar initially relied on its JV partner's estimates as the Jiliang Group had two of China's largest plants for starch products. Yet these estimates proved grossly erroneous and misinformed. Also, publicly available market information was at least two years out of date. Delphin eventually obtained the market information she needed through exhaustive hands-on research, which was begun late in the JV's life. Delphin and her staff compiled a list of thousands of possible starch users, then began cold calling, eliminating trading firms, distributors and representative offices, none of whom use starchy products directly. Her information-gathering stalled repeatedly because of disconnected telephones, bankrupt companies, and companies that had moved. Many on Delphin's list refused to speak with strangers. Finally, fewer than 10% emerged as genuine, potential customers.

Cerestar also had poor information on available transportation to deliver its products to customers. The JV could not transport its liquid sweeteners, such as glucose, a product used in beverages, through current means. A highly viscous substance, glucose thickens as the temperature drops. In Europe and the US, Cerestar shipped glucose in giant steam-jacketed tanks that maintain the temperature, so the glucose stays liquid until it reaches its destination. But the company could not obtain food-grade large tanks in China, even without steam jackets. Cerestar pondered importing the tanks from Europe, but the roads leading south from the plant, two-and-a-half hours' drive north of Changchun in Northeast China, could not accommodate 20-ton shipments of liquid glucose in heavy tanks on even heavier trucks. The JV is currently considering transporting the glucose in small drums to Southern China, where most of the plant's customers may reside. Delphin has estimated that customers can heat up the glucose when they receive it. However, this option would increase costs and reduce profits even further. In April 2002, still having a tough time in China, Cerestar was acquired by Cargill of the US. More recently, in December, 2003, China Resources Bio-Chemical Co Ltd tendered a US$49 miilion offer to acquire the interests of Cerestar's Chinese JV partner, Jilin Foods Group Co, Ltd in the JV. Cerestar still considered business in China as "tough".

DECISION-MAKING IN CHINESE STRATEGY

Successful Chinese and Overseas Chinese managers from South-east Asia have similar decision-making styles,[19] both being strongly influenced by Neo-Taoism and Confucianism, and both operating in information-scarce environments or "blackholes".[20] However, China's historical circumstances, culminating in its present Communist regime, have amended many of the decision-making strategies that include:

- hands-on experience;
- lateral transfers of knowledge;
- reliance on qualitative information;
- holistic information-processing;
- action-driven decision-making; and,
- emergent planning.

▲ Hands-on experience

Chinese companies make decisions quickly and work hard to implement their decisions quickly. Stan Shih of Acer underscored, "It's all in the implementation". Making decisions quickly, without detailed analyses of hard, often non-existent data, requires intimate experience. Hands-on line managers have a fuller understanding than staff of their companies' work routines, processes, products, markets, business environments and industries. Formal education and in-house training do not provide sufficient preparation for operating in China. YY Wong,

Chairman, CEO and founder of WyWy Group, also emphasized hands-on experience as a necessary component for success in China: "I think what we need, whether it's an Overseas Chinese company [or] a Western start-up company ... is how to practice business, and this is a real-life thing. It's not something for lecture or debate; it's something that one has to do and get results with."

Without hands-on experience, managers will not have the necessary knowledge, experience and insights to make timely, high-quality decisions in China. Such experience compensates for the lack of the supporting information most Western managers find highly desirable. Hands-on experience also builds necessary knowledge of industries, markets, and environments to make accurate market projections; it facilitates the building of networks and helps managers to bring projects to fruition.

All successful Chinese managers highlighted the importance of knowing whom to approach in the government for support with projects, and what government agencies could influence their projects. For foreign managers, just identifying personnel in the CCP's key committees — the individuals with real power and with whom they should interact — becomes a daunting task. The government guards information on the Party's personnel from foreigners. For example, in 2002, the outside world saw, Tang Jiaxuan (now State Councilor) as the PRC's Foreign Minister; only cognoscenti knw that then vice-minister, Li Zhaoxing (now Foreign Minister), headed the Foreign Ministry's Party committee and thus wielded - more power. Foreign managers may spend months negotiating with government officials only to discover that their contacts have no power to make decisions.

Chinese managers also emphasize that one has to know the goals of the governments with primary jurisdiction over a company's projects. Aligning these projects with government goals greatly facilitates implementation and completion. This alignment can also reduce operating costs, as governments often provide land and utilities at heavily subsidized rates to these projects. However, government goals have more to do with per-ceived strategic importance than market demand or supply. For example, in the mid 1990s, the Chinese government decided to establish a globally competitive semi-conductor chip industry and aggressively built up capacity through JVs with foreign companies. China currently accounts for over US$10 billion of the Asia-Pacific's US$42.8 billion industry, and has become the region's largest chip market. But semi-conductor sales have dropped by about half, and the price of chips dropped to one-tenth of the 2000 price. The price of Dynamic Random Access Memory Chips (DRAMs) dropped from around US$15–20 to US$2 per chip over the same period, as Samsung and Hyundai slashed prices to pay bank loans. Shanghai Hua Hong NEC, China's largest chip manufacturer, lost over US$800 million in 2001. China still plans to build 19 new semi-conductor fabrica-tion plants in the next decade, which will probably contribute to significant excess global capacity. China does not have the technology to manufacture high-end 12-inch chips, and so the plants will concentrate on 5–8-inch chips. The Chinese govern-ment has assumed that the chip market will grow 10% every year and swell to US$21 billion by 2005, but these assumptions may not hold true.[21]

Many successful Chinese managers hold the view that the complex three-network system described in Chapter 5 demands unprecedented, continual involvement from managers. Many Overseas Chinese managers confess that they have difficulties managing this complexity. Kwek Leng Joo, managing director of City Developments, Ltd., and president of the Singapore Chinese Chamber of Commerce and Industry, said that "build-ing these relationships is a full-time job. You can't just go there and build relationships every once in a while. It helps to know people and have their confidence. But, I have a full-time job right here in Singapore and just cannot do it. I have to bring some value-added to the table to make up for it." The value-added often relates to hands-on line experience.

CHANGZHOU KOOSHIES: LEARNING BY THE SEAT OF THE PANTS [22]

In 1996, Kooshies Baby Products, a family-run Canadian company, formed a JV with Diqui, a Changzhou-based SOE, famous in China for its dying and flannel, and Ray Perez introduced his family's business into China. Kooshies had just launched a range of non-disposable diapers and China, with 20 million babies born each year, seemed like a huge market. It turned into what Perez described as "a rollercoaster".

Neither Perez, nor the Shanghai-based consulting company that had done due diligence for Kooshies, knew of Diqui's bankruptcy. After contributing the plant and some flannel, Diqui reneged on its agreed financial investment. Perez had to run the business with 40% less operating capital than he planned. The JV struggled for a year before Kooshies bought out Diqui's stake. Unable to access credit locally or to get capital from Canada, Perez kept Kooshies afloat by insisting that all distributors pay up-front in cash.

Diqui's management team greatly hindered the acquisition of market information. "The SOE gave me all the riff-raff, people who had just slept for 10 years," Perez recalled. When he arrived in Changzhou, Perez drew up a list of raw materials that the JV could source locally. Diqui's procurement managers assured him that no one could find these raw materials in China. At first, Perez deferred to their experience; but, then, on regular to trips to Shanghai, began to source the raw materials himself.

Perez started firing local managers. Within two years, he had replaced all of Diqui's managers with people under 25 — "people with fresh minds, uncorrupted and easy to train". He has had difficulty finding creative people such as designers. He has had even greater difficulty finding people he can trust: secret information, such as salespersons' commissions, often became common knowledge in the business.

With few resources at its disposal, Changzhou Kooshies' marketing relied on Perez and one assistant. Traveling around China, within 18 months they personally placed Kooshies' products in 200 department stores in 14 provinces. Experience helped Perez to adapt his products to China's markets. For example, in Western markets, Kooshies promotes its non-disposable diapers as environmentally friendly; but in China, health and cost override environmental concerns. Flannel is Kooshies' main product in 45 countries around the world, including Hong Kong; but the Chinese perceive flannel as being of poor quality and prefer brushed cotton. "Kooshies Ultra", made from flannel, sold poorly. As Diqui's contribution had included 100,000 meters of flannel, Perez could not easily change the production line. While Canadian customers preferred diapers with white waistbands, Chinese pattern-makers had warned Perez that local consumers would associate white with funerals, and so he changed this feature. Within China, provincial product markets differed. Popular Western designs featuring animal prints did not sell well. Guangzhou and Shanghai, though, were more open to Western designs.

In 1999, Perez teamed up with Chen Quio Yu, the owner of a local private company that made beach chairs for major US retailers, including Wal-Mart. Chen bought a 49% stake in Changzhou Kooshies and Perez started a new factory in Wujing. Perez also tied up with a US mail-order company in Guangzhou. He has taken risks he would consider too costly in Canada: he has diversified into new product ranges such as educational toys, branded shoes and sunglasses; and he has operated on "gut" feelings.

In 2000, Changzhou Kooshies finally made a profit. Perez has learned enough Chinese to dispense with an interpreter. However, he confessed, "I feel everything is on my shoulders, from the way the receptionist answers the phone to the packaging". He has also been unable to find someone he could trust to run the business in his absence.

▲ Lateral transfers of knowledge

According to Chinese government statistics, private companies now contribute about half of China's GDP and employ over 130 million people. Many of these Chinese managers appear to acquire, and to manage successfully, companies across sectors with few overt similarities or synergies corresponding to industrial structure. For example, Li Ka-shing's companies operate in property, ports, utilities, retailing, telecommunications and oil. Yang Bin, the flower tycoon, also epitomizes such lateral transfers of knowledge. *Forbes* magazine estimated his wealth at around US$900 million, making him the richest man in China. [23] As we will see later, Yang's companies operated in greenhouses, property, theme parks and even independent diplomatic and economic missions!

Many researchers and managers have attributed the rapid growth of networks in Asian business to their unique processing and channeling of information. [24] Western managers often have difficulties making decisions within new environmental contexts without considerable, time-consuming research and analysis. As we argued in Chapter 1, cognitive research has shown that Asian managers may process information differently from Western managers. For example, unlike Westerners, who concentrate on the particular and move to the general, East Asians appear to follow the reverse process. Asians often begin with viewing whole situations and move on to particulars; they move from observing single objects to similar ones, and notice overall environmental similarities or dissimilarities. These abilities to perceive overall similarities between disparate situations may explain why some Asian companies are able to transfer knowledge laterally across industries and markets.

Edward Zeng, founder, chairman and CEO of Sparkice in Beijing, carries two business cards; one short, another long. The long business card presents all his titles and all the organizations with which he is affiliated. In addition to running www.SPARKICE.com — a global E-commerce site promoting business between China and the world — he sits on several government committees, serves on the faculty of China's most prestigious business school and hosts his own television program. The skills and markets for each position vary tremendously:

- Commissioner — Global Information Infrastructure Committee (GIIC)
- Visiting Scholar — China State Planning and Development Commission (SPC)
- Visiting Professor — The Business School of Tsinghua University
- Project Leader — China National Pilot Project of E-Commerce, Ministry of Information Industry (MII)
- Special Consultant — China State Administration Bureau for Industry and Commerce
- CEO — China West Network, www.21CWN.com
- Chairman — China EC Network
- Deputy Chairman — www.21DNN.com
- Host — China Education TV E-commerce Program
- Chairman & CEO – www.SPARKICE.com

Zeng has transferred and applied knowledge and understanding laterally between global markets (business-to-business), local markets (both business-to-business and business-to-consumer), and education and government markets.

YANG BIN[25]: TULIPS, THEME PARKS AND ECONOMIC ENCLAVES

Born in 1963 and orphaned at age five, Yang Bin, China's richest man, studied and taught politics at a naval college in China before winning a place at Leiden University in the Netherlands. The Netherlands had adopted a lenient policy towards Chinese students following the Tiananmen Massacre, and Yang was granted political asylum and gained Dutch citizenship. Leaving politics behind, Yang began importing silks and other textiles from China, but soon discovered a more lucrative trade: exporting orchid seedlings to China's burgeoning flower growers. In 1994, he returned to China to establish his own orchid-seedling greenhouses. He used his Dutch passport to gain JV status for his companies and to import equipment duty free.

Within a few years, Yang dominated China's orchid-seedling market, with greenhouses in eight provinces. His biggest operation, in Sichuan province, received a listing on the Shanghai Stock Exchange in 1997. Two years later, he sold his stake to his partners at a huge profit. Controversy surrounds the deal, as the stock prices rose sharply prior to his sell-off.

Later, Yang concentrated his business in the northern city of Shenyang, which, he explained, provided a suitable venue for greenhouse agriculture despite its short winter days, because of its cool summer days. His close friendship with the provincial governor, Bo Xilai, perhaps better explains Yang's choice of this unlikely locale. In July 2001, Yang listed his orchid businesses on the Hong Kong Stock Exchange as Euro-Asia Agricultural Holdings, a wholly owned foreign company. With Singapore-listed fruit distributor FHTK Holdings, Yang bought a US$10 million fruit-and-vegetable greenhouse in Shandong province. He was also negotiating to buy a minority stake in a Japanese supermarket.

Greenhouse agriculture forms only a small part of Yang's business and personal wealth. He retains stakes in flower companies across China and some property in Beijing and Shanghai. However, Holland Village remains his most inexplicable business: the 1000-acre multifunctional development surrounding his Shenyang greenhouse comprises a theme park, an office, a trade-fair center and residential buildings. Rising above Manchuria's windswept plains, the incongruous project includes replicas of the International Court of Justice and the Amsterdam train station, windmills and an indoor beach, as well as 300,000 square meters of residential space in 50 European-style buildings. Holland Village had drawn over US$360 million in investment by the end of 2002; Yang's long-term plans included doubling the total investment to $850 million.

Yang's most daring business deal occurred when he accepted a North Korean invitation to govern a special administrative region (SAR) in Sinuiju, North Korea, on China's border. The North Koreans offered Yang unprecedented total administrative control. North Korea had chosen Yang to begin its experiment with capitalism and to save its ailing economy. This 70-mile, walled capitalist enclave, with its own economic, political and economic system, surprised everyone; most especially, the Chinese government.

Yang's strengths are centered on his political contacts and his skill at synchronizing his diverse business ventures with government goals. For example, he promoted his greenhouse business as a model of Chinese agriculture, but the broader applications of its capital-intensive, labor-scarce approach seem unlikely in China. Widespread greenhouses appear even more unlikely in financially strapped North Korea; yet Yang used them to gain regional power and to forge links with the mysterious Korean leader Kim Jong II. Kim offered Yang prime plots of land to build greenhouses for fruit and vegetables and to overcome food shortages. Later, Kim chose Yang to lead North Korea's experiment with capitalism.

However, as we will see in the next chapter, even Yang may have slipped up: the North Korean government had chosen him to head its economic enclave without Beijing's permission. In October 2002, as the flamboyant Yang had just finished elaborating on his new economic eminence in North Korea to international reporters, the Chinese government placed him under house arrest pending an investigation into possible criminal activities. In July of 2003, Yang Bin was sentenced to 18 years in prison.

▲ Qualitative information

Chinese managers appear to take unnecessary risks by not doing sufficient research or analysis before acting. As we saw in Chapter 4, Beijing Jeep designed the Heroic without first developing a portfolio of desirable product characteristics for the model through a phalanx of market-research projects. The JV also had only about 100 product-design engineers on its staff. As a result, Chrysler's executives that visited Beijing to ascertain the project's feasibility, ruled against the project. However, BJ's managers had processed myriad bits of information and considered several alternatives before designing the model. They gathered this information through consumers' comments on existing products, their executives' and engineers' personal experiences and opinions, and their observations of the products of competitors and potential competitors. Though imperceptible to the Americans, the data gathered and analyzed by the JV's managers was the best available.

Chinese managers often conduct their analyses almost entirely internally and transfer understandings across product markets to compensate for unreliable secondary data. Their analyses draw on data that they import laterally from other, similar situations, and generate from qualitative sources that Western managers often regard as illegitimate. Philip Ng, executive director and CEO of the Far East Organization, Singapore, elaborated: "You need someone who knows. Someone who knows when a project is going right on and when it is not. Someone who can see that a project that was going right last week is now going wrong, and how to get it back to going right. Only hard work and experience can tell you this so quickly."

Chinese managers seek out critical information that will affect their strategic decisions.[26] They often prefer qualitative, even subjective, information supplied by friends, business associates, government officials, and others in whose judgment and character they trust. Local contacts can supply up-to-date, accurate, unpublished information superior to available, published or traditional, primary research alternatives. For example, Pan Shi Yi, founder and CEO of Redstone Development, the largest property developer in Beijing, admitted that before drafting proposals for the development of major properties, he always queried local political officials and government ministries. This informal data-gathering helped him to determine what the policy-makers desired, and to identify any concerns they had about the properties. By incorporating such qualitative data, Pan had a far greater probability of developing acceptable, desirable and profitable proposals than by conducting market studies or by using available market data. His data, however, frequently appeared subjective, and he did not collect them in accordance with scientific principles of sampling and marketing research. Pan categorized his data, and judged their validity, through his experiences in dealing with individuals he knew through his business dealings. His trust in his contacts' judgment permitted him to exercise their knowledge to satisfy the markets, and to garner significant profits.

Wai Kwok Lo, managing director of Artesyn Technologies, Asia-Pacific, Ltd., threw some light on how his Florida-based company used data in China's informational void: "We follow the same planning procedures here as we do at HQ. We collect all the data, but we recognize that our data is neither of the same quality nor the same quantity as in the States. We take every step possible to confirm it before using it, and if we can't confirm the data, we use alternative means to try to confirm the results of our analysis. If we can't confirm the results of our analysis either, we earn our pay and have to use our knowledge and experience to make the best decision possible."

▲ Holistic information-processing

The West's conventional, analytical problem-solving emphasizes a sequential, systematic, and step-by-step approach to decision-making. It works best in relatively information-rich situations, in stable and mature economies and industries. In the informational-void situations that managers often find in emerging markets and rapidly evolving markets and industries, conventional analytical models often prove unworkable; indeed, experience-based intuitive models often work best. With experience-based intuitive models, managers take a general approach to problems, define parameters intuitively, and explore solutions holistically.[27] Goh Hup Jin, chairman of Nipsea Holdings and director of the Wuthelam Group, vividly described holistic information processing when he told us:

> "We have a history to refer to and we draw on the similarities. Sometimes you look at the market and say, 'This

is something I saw before' ... little, little things. The real, the key, pieces of information are very difficult to record. A lot has to do with listening to the whole story, the story you pick up from China, the war story. The enemy is coming this way. From memory, you see something like this. What do you do? I tell you, 'We [had] better turn left.' 'Why?' you say. Actually, I don't know. From a hunch, I say, 'Turn left' ...You turn left, and it's [correct]. So how to record this? There is no way. It's a hunch, and it's right many times. This is the real story."

Chinese top managers, once they establish themselves and their companies, almost never invest amounts that could endanger the survival of their company. Compartmentalizing risks allows them to view business situations in their entirety, and to judge leverage. This investment strategy draws on holistic approaches that complement the managers' information-processing strengths. The managers invest based upon general perceptions of entire product markets, then react to market events that occur in the daily conduct of business. For example, Yang Bin's US$360-million investment in a Dutch theme park in Manchuria, in a city with over 20% unemployment, has caused analysts to question his business acumen. The entrance price (US$18) for one-day passes appears steep and China is littered with failed theme parks. But, Holland Village also includes 300,000 square meters of residential housing. The sale of the residential housing should provide Yang with some US$60 million in net profits (this assumes a conservative selling price of US$400 per square meter, after repaying a US$60 million loan). If Holland Village achieves success, possibly through a US listing, Yang's wealth could quadruple. If the theme park flops, Yang would still have about US$350 million, making him China's 10th-richest man.

If Chinese managers do well and prosper, through controlling risks, they learn more about the product markets, they refine their strategies and enlarge their investments. Li Ka-shing presents a vivid case of holistic decision-making and learning. Investors in Hong Kong label Li as *Chiu Yan* or "Superman". When Li launches a company, with or without a business plan, and lists its shares, they rush to buy. In part, Li's success stems from luck. From the 1980s to 1997, Hong Kong's property provided a one-way ticket to wealth as the British government restricted the supply of new land for development. Li, and several other developers, rose with land prices. Once he secured his niche in the container port, Li piggybacked on Hong Kong's rise as a trading hub. In 1997, during the Asian financial crisis, Hong Kong's peg kept its currency artificially high and saved Li once again. Luck, however, fails to explain why Li branched overseas when he did and, most importantly, how and why he spots opportunity. His record has blemishes, though few remember them: Li recouped and never invested enough to ruin himself or his companies financially. For example, in mobile telephony, Li's first foray into Britain, Rabbit, flopped. Learning from this failure, Li built another British mobile-telephony operator, Orange, which he sold for a US$22 billion profit .[28]

Holistic information processing explains why Chinese companies successfully diversify into very different, non-core businesses, in contravention of Western business wisdom of related diversification. To succeed in diverse industries and ventures, managers must generalize past experiences in industries and markets to their new contexts in other industries and markets. As discussed in Chapter 1, the managers' abilities to tackle new problems in different situations involve conceptualization skills different from analytical skills.[29] This holistic approach to information processing reduces the importance of the hard data that Westerners demand to analyze new and unfamiliar industries and markets. Consequently, it aids speed in strategic responses.

▲ Action-driven decision-making

Superficially, Li Ka-shing, Hong Kong's "Superman", appears a lot like Warren Buffet, "the Sage of Omaha". Both look for value and both bottom-fish. Yet, there the similarities end. Buffet crunches piles of numbers in search of undervalued companies and holds their assets indefinitely. Li tries to time the market, shows patience, but moves with phenomenal speed when opportunities arise.

Li's legendary timing has become visible in his forays into the telecom industry. His company, Hutchison Whampoa, sold Orange to Mannesmann at the peak of the telecom boom, making US$22 billion in profits. That windfall gave Li the cash to get into a new technology without the debt with which his competitors were burdened. On April 27th, 2000, Hutchison, and a little-known, cash-short Canadian company, Telesystem International Wireless (TIW), won a hotly contested British government license to offer a next-generation mobile system, 3G, that offers high-speed Internet connections and video for mobile phones. Hutchison stayed behind the scenes while TIW used its status as a first-time market entrant to make the bid. Surprised competitors, including a JV between France Telecom and NTL, remained ignorant of Hutchison's big bankroll behind TIW. Consequently, Hutchison paid US$2.5 billion less for the license than its competitors in a higher category designated for experienced players. Moreover, Hutchison paid far less — US$6.9 billion up front, and up to US$7.8 billion to construct the network — than the profits it made by selling Orange. "We sold at full value, and we came back in on the ground floor," said Hutchison Group managing director Canning Fok. "When it comes the time to sell, we have no hesitation." Similarly, in 2000, Hutchison got US$5.9 billion for its share of US cellular carrier VoiceStream Wireless — which it had bought control of in different transactions made in 1998 and 1999 for just US$1.3 billion.[30]

Speed constitutes a key characteristic of decision-making in Chinese business. Top Chinese managers prefer action to discussion. These managers also prefer action to analysis. Indeed, most Western managers would characterize these Chinese preferences as action without discussion or analysis. Y Y Wong of

WyWy Group, a major distributor of both consumer and business electronics, emphasized the importance of these characteristics. "The secret of this business is speed," he said. "The secret of this business is flexibility, adaptability, the speed of new looks..."

This speed reflects the power given to Chinese managers and the accountability expected of them. Managers often have great latitude in deciding matters; long debates and committee meetings rarely occur in private Chinese companies. Most investors and other stakeholders assume that top managers in Asia generally, and in China particularly, make mistakes. Consequently, once the managers establish their reputations, most investors analyze their overall records for success, not whether their latest decisions failed or succeeded. Early in their careers, of course, managers must build a record of success to establish favorable reputations.

▲ Emergent planning

The Chinese networks engage in what Henry Mintzberg termed emergent planning.[31] Strategies bubble up through individual companies and also collectively through the networks. Typically, news, rumors or inside information will reach the networks' managers and create interest. The managers will then seek confirming evidence, gauge available resources, make and implement decisions. As further information becomes available, the managers will modify strategies. The companies' strategies emerge from the learned business behaviors of the companies and their managers.

Steven Chan, executive chairman of Superior Multi-Packaging Ltd., Singapore, explained his company's perspective like this: "We've got a five-year plan that we revise every year. All our people involved in our China operations will have some ideas. They will have ideas of why we did not achieve the growth we want; they will have ideas of how to achieve 20% growth, and we revise our plans accordingly." This bubbling-up process takes advantage of line managers' experiences and knowledge. These line managers often lack training in business technologies, but their experiences and abilities to process information holistically help them to outperform headquarters' staff analysts. Chan identified one line manager that his company values and who shows significant managerial potential as a "mid-level engineer". The manager appeared highly intelligent and well trained, but not in traditional business techniques and terminologies. Without Superior Multi-Packaging's proactive efforts to acquire and to understand his strategic suggestions, the company would have lost his potential contributions.

Chinese companies also display emergent planning when searching for local JV partners. Partnership possibilities emerge, preferably within the originating partners' business networks. The potential partners' decisions to join hinge largely on their confidence in the proposing managers' judgment and abilities. The proposing managers' suggested strategies bubble up within their companies, through their top management, seep through their JV partners, and could bubble up through the entire business network. In effect, Chinese companies have enlarged Henry Mintzberg's emergent planning beyond the boundaries of individual companies to include associated groups of companies.

HAINAN AIRLINES[32]: THE LITTLE AIRLINE THAT COULD

Hainan Airlines appears like no other in China — quick and driven. It has filled a market, mainly tourist flights and feeder routes from smaller Chinese cities. Unlike its competitors, the airline has also consistently posted profits.

Action-driven decision-making and *guanxi* fueled Hainan Airline's development. Hainan Airline's founder and chairman, Chen Feng, worked in the airforce, Lufthansa's flight-training school in Germany, and economic and aviation bureaus in Beijing, before coming to Hainan in the early 1990s. He became the provincial government's deputy head under Liu Jianfeng, the current director of the Civil Aviation Authority of China (CAAC). "I'm very lucky," Chen said.

In 1992, the Hainan provincial government gave Chen US$1 million to start an airline. Hainan's status as a special economic zone (SEZ), and Chen's connections, enabled his quest for more capital. The company raised funds from the stock market and ran its first flight in 1993.

In 1995, Chen caught his next big break. The American financier George Soros had invested in Phoenix Information Systems, a small Nasdaq-listed company selling outdated ticketing systems to Chinese airlines. Chen was also helping Phoenix. Phoenix went bankrupt, but their mistakes allowed Soros and Chen to meet. Over a three-and-a-half-hour meeting, Soros provided Chen with US$25 million for 25% of the airline. Through successive share placements, Soros' stake fell to 14.8%.

China is one of the fastest-growing air-travel markets in the world, but the fragmented airline industry has been losing money. In 2001, the Beijing government announced its intention to consolidate the nine CAAC and 14 provincial airlines into three large groups. Hainan Airlines faced a choice: to remain a regional, niche carrier or to become something bigger. Chinese tourism is growing rapidly and Hainan is a very popular tourist destination — the eight-year-old company chose the riskier path and decided to grow.

In 2001, Hainan Airlines bought three regional airlines, establishing six hubs across the country, including Beijing, Xian and Lanzhou. These acquisitions broadened its network to 300 routes, including Seoul, Macau and Kuala Lumpur, and cemented its position as China's fourth national airline. It had a 68-aircraft fleet and planned to raise that to 90 by the end of 2002. Hainan Airline's load factor was approximately 68%, topping other Chinese airlines, and the average for US carriers flying international routes.

Hainan Airline's six-aircraft subsidiary in Beijing, Deer Jet, leased corporate jets. In December 2001, the airline started Yangtze River Express, China's second air-cargo operator. It owned a majority stake in the busy airport at Haiku and planned to invest in two others. By the end of 2002, it bought three new Gulfstreams, and three new helicopters. Despite its expansion, Hainan Airline's debt comprised 75% of operating capital — low in the Chinese airline industry. Since mid 2002, external sources of investment have also arisen through A and B shares on the Shanghai Stock Exchange. Chen planned a US listing for his company. However, in August 2002, the Chinese government ruled that single foreign companies can hold up to 25% (reduced from 35%) in any Chinese airline.

In October 2002, Beijing announced that it will consolidate the industry around Beijing-based Air China, Guangzhou-based China Southern, and Shanghai-based China Eastern. Hainan Airlines would continue at number four, with just 9% of the market. China Southern would compete on Hainan's core businesses, key routes from southern cities to Hainan. Li Weijian, Hainan Airline's CEO, sketched the company's next steps: moving away from Hainan and into JVs for short-hop carriers or helicopter services from Hong Kong to Guangdong province. He has also considered changing the airline's name, which was the reason why, in 2001 another province's officials refused the airline's bid for their carrier. Li wanted to position Hainan as a national brand. In 2004, Hainan Airlines has retained its provincial name, but now also aims at international skys. It has 94 aircraft in its fleet and operates about 500 domestic and overseas air routes. On February 18, 2004, Hainan signed a cooperation agreement with Malev Hungarian Airlines to operate the fixed-time Beijing-Budapest Flight Line (BBFL) before September 2004. It will be Hainan Airline's first intercontinental fight.

MANAGERIAL FUNCTIONS

Shifting objectives, contracts and government regulations affect managerial goals in China, making it necessary to be both responsive and flexible.

▲ Altering goals and objectives

In 1998, a survey of 229 foreign-invested companies by management consultants A. T. Kearney showed that only 38% of all manufacturers were covering their operating costs. If the companies had included their borrowing costs, or costs of capital, fewer still could have claimed to have broken even.[33] To achieve profitability, companies may have to leave loss-making businesses in a timely fashion. Li Ka-shing, of Hutchinson-Whampoa highlighted this point: "A big mistake that people make is to like a business too much. You must know when to get out of a business and be willing to act on your decision."

As companies expand their Chinese operations, China's geographic diversity will contribute to changing goals and objectives, as indicated by Austin Hu of the World Bank, Beijing. Hu emphasized that China is moving from state-driven to market-driven planning systems; analysts cannot determine the ultimate influences these two approaches will have on business planning, including the kind of data that companies should seek. Hu also emphasized that today geography primarily shapes business planning in China:

> "[Chinese business planning] really depends [on geography]...China in many ways is a big country, and very diverse. You have so many provinces, you have such disparity in provincial GDPs and cultures — the way they do business is very different. For example, large enterprises, especially the ones in the north, are quite different from those along the coast. Most of the large northern enterprises are quite traditional. They have inherited the SOE in their planning."

Pan Shi Yi of Redstone delineated China's geographic diversity by advising, "You cannot truly know China just by visiting Beijing, Shanghai and the business centers. You must visit and study all the 56 Chinas, the China of each minority race, to truly understand all of China."

Kwek Leng Joo, managing director of City Developments, Ltd (Singapore) and president of the Singapore Chinese Chamber of Commerce and Industry, noted that changing demographics will also affect China's business environments and should affect companies' goals. Kwek stated that the coming generation differs greatly from its predecessors and business as usual may not continue:

> "...they are the first generation of China's single-child policy, and hence do not have the experience of siblings. They grew up in China during a period of such great and rapid change, and had to adapt to it at an early age. They are the first generation to go to China's best universities and then, in significant numbers, go on to study further in the West's best universities, and gain experience working in Western companies and environments — and then come home to China and make use of their Western training and work experience. Just talk to them; I think the impression is very distinct. You talk to them and you can feel that they are at a very different level of maturity than previous generations, and Overseas Chinese [of] the same age. There are not many in China like this now, but their numbers will grow every year."

Access to technologies such as the Internet have changed local companies' goals and business objectives. For example, in the mid to late 1990s, the Internet radically shrank the distance between buyers and sellers, and some Overseas Chinese intermediaries recognized the warning signs. Hong Kong-based Li & Fung successfully adapted to the game's new rules. Traditionally a procurer of Asian textiles for Western clothing manufacturers, Li & Fung has become a one-stop shop for big Western retail stores such as Abercrombie & Fitch and Espirit, USA. To add value to its operations, Li & Fung manages everything from design to tailoring and delivery of clothes on behalf of its clients.

For many foreign companies, the realities of China's markets force changes in goals. When Philips Electronics began operating in China in the early 1980s, the Dutch company adopted an obvious strategy at the time: sell products to a billion Chinese. China, however, did not go according to plan. Instead of becoming a market of boundless demand for Philips's irons, televisions and consumer electronics, China became a place where the company made its products to ship elsewhere. In 2002, Philips operated 23 factories that produced about US$5 billion-worth of goods in China each year, but exported nearly two-thirds. "Our initial vision was to sell in China," said Johan van Splunter, the head of Philips' Asian operations. "Things turned out a bit differently."[34]

Often foreign companies introduce new products into China, and within months a throng of manufacturers, many of them private Chinese companies, start cranking them out. Raging competition sets in, sending prices sliding. Before long, the foreign companies look to new markets, increasingly overseas. Besides Philips, other foreign companies such as General Electric, Samsung Electronics and Toshiba, as well as thousands of Chinese companies, have found that using China as an export base provides more profits, and takes less effort, than selling goods inside the country.

China's manufacturing prowess is forcing companies around the world to scrap old business strategies — and some businesses altogether — and to devise new ways to compete. Indeed, China has become a powerful, global, deflationary force affecting a broad cross-section of industries. In June 2002, exports of electronic products from China to the US hit US$1.2 billion, up 12.3% from May. China's hi-tech exports to the US are growing faster than any sector, up 47% in the first seven months of 2002 over the previous year. Televisions and audio equipment rose at 13% annually between 1998 and 2001, to US$6 billion in 2001; tools and metal implements grew by 23% annually, to more than US$1.5 billion; sporting goods rose by 16% annually, to US$2 billion. As imports from China are rising, US retail prices in these sectors are falling. TV prices have fallen on average by 9% each year since 1998, according to the US Labor Department. Tool prices have fallen 1% each year on average. Sports-equipment prices have dropped by 3% annually.[35]

China itself is experiencing one of the most powerful deflationary periods in modern history. In the past seven years, average prices have declined by nearly 20%. A decade ago, a 21-inch color TV in China sold at over US$400; in 2002, it sold for US$80 and the price is still falling. "China's rise as a manufacturing base is going to have the same kind of impact on the world that the industrialization of the US had — perhaps even bigger," said Andy Xie, an economist with Morgan Stanley in Hong Kong.[36]

▲ Managing relations with the CCP

The CCP pervades business and social environments and yet many foreign companies have no knowledge of its reach. For example, many foreign managers do not know that some of the staff they hire may indirectly receive political instructions that contravene their companies' goals. These same staff may hold high-ranking positions in the CCP that do not correspond to their workplace roles. Foreign companies also have to cope with local labor pools that avoid risk taking and initiative for fear of contravening the CCP's rules that emphasize "unifying thinking".

The CCP's committees and branches provide the outlet through which the Party's 64 million members lead their lives. All government departments, state-run academic institutions and SOEs have Party committees. In foreign JVs, the Chinese partners contain the Party committees; in foreign representative offices, the Chinese employment agencies where Chinese staff register, contain the Party committees. Foreign managers may have great difficulty identifying Party members in their companies as even Chinese employees often do not have comprehensive information.

The *dang'an*, or personal dossier, is the Party's most convenient tool to ensure loyalty in companies. Every Chinese citizen has a *dang'an*, a thin sheaf of paper in a big envelope, which shrinks his or her life to school reports, employment and marriage history and, significantly, political record. No one can see his or her own *dang'an*. When a citizen changes jobs, the new employer's personnel department will formally request the *dang'an* from the old employer's personnel department. Foreigners cannot see or control the *dang'an*. In Beijing, five employment agencies, including the Foreign Enterprise Service Corp., exist primarily to store the *dang'an* of Chinese working for foreign companies. These employment agencies contract out to foreign companies the services of those whose *dang'an* they hold.[37]

If a citizen's employer refuses to release the *dang'an*, he or she can never return to state employment and can only join the informal private economy. Employers routinely withhold political-evaluation letters from employees who do not co-operate, politically or otherwise. In return for the evaluations, employers may demand that employees sign statements surrendering certain benefits — including housing and pensions.

For Chinese private companies, Party connections help a lot. For example, Zhou Furen, one of China's richest men, with a fortune of about US$125 million, owned and ran the Xiyang Group, a manufacturing conglomerate. He served as the CCP's secretary of Xiyang Village and an adviser to the provincial legislature. These connections have helped Zhou. In 1997, he discovered an ailing state-owned sulphuric-acid factory in Jinzhou. The government leased it to him for less than US$700,000 a year, and assumed responsibility for all debts and pension liabilities. Zhou used the sulphuric acid to produce fertilizer and turned the factory into the biggest compound-fertilizer manufacturer in the northeast. However, when he applied to list his fertilizer companies on the Shanghai Stock Exchange, the government applied a quota system; it opted to approve ailing SOEs rather than the Xiyang Group that employed 7,000 people, had assets of 2.5 billion yuan (US$300 million) and was the province's biggest taxpayer. The government scrapped the quota system in 2000, but with the large number of SOEs on the waiting list, Zhou would have to wait for years. He decided to list on the Hong Kong Stock Exchange, instead.[38]

Party connections help to ameliorate the innate hostility towards private companies, but the interests of provincial governments often intrude. Figure 6.1 breaks down some 1,216 companies listed on the Shanghai and Shenzhen Stock Exchanges: SOEs which list only a minority of their shares, and Collectives, or state enterprises run like private companies, dominate these listings. Provincial governments pressure government regulators to discriminate against private companies and give the precious slots to their ailing state dinosaurs.[39] Consequently, private companies, despite excellent Party connections, also have to demonstrate repeatedly that they "play ball" with provincial governments and respond to their interests. Pan Shi Yi, of Redstone, indicated how, whenever possible, he sought to satisfy government goals in his land developments to enhance profits or to build goodwill for subsequent projects. Similarly, in 2000, Zhou invested 900 million yuan (US$109 million) in a Guizhou fertilizer plant in response to national campaigns to develop Western China. To please government officials in Haicheng, close to Xiyang Village, he abandoned his plans to build a steel factory in the southern port of Beihai where he could easily access ore from Australia. The factory's new inland location in Haicheng would reduce annual profits on his investment of 500 million yuan (US$60 million).

FIGURE 6.1: CHINESE COMPANIES LISTED ON SHANGHAI OR SHENZHEN STOCK EXCHANGES

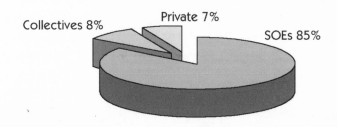

Collectives 8%   Private 7%   SOEs 85%

▲ Extracting contractual obligations

Historically, Chinese managers entered into and maintained contractual relationships with expectations of quick profits. The Chinese merchant classes, both PRC and Overseas Chinese, seek fairly immediate, tangible returns and maintain substantial holdings of liquid assets.[40] Many will not honor contracts, especially with foreign companies, which appear as loss-making propositions.

Prompted by national duty and a desire for profit, present-day Chinese companies frequently seek to accomplish both their own and governments' goals, which can also hurt written contracts. The PRC's companies, for instance, operate under government policy directives to acquire advanced technologies at every opportunity. However, many of their competitive advantages revolve around labor-intensive rather than the capital-intensive technologies which the Western companies possess. Consequently, this directive violates the Chinese companies' economic interests and may lead to contractual violations. As indicated in Chapter 4, many foreign companies have found their local partners violating their brand names to sell inferior, but cheaper, products for the local markets.

As we saw in Chapter 5, in Chinese companies, signed contracts may signal the beginning, rather than the end, of negotiations. Traditionally, significant changes in business situations, or the discovery of new facts as managers learned about new markets, justified renegotiating contractual terms.[41] Consequently, commercial partners should expect periodic quibbling over contractual terms as their business relationships evolve. For instance, many SOEs requested renegotiation of their loan agreements with Western banks, or loan-payment sabbaticals, due to difficulties stemming from the restructuring of the Chinese economy. When Western banks, such as Deutsch Bank, declined or protested, the SOEs refused to render payments. Western banks sometimes roll over debts when their major corporate clients cannot meet obligations; however, in Chinese business practice, this rollover stems from the client's reputation and history of dealings, not their relative size and importance.

Conflicting government goals have also resulted in forced renegotiation and reinterpretation of large-scale signed contracts. These renegotiated contracts have especially hit foreign companies in the power industry, which has displayed great vulnerability to renegotiated contracts. As Raymond Vernon outlined over four decades ago, companies in this sector fall prey to the "obsolescing bargain" with governments; the companies lose power over time because of large fixed investments and an inability to leave without incurring large losses.[42] Investors in the power industry must put up hundreds of millions of dollars before they see any return; since electricity constitutes a public good, the investors base their calculations on negotiated long-term agreements with provincial governments rather than market expectations. In China, power plants supply provincial rather than national electricity grids. Provincial power bureaux negotiate contracts and buy the power. These bureaux also obey provincial regulators and provincial government officials who respond to the concerns of local citizens, especially on prices. As Chinese contract law remains underdeveloped, foreign companies can leave China, or continue to operate in loss-making conditions, if the provincial governments renegotiate their contracts offering unfavorable terms.

Begun in 1998, and involving 17 high-profile international creditors, the Meizhou Wan power plant illustrates this obsolescing bargain. Built as a build-operate-transfer project, the investors planned to transfer the plant to the Fujian government in 20 years. With a US$755 million investment, the power plant served as a model for Beijing's efforts to promote clean, coal-burning thermal power. The State Development Planning Commission approved the 100% foreign-owned high-profile power plant in coastal Fujian province — the first time that a wholly foreign-owned company had received such approval. The Asian Development Bank (ADB) provided funding and equity. The plant's consortium included some of the biggest names in the global power industry. The investors built an elementary school and provided money for community projects. The plant started producing electricity in March 2001, with provincial and central government officials present at the opening ceremony.

The 720MW plant uses low-sulphur coal and expensive electrostatic precipitators to control emissions. This production technology contributes to Beijing's stated goals to clean up power plants and to control environmental pollution. The technology also costs money, and Meizhou Wan became one of the three most-expensive power plants in Fujian. The provincial government found several cheaper options that hurt the Meizhou Wan project. Fujian got half its electricity from hydroelectric plants and received a lot of rain in 2001. With plenty of hydropower, the provincial government could choose whose output it wanted to buy. Simultaneously, Wang Yuan-Chin, chairman of Taiwan's Formosa Plastics group and one of Fujian's largest investors, was bringing his US$3.2 billion operations on stream. These operations included a polluting, coal-fired plant, from which Fujian could buy power. The Fujian provincial government stated that Meizhou Wan's 0.56 yuan (6.7¢) per kwh proved too expensive given the oversupply of power, and offered 0.44 yuan per kwh. In January 2002, Meizhou Wan's four consortium members — InterGen, a JV between Shell and Bechtel; El Paso Gas; Lippo China Resources; and the ADB, whose cumulative lending to China exceeded US$10 billion — began negotiating with the Fujian Power Bureau to lower prices and to keep the plant operating. Till April 1, 2003, Meizhou Wan reached a temporary agreement with the Fujian government to receive .42 yuan per kwh to avoid default on its loans. In April 2003, Mark Takahashi, China Managing Director for InterGen admitted that the long-running negotiations had reached an impasse, threatening to leave the project in limbo indefinitely. "The rate of return isn't very high. It's not what we anticipated when we made this investment", he said. "I don't think investors have reaped the returns that they anticipated when they made their original investments in China. [The Chinese governments] say they will continue to honor contracts. But, what they want the foreign investors to do is to take stock of the situation and adjust accordingly. [43, 44]

The next chapter analyzes the strengths and weaknesses of Chinese strategies.

endnotes

1. Adapted from Lu, Y., *Management Decision-Making in Chinese Enterprise*, p.13.
2. Studwell, J., *The China Dream*.
3. Haley, U. C. V., "Here There be Dragons: Opportunities and Risks for Foreign Multinational Corporations in China."
4. Liu, M and P. Mooney, "Why China Cooks the Books: The Reputation of the People's Republic as an Economic Powerhouse is Based in Part on Pure Bunk," p.40.
5. *The Economist*, "How Cooked are the Books"; Rawski, T. G., "Beijing's Cooked Books", p.A9.
6. Rawski, op.cit., p.A9.
7. *The Economist*, op.cit.
1) Liu and Mooney, op.cit., p.40.
9. Ibid.
10. Piore, A. and P. Mooney, "China's Statistics are Fishier than its Oceans".
11. Haley, op.cit.
12. Studwell, J., *The China Dream*.
13. Ibid.
14. Ibid; Kurlantzick, J., "Making it in China".
15. Fukuyama, F., *Trust: The Social Virtues and the Creation of Prosperity*.
16. Chu, C. N., *Thick Face, Black Heart: The Path to Thriving, Winning & Succeeding*, p.184.
17. Lu, Y., *Management Decision-Making in Chinese Enterprise*.
18. Haley, op.cit.
19. Haley, Tan and Haley, *New Asian Emperors: The Overseas Chinese, Their Strategies and Strategic Advantages*.
20. *The Economist*, "From bamboo to bits and bytes", Survey of Asian Business, p.8.
21. Clendin, M., "China starting to lure back its best brains"; Yi, M., "Land rush to the East", *San Francisco Chronicle*, p.G-1.
22. Gamble, J., "Inside Track: The struggle to get nappies off the ground".

23. Gilley, B. (2002), "Is Yang Bin the Richest Man in China?".

24. Gidoomal, R., and D. Porter, *The UK Maharajahs: Inside the South Asian Success Story*; Haley, G. T., and C. T. Tan, "The Black Hole of Southeast Asia: Strategic Decision-Making in an Informational Void".

25. Compiled from Kahn, J. "China Holds Capitalist Chief of North Korea Trade Zone"; Gilley, B., "The Perils of Flower Power".

26. Haley and Tan, op.cit.; Haley et al, op.cit..

27. Haley et al, op.cit.

28. *The Economist*, "Asia's Superman Swoops Again".

29. Haley, G. T., "A Strategic Perspective on Overseas Chinese Networks' Decision-making."

30. Compiled from Clifford, M. L., H. Filman and S. Reed, "Li Ka-shing Sneaks Back into the Wireless Game," and Clifford, M. L., A. Reinhardt and K. Capell, "Li Ka-shing's Long Shot — or Sure Thing?".

31. Haley et al,; Haley, U. C. V., "The Myers-Briggs Type Indicator and Decision-Making Styles: Identifying and Managing Cognitive Trails in Strategic Decision Making"; Mintzberg, H., "Crafting Strategy"; Mintzberg, H., "The Fall and Rise of Strategic Planning"; Mintzberg, H., and J. Waters, "Of Strategies, Deliberate and Emergent".

32. Dolven, B., "The Best Little Airline in China"; *AFX News*, "Focus. China Airline Industry Restructuring Seen Easing Competition"; *Asian Wall Street Journal*, "Hainan Airlines Posts Higher Net"; *Aviation Daily*, "China Limits Foreign Investment by Single Company to 25 Percent".

33. Studwell, J., *The China Dream*.

34. Leggett, K., and P. Wonacot, "China-Trade — Burying the Competition".

35. Ibid.

36. Ibid.

37. Lawrence, S. V., and D. Murphy, "China-Repression — Appearances can Deceive".

38. *The Economist*, "Not in the Club".

39. *The Economist*, "Set them Free".

40. Haley et al, op.cit.

41. Ibid.

42. See Haley, U. C. V., *Multinational Corporations in Political Environments: Ethics, Values and Strategies,* for a review of shifting power between businesses and governments.

43. Dolven, B., and S. V. Lawrence, "Power — Playing by The Rules," *Far Eastern Economic Review*, January 31, p.52; Kynge, J., "Survey — Energy and Utility Business".

44. Batson, A. "InterGen's China Plant at Impasse in Talks".

7

EVALUATING CHINESE STRATEGY

"The way of heaven
Excels in overcoming though it does not contend,
In responding though it does not speak,
In attracting though it does not summon,
In laying plans though it appears slack."
Tao Te Ching
Book 2, Chapter 73, Stanza 179

INTRODUCTION

"I recognize the weakness of the Chinese," said Stan Shih, the founder, chairman and CEO of Acer, the large Taiwanese computer manufacturer. "I'm talking about business values."[1] Shih identified those values, expelled them from Acer and replaced them with what he perceived to be international best practices. He banned his daughter and two sons from ever working in Acer; his second son got a summer internship, but the working relationship ended there. In a related move, Shih addressed issues of corporate governance before any other Asian company did. He invited outside directors onto Acer's board, began releasing detailed audited accounts every quarter (although Taiwan requires only annual statements) and paid his managers in shares. He told his employees regularly and loudly that he expected them to disagree with him openly; and that they could fail provided they did so for the right reasons. Then Shih committed the ultimate Chinese iconoclasm by stating that Acer's principle encompassed "No control". He transformed the Acer group into a flat rather than a pyramidal organization. The holding company owned no more than 30% of each subsidiary, and Shih controlled no more than 5% of the holding company. As this chapter later elaborates, Acer has continued to evolve in anticipation of problems and opportunities.

Shih pressed the above argument in his 1996 book, *Me-too is Not my Style*, and he has served as a pioneer among Chinese managers despite displaying many traditional characteristics. The quote from the *Tao* at the head of the chapter illustrates that Chinese managers plan; yet, as we discussed in Chapter 6, their planning and cognitive styles differ significantly from those of Western companies.

In this chapter, first we discuss the competencies of Chinese management. The ensuing sections explore some strengths and weaknesses, as well as successful and unsuccessful strategies, of Chinese companies. The final section highlights some aspects of Chinese strategic planning that may lead to crises.

CHINESE CORE COMPETENCIES: SPINNING WEBS

C. K. Prahalad and Gary Hamel indicated that by design or co-incidence, successful companies develop collections of skills at which they excel and which constitute the bases for their success. These key skills they termed the companies' core competencies.[2] Successful planning occurs when companies exploit these core competencies. As core competencies span both Chinese and Western companies, we will cover these in more detail in Chapter 8. Suffice to say here that their core competencies must provide Chinese companies with potential access to multiple markets, must provide their customers with perceived benefits and must prove difficult for their competitors to imitate.

The chairman of a Western agribusiness company's Chinese venture noted that successful PRC and Overseas Chinese companies reacted differently from their North American and European counterparts to market opportunities in China: the former came with a shotgun approach and pared back to what worked; the latter emphasized their core competencies.[3] Haley, Tan and Haley[4] also noted that Overseas Chinese companies pursued conglomerate diversification. Similarly, many of the PRC's companies seem to make nearly everything but the kitchen sink. For example, Haier has some 70 product lines. The Western agribusiness manager observed well but erred in his interpretation. The Chinese shotgun conglomerate approach does draw on core competencies, as this chapter reveals; it also helps the companies to spin webs of influence.

The core competencies of Chinese companies include their decision-making styles, their control over information, and their networks.

▲ Decision-making styles

In Chapter 6, we elaborated on the decision-making styles of Chinese managers. Many researchers have attributed the rapid growth of Overseas Chinese businesses in Southeast Asia to their decision-making styles, especially to their speed of decision-making.[5] This, together with control of information, enables these managers to seize business opportunities before their competitors sense they exist.[6]

Chinese decision-making combines special and readily available market information, with their own experiences and additional subjective data gathered from friends and associates to arrive at business strategies. Their decision-making styles provide the managers with access to various markets (a requirement for a core competency) with scanty data for making analytical decisions, and thereby allow them to avoid competition from at least some Western companies. Their network of information-gathering associates also helps them exploit multiple opportunities (another requirement for a core competency), including present and future scarcities in goods and services, by granting time to stockpile inventories to supply these markets. Competitors, especially Western multinationals with decision-making techniques developed in information-rich environments, and less-well connected local companies, have difficulties imitating this decision-making style (a third requirement for a core competency).

The PRC's managers also display speedy decision-making and reaction times. In addition, they constantly, almost unthinkingly, incorporate the central or provincial government's goals and desires into their planning. The best PRC entrepreneurs wield government plans and goals to their own benefit, to grease their strategic moves as well as to consolidate their control of special market information. As Pan Shi Yi of Redstone told us, "If you recognize the government's needs on one project, it will help them remember you on another." To illustrate this, he provided the example of one of his largest construction projects, Soho, a combined residential/commercial development, across from Beijing's World Trade Center in an area that Beijing's municipal planners have slated as equivalent to New York's Wall Street. The municipal planners wanted to maximize green space and to minimize children's, especially primary school children's, commute to schools. When Pan proposed his development, he incorporated underground parking and the building of a primary school at his expense within the development, something no competing developer offered. Though more expensive upfront, underground parking allowed Pan to maximize green space in the development, to dedicate some of Asia's most valuable land to non-economic purposes (the school), and yet to develop more commercial and residential space. Thereby Pan satisfied the Beijing municipal planners and won the development project. Despite the adjustments to his original plans, he has calculated that his profits should improve slightly overall. The municipal planners have also given Pan more leeway on another current luxury-home development outside the Great Wall near Beijing.

▲ Special market information

Both the Overseas and PRC Chinese maintain control over special market information through their networks. Much of what the Chinese consider special market information would pass as insider information in the West.

In most of Southeast Asia, the Overseas Chinese maintained an informational void or black hole, thereby keeping competitors in the dark and thwarting their strategic plans.[7] In China, the central government deliberately controls and disseminates information that it considers of strategic importance. As we noted in Chapter 3, the central government depends almost entirely on notoriously poor-quality statistical reports from the provinces for its data. The provincial bureaucracies have traditionally manipulated data to curry favor with the national bureaucracies and work hard to align their estimates with national projections. However, many managers have told us that industrial associations are now endeavoring to provide relatively accurate and timely economic statistics for their industries, which belie many official figures. For example, despite China's official growth rate of 8%, independent surveys of industrial capacity, energy use, employment, consumer income and spending, and farm output indicate much slower growth. The Chinese government had long known this and, in 1999, Prime Minister Zhu Rongji complained that "falsification and exaggeration are rampant."[8] Ironically, because of their difficulties in maintaining their *guanxi* contacts in the PRC, the Overseas Chinese — until recently the largest single group of investors in China — are major participants in many of the associations that are gathering market data for China. Despite these efforts at the sectoral levels, conducting due diligence on individual Chinese companies remains difficult and will probably remain so for the foreseeable future.

▲ Networks

While the Overseas Chinese consolidate their networks to span business, governmental and familial concerns, the PRC Chinese differentiate between private-business, government and traditional family networks. In both instances, their mastery of building, maintaining and using networks shows the characteristics of a core competency. The networks provide access to various markets, as the conglomerate diversification and geographic expansion of Overseas Chinese companies reveal. Competitors have difficulty emulating network relationships, which take time to form and to maintain. Finally, the networks provide members with greater perceived security, reduce perceived risk, induce greater flexibility in dealing with business crises, and generate other efficiencies and benefits that companies can pass on to customers.

Importantly, the networks contribute to creating harmony, as Cheung Kim Hung, editor-in-chief of Hong Kong-based *Next Magazine*, has pointed out: "In Chinese business circles," he said, "the emphasis is on harmony. People agree to compete or not to compete." This statement reflects the Taoist belief that societies and individuals prosper when cooperation rules and social harmony prevails; uncontrolled competition can lead to disastrous results. The Chinese empire endured because it cultivated the secrets of harmony, though not without considerable effort. As Etienne Balazs noted,[9] the emperors kept tensions under control by force. Chinese imperial courts continually engaged in battles to maintain harmony, and "the Way" defined a mythical center of gravity for the Chinese polity.

In Taoism, one owes no ethical duty to a competitor, unbounded by familial or friendship ties, than the duty to preserve social harmony. Thus, uncontrolled competition can lead to highly destructive, even self-destructive, behavior. As Maoism declines, the strict harmony that the government has maintained through imperial times has begun to flicker. Erik Eckholm[10] reported an incident where a fight between school children rekindled a rivalry between the dominant clans of two villages. The clans built earthwork defenses, armed themselves with homemade cannons, and waged war against each other. Their duty to maintain social harmony had collapsed under the weight of historic enmity.

"LITTLE SMART":[11] UTSTARCOM EXPLOITS ITS CORE COMPETENCIES

Founded in 1991 by Chinese entrepreneurs Hong Liang Lu and Ying Wu, telecommunications company UTStarcom saw its revenues soar from US$76 million in 1997 to US$925 million in 2002; 85% of these revenues came from China. Since its IPO in March 2000, the company has achieved 12-month profit growth of 47% on net income of US$78.4 million for the same period. UTStarcom's success underscores its managers' opportunistic decision-making styles, their access to special market information and their government networks.

By the mid 1990s, China Telecom, the state-owned telephone monopoly, had undertaken a massive program to build high-capacity voice and data network infrastructure in China. But, the high cost of bridging the last mile from network to handset thwarted its ambitions. Meanwhile, the central government had granted UTStarcom one of only eight licenses to sell equipment to connect cities to the nation's long-distance network. To foster competition, the central government had also spun off wireless carriers China Mobile and China Unicom from China Telecom and refused to grant the latter a license to sell lucrative cellular services.

Spotting an opportunity, UTStarcom devised its personal-access system (PAS) to connect mobile phones to existing copper-line networks while avoiding expensive wiring of buildings. By sending signals through regular phone lines and then through antennae to mobile phones, PAS operates like a heavy-duty cordless phone; it also costs much less than the two main wireless technologies, GSM and CDMA. In December 1997, the Yuhang Telecommunications Bureau, China Telecom's southeast operator, offered PAS as Xiao Ling Tong, literally meaning "Little Smart". With only 175 million fixed-line subscribers in China, 50% of China Telecom's state-of-the art network had been lying fallow; Little Smart allowed the company to use its existing capacity and to satisfy existing demand for wireless services.

Little Smart is the fastest-growing phone service in the world, with subscribers doubling to over five million in 2001. China Telecom and China Netcom (China's second fixed-line telephone company spun off by China Telecom in early 2002) have operated Little Smart through their fixed-line networks. Available in 300 Chinese cities (though not in Beijing, Shanghai and Guangzhou), Little Smart sells on price. Handsets and one-time set-up charges approximate those from cellular services, but subscribers can save more than 70% on calls. As PAS draws on fixed-line networks, it cannot provide roaming services to other cities, and the speed of cars or trains can disrupt its signals. But, Little Smart's target market of middle- and lower-class residents in small towns mostly own bicycles. In effect, Little Smart provides about 80% of cellular service for about 20% of the price. As they piggyback on existing fixed-line networks, PAS networks cost much less than cellular networks and can turn profits in about three to five years; no cellular network reaps profits so quickly. Yet it is provincial and local managers, rather than national managers, who decide on whether to launch the mobile service and what to offer. Huang Wangshun, head of China Telecom's Xiao Ling Tong division, said, "Our attitude towards the future of Xiao Ling Tong is 'go and see', based on how much it costs and how much we benefit from it."

China Mobile and China Unicom, the nation's two licensed cellular operators, tower over Little Smart with 140 million customers. But with over 10% of the market owning cellular phones, the high-end market appears to be saturated. Some 96% of China Mobile's new customers chose cheap pre-paid plans without roaming services — Little Smart's target market. Consequently, Little Smart has engendered fierce opposition from the cellular operators and their supporters in the Ministry of Information Industry (MII). In 1999, competitors argued that China Telecom lacked a license to sell wireless services and UTStarcom lacked one to sell PAS equipment. After fierce lobbying by China Telecom, MII agreed to let Little Smart operate in small and mid-sized cities. Again in May 2000, immediately before China Unicom's listing on the Hong Kong Stock Exchange, MII responded to pressure by halting Little Smart. However, after a month, and because of China Telecom's petitions, MII lifted the ban and allowed Little Smart to operate in small and mid-sized towns, as technically it did not offer cellular service.

As China's market for phone services evolves, UTStarcom is facing other problems and opportunities. Some customers see PAS as an old technology. Yet PAS offers download speeds of between 32 and 64 kilobytes per second, compared to less than 10 kilobytes per second on NTT DoCoMo's iMode in Japan. In response to changing consumer tastes in some cities, China Telecom is offering a premium Little Smart service that emphasizes high-speed data capabilities rather than low price. For example, in Xian, it has launched a value-added subscription plan that provides location-based services and an option called "c-mode", which is similar to NTT DoCoMo's iMode.

Despite Little Smart's popularity, the central government has refused to grant full approval to the PAS technology, or to let UTStarcom enter China's largest and most lucrative cities. While UTStarcom enjoys considerable *guanxi*, it noted in a recent Securities and Exchange Commission (SEC) filing that a single stroke from a bureaucrat's pen "could substantially harm our business, financial condition and results of our operations".

THE STRENGTHS OF CHINESE STRATEGY

The strengths of Chinese strategy derive from their companies' core competencies and include speed, knowledge and *guanxi*.

▲ Speed

The speed of decision and action in Chinese companies stems from their managers' decision-making styles, a characteristic we have previously identified as a core competency. Chinese businessmen often mention speed as a key strength they enjoy. Stan Shih of Acer Computers told us, "We believe in doing things quickly …We implement and change things quickly. It's all implementation in the market place." Simon Murray, former group managing director of Hutchison Whampoa, also emphasized speed when he analyzed Li Ka-shing's legendary decision-making style. "One of the reasons that he is very successful is his timing. He buys when the markets are flat because he has a good balance sheet, and [because of] his speed. Good deals do not stay around for a long time. Everyone wants them. So the man who is quick, who can make decisions quickly, will get the good deals. His story is about a series of good deals." Y Y Wong, chairman of the WyWy Group, reiterated the increased importance of spotting opportunities in the "digital world" in which we live, as opposed to the "analog world" from which we evolved: "I feel that there is a premium now to be able…to identify opportunities before they become obsolete."

Speed in Chinese companies arises through the data their managers use and through the companies' formal structures. First, despite their increasing use of Western-style analytical tools, Chinese managers still use subjective and experiential data which can speed their strategic decision-making. This ability to use both quantitative and subjective decision-making technologies offers a tremendous strength when managers cannot undertake research (as data prove unreliable or nonexistent), or do not have the time to do so. Second, in Chinese companies, strategic decisions generally involve very few levels of hierarchy and people. Consequently, Chinese companies possess a nimbleness of action that most major Western companies envy.

▲ Knowledge

In business situations, knowledge for Chinese managers stems from their control of information, one of their core competencies. Overseas Chinese companies historically conducted business by developing their sources of information through building networks. Their networks provided market research and information; and the managers' talks with trusted members, as well as their own experiences, provided analysis for informed decision-making. However, the large Chinese market complicates the use of networks for information and analysis. In China, unlike Southeast Asia, power seeps through central, provincial and municipal governments as well as various levels of the CCP. Consequently, PRC Chinese managers can rarely access the same kind of knowledge that is available in, say, Malaysia or Thailand. Additionally, hard-line Communists in positions of power often hinder private entrepreneurial ambitions. Despite China's official embrace of free-market philosophies, private businesspeople still suffer from discrimination. For example, they have difficulty getting loans from state-owned banks or listings on one of China's two stock exchanges. Yet, Chinese managers are still able to control their business environments through knowledge more than their Western counterparts can.

First, the networks in China and Southeast Asia control market and business information through excluding outsiders from key listening posts. They accomplish this strategy through supporting their friends in government service for higher offices. Consequently, competitors and non-associates cannot obtain the timely levels of policy information necessary to compete effectively. Second, the Chinese maintain their strength in knowledge through inaction. Business communities in Southeast Asian countries have never desired more readily available market and business information. Until recently, multinational corporations did not lobby for better, or more timely, market information in Asia either. Local Chinese companies generally prefer the strengths that dispersed information and specialized knowledge gives them over outsiders, and also do not lobby for better market information. Asian governments, including the Chinese, do provide information for both consumer and business-to-business markets: however, the freely available data have little competitive consequence; and only insiders and network associates can access the strategically valuable "special market information" that includes government plans for changes in economic policy.

Chongquing Lifan Industries demonstrates[12] the strategic opportunities that knowledge provides and the maze that well-connected managers have to navigate to get it. The company has interests in winemaking, mineral water, sports shoes and a top-ranking soccer team. The company's founder and CEO, Yin Mingshan, considered entering the auto industry, which is enjoying rapid growth but also intense competition. Consequently, he shifted his interests to financial services, which he wants to place at the summit of the "Lifan pyramid". He thinks the government could approve the formation of several private banks in 2003 and 2004. Officially, China has only one private bank, the Minsheng Bank, an organization with strong links to the government.

In 1992, with US$36,000 and nine employees, Yin began as a small producer of motorcycle components. His pursuit of new technologies and export markets quickly turned his company into a giant — and a big contributor to the government's coffers. In 2002, Lifan paid US$15 million in taxes. In 2003, as one of China's wealthiest private entrepreneurs, Lin employed more than 5,000 workers. He carefully curried favor with the CCP and in 2002 told Party officials that he wanted to join. His timing proved opportune: the CCP was trying to woo private businesspeople. In January 2003, the party approved Yin's appointment as deputy chairman of an advisory body to the government of Chongqing municipality, from where he manages his company,. Yin became the first private businessman in China to hold such a high office. One official magazine called his political abilities "the acme of perfection".

Through his position and connections, Yin has garnered strategic information and has tried to influence the business landscape strategically. He has lobbied the government to allow private companies to operate banks, arguing that private banks would promote institutional development and cater more effectively to small and medium-sized enterprises than the big four state-owned giants or the 111 city commercial banks, which are similarly laden with bad debt. The Lifan Group has joined 15 other big private companies in Chongqing in a "study group" to review the establishment of their own private bank in the city. Yin has contended that, since China is allowing foreign banks to expand in accordance with its WTO pledges, it should give domestic non-state investors the same privileges. "We often say that foreign investment is like a son-in-law: it's no good acquiring one if it makes your son walk off in anger," he said.

Because of his connections, and his ability to ascertain the CCP's policy directions, Yin had chosen the right moment to make his case. At its 16th Congress in November 2002, the CCP announced that private capital would be able to access all areas open to foreign capital — but did not specify any dates. The Lifan Group would particularly welcome new opportunities, as it needs to diversify. Competition in motorcycles has become intense, and profit margins are falling. The group has a big share of the export market to Vietnam, but there too it faces rapidly growing competition and vicious price wars. However, the Chinese government has been slow to experiment with private banking. Yin, ever sensitive to official moods, has also urged caution. "We should have [private banks], but not too many at once. Those who fulfill the conditions should be allowed to go first," he said. Nevertheless, Lifan will likely emerge as one of the first private Chinese banks because of Yin's timely strategic knowledge.[13]

▲ *Guanxi*

No exact English translation exists for the Mandarin term *guanxi*, but it incorporates trust, as well as the ability to project uprightness and to build relationships. "Uprightness" captures the notion of individuals comprehending their respective position and stature within networks and their proper behavior in social or business situations. *Guanxi*, often culturally specific, constitutes a significant strength for the Chinese throughout Greater China (East Asia outside of Japan and South Korea), and Southeast Asia.

During the course of our research, many managers informed us that rather than diminishing in importance in China, maintaining *guanxi* has assumed more complexity. Because of the three semi-autonomous networks operating in China — family, government and private business — managers often have to reside in China and to work continuously to maintain *guanxi*.

Kuok Khoon Ean, executive chairman of Kuok Ltd. (Singapore), a subsidiary of the Kerry Group, identified *guanxi*, along with perseverance and patience, as being key to success in China. Of *guanxi*, Kuok said, "I think it is important; it means you have good relations; but I don't think it is the only ingredient that can bring about success. I think integrity, perseverance, patience and, of course, good relationships help a lot." The Kerry Group was among the first private companies to enter China and has one of the longest and greatest records of success in the country. Indeed, when Coca-Cola was floundering in China, it turned to the Kerry Group for assistance and *guanxi*.

XINHUA FINANCIAL NETWORK[14]: FUSING KNOWLEDGE AND *GUANXI*

Fredy Bush, the American founder and CEO of Xinhua Financial Network (XFN), is pioneering the spread of Western-style financial information in China. Until she founded XFN in 2000, China had had no independent market intelligence. Xinhua, the country's only official news agency, forms part of China's propaganda ministry.

China's estimated 10 million individual investors (the government claims 69 million, but no independent reports can verify this figure) use news websites that concentrate on market gossip. Institutional investors had no dedicated wire service, nor could they rely on common benchmarks or indices. For example, China's two stock exchanges, in Shanghai and Shenzhen, calculate market averages without adjusting for the shares that investors can actually buy — an important omission as the Chinese government generally owns about two-thirds of the listed companies. Investors also could not garner industry-specific averages. In addition, foreign companies that wanted to enter JVs had no standard way of gauging their potential partners' risk because no credit ratings existed.

In 2003, XFN dispatched over 300 wire stories a day to Chinese fund managers. The company issues credit ratings, which forces Chinese companies to adhere to some standard Western reporting practices. It also issues a series of indices, properly weighted by the free float of shares. In April 2003, one of China's mutual-fund companies launched the first family of funds linked explicitly to XFN's indices, including those for high-tech shares and cyclical stocks.

To extract strategic market information, XFN needed modern Western-style technical know-how and traditional Chinese *guanxi*. For technical know-how, Bush brought in FTSE, a British company that calculates London's FTSE 100 index. For *guanxi*, she formed a partnership with Xinhua but has emphasized that Xinhua provides no capital and no employees, which could undermine XFN's credibility with institutional investors and unduly influence the company's reporting. Rather, Xinhua opens doors for XFN, shields the company from bureaucratic and regulatory hazards, and protects it from other Western competitors that need Xinhua's approval to expand their reporting in China. Xinhua has also promised not to launch a rival service for 20 years.

THE WEAKNESSES OF CHINESE STRATEGY

Perversely, the weaknesses of Chinese strategy also stem from the core competencies of companies and include their home-turf-only dominance, their susceptibility to be blindsided, their poor proprietary capabilities, family limits and a lack of institutional memory.

▲ Home-turf only

The home-turf-only weakness stems from the core competency of the control of information. The Chinese remain extremely competitive in some industries, such as real estate and hotels, regardless of where they compete. However, when they have moved into other areas of business, such as packaged consumer products and services, they have initially had significant difficulties competing effectively. Hong Kong property developer Lee Shau Kee's travails provide an example of an inability to diversify successfully outside property development. In 1994, *Forbes* magazine identified Lee as Asia's richest man and the world's fourth-richest, with assets of US$15 billion. Even before the apogee of his career, Lee had realized that he needed to find new growth sources for his flagship company, Henderson Land Development. Yet with the exception of Hong Kong and China Gas of which he became chairman in 1983, his sorties outside property development have proven unsuccessful: these include Hong Kong and Yaumati Ferry, Henderson China and Henderson Cyber.[15] Poor understanding of the businesses, little say for outsiders including those with expertise, and strict family control appear to have stifled these businesses.

Li Ka-shing, although immensely successfully, also faltered initially in two mid-1980s ventures into Western markets.[16] First, in Canada he bought Husky Oil, Ltd., and incurred losses of US$183 million before his acquisition showed profits in 1993. Second, in Britain, his company Hutchison set up Rabbit, a cordless-phone company that sputtered; Li again incurred losses of US$183 million before he walked away from the company. Subsequent investments in the European telecom industry, however, have proven much more successful for Li. True to his doctrine of never forming too strong an attachment to any investment, Li sold his European telecom interests, Orange, to fund the development of one of Asia's most successful Internet-based companies, Tom.com.

Many Chinese companies fail when not on home turf because managers depend on intimate knowledge of their businesses and markets for their decisions, and also on the significant superiority of this knowledge over that of their competitors. These Chinese managers often cannot compete effectively on the relatively level playing fields found in the information-rich market environments of the industrial democracies. Also, as they gain their knowledge through the trials and errors of personal experience, the managers sometimes have difficulty transferring it to Western or otherwise diverse markets where few similarities with their traditional markets exist. Consequently, when Chinese managers leave their home markets, they lose their knowledge-based core competency and strength and have to work hard to recover and to re-establish it.

▲ Susceptibility to blindsiding

Any trust-based system such as the Chinese networks falls prey to blindsiding. Though trust provides enormous economic benefits,[17] it also exposes those employing it as a primary competitive tool to significant losses when others betray that trust. The collapse of Hong Kong-based Peregrine Investments Holdings presents the classic example of blindsiding. Peregrine grew to be non-Japanese Asia's largest and most respected homegrown investment house over a 10-year period. Peregrine's collapse came after the Indonesian government allowed the rupiah to float and to plummet in value, losing about 80% of its value within a six-month period in 1998. Because of the devaluation and problems with governance, a major Indonesian debtor, Steady Safe, defaulted on the US$260 million bridge loan it had obtained from Peregrine. Peregrine could not extract any payment on the loan. Neither the Hong Kong government nor the

Indonesian government investigators could determine what happened to the US$260 million, which had disappeared without a trace. The traditional trust-based relationships that it had employed completely broke down and destroyed Peregrine.

▲ Poor proprietary capabilities

The poor proprietary capabilities of Chinese companies stem from the often reactive nature of traditional strategic decision-making.[18] Reactive managers rarely innovate products or technologies or seek to build brand equity. They only adopt new products, technologies and strategies once their competitors succeed through their proprietary capabilities. Stan Shih of Acer recognized this major potential problem when he said, "Branding is ... unusual in this part of the world."[19]

Aware of this problem, the best Chinese companies are developing respected brand names, such as Haier, Legend Computers, Tiger Balm, San Miguel Beer, Shangri-La Resorts and Hotels, Banyan Tree Resorts and Sound Blaster. In 1999, Far East Organization moved quickly to acquire Singapore's Yeo Hiap Seng food and beverage division. A household name in Singapore and Malaysia, Yeo Hiap Seng is a leading producer of carbonated and non-carbonated beverages, including the Yeo and H Two O brands and drinks such as Pink Dolphin and SoyRich. Many Chinese analysts argued that Far East had overpaid for the division. Yet, Philip Ng, executive director and CEO of Far East told us, "We went after Yeo Hiap Seng because it was a company that had family problems,[20] and it had a brand name which we all appreciate ... Yeo Hiap Seng is one of the few homegrown name brands. We also saw that Yeo Hiap Seng had a component of property to it that we could value and other people that were looking at it could not. They saw Yeo Hiap Seng as a food processor." Far East has built on the reputations of these brands so that it can compete successfully against Western icons such as Coke and Pepsi.

As we saw in Chapter 4, the proprietary capabilities of Chinese companies have been shaped by China's regulatory environment and legal history. Though exceptions exist, most Chinese companies, even those in high-tech industries (such as Sparkice), have not invested heavily in the development of cutting-edge technologies. Instead, their managers have worked to acquire Western technologies to compete effectively and swiftly with Western competitors. Consequently, few Chinese and Overseas Chinese companies worry about protecting technologies through building brand awareness and demand in home markets.

Through the 1990s, policymakers and businesspeople in China generally looked on the protection of intellectual property as simply a trade dispute pitting the wealthy West against the developing East. Currently, many Chinese also see intellectual-property violations as a serious domestic problem. In particular, the failure to enforce copyright and patent laws has severely affected China's creative industries. Consequently, Chinese artists have begun to join Western companies such as Microsoft and AOL Time Warner to protest against China making cheap knockoffs across a broad spectrum of production areas. For example, Zhang Yimou's big-budget martial-arts film "Hero", a movie with an all-star cast led by Jet Li, cost US$30 million to produce, making it China's most expensive film production. Unprecedented security including security guards, metal detectors, and identity-card numbers, accompanied its Beijing preview in October 2002, along with requests not to make illegal copies. "After the release we often have only three days before the pirate copies hit the market," said Jiang Wei, of New Pictures, the distributors that handled the movie's release in China.[21]

Artists and their lawyers have stated that piracy has worsened since China joined the WTO in 2002 and pledged to meet international standards for protecting intellectual property. "The Touch", an action-adventure film was another recent casualty. DVD copies appeared on the Chinese black market four days after the nationwide release in August 2002 and ticket sales slid fast. A popular folk-music group, Yi Ren Zhi Zao, had an even shorter run with its latest CD. A pirated disk made from an earlier tape release hit the market before the authentic version appeared in stores. In 2003, 41 pirated versions of the album existed, and many top Chinese department stores openly sold the pirated versions. The legal CD had a 1.2% market share.

A flurry of domestic lawsuits on patent and copyright protection has highlighted the problems that some Chinese companies face. The country's two leading Internet portals, Sohu.com and Sina.com, sued each other for stealing each other's content. Zhou Yaping, who runs Yi Ren Zhi Zao's production company, sued Chinese factories for manufacturing the illegal CDs. He won damages of 300,000 yuan (about US$36,300) in a Beijing court. Even the Buddhist monks of the famed Shaolin Temple that pioneered Shaolin boxing have joined the fight. The monks are trying to trademark their name and have filed suits against companies that use Shaolin as a brand, including one local manufacturer of canned pork.

▲ Family limits and corporate governance

The weakness of family limits still exists among the Overseas Chinese companies, but is diminishing as the families professionalize their approach to managing their companies. The historical family limits on Overseas Chinese companies originated from Chinese businesses resembling a Chinese family. In our book, *New Asian Emperors*,[22] we characterized the traditional Chinese perspective on business management as a case of "Not the family business, but the family as a business". China's present single-child generation, with no large group of siblings or cousins, may change this perspective of family control. As Steven Chan, executive chairman of Superior Multi-Packaging, mused to us, China's growing young elite is the first generation that has grown up without siblings and it remains to be seen how seriously this will affect their behavior and predilections.

When Chinese companies have talented family members running their businesses, they often take risks and prosper;

however, they could also flounder if control passes to lackluster scions of controlling families. Consequently, any period of succession poses significant uncertainties for family-controlled businesses. Despite the risks, some companies have effected smooth transitions of all-in-the-family leadership including the United Overseas Bank (UOB) and Wuthelam Group of Singapore; Hutchison Whampoa/Cheung Kong Holdings of Hong Kong; The Kerry Group of Hong Kong, Singapore and Malaysia; and Hong Leong City Development of Singapore.

THE FAMILY PERSPECTIVE[23]: WHEN THE OVERSEAS CHINESE OVERCOME

Li Ka-shing is one of China's most trusted and farsighted businesspeople. His elder son, Victor, sits on Li's boards and Li is grooming him for succession. His younger son, Richard, has become a telecom tycoon in his own right. On the surface, Li's companies seem to embody many of the weaknesses of Chinese management. Li senior's leadership style seems secretive and strict. Li has also designed his corporate structures to maximize his family's control with minimal capital; the structures are among the most complex pyramids in Asia. Analysts have found monitoring transactions within this empire to be a daunting task.

Nonetheless, Li's companies rank among the few that international investors have consistently trusted with their money, even through the Asian financial crisis. Family considerations have not interfered with Li's ability to choose and to attract the best Chinese or Western managers. Even if minority shareholders have little say in the running of his empire, Li has resisted the temptation to exploit them. "He always leaves enough for us on the table," one investor stated. "We operate the company Western-style, although with an Eastern touch," said Canning Fok, who runs Hutchison Whampoa and is one of Li's most trusted managers.

Charoen Pokphand (CP Group), the largest conglomerate in Thailand, presents another encouraging example. The CP Group's interests range from chicken feed to telecoms. In the boom years leading up to 1997, the ethnic-Chinese Chearavanont family that controls CP Group, expanded into several unrelated businesses. Since the crisis, the family has changed its ways. The family now focuses the group more tightly, and has sold supermarkets, a brewery, a motorcycle maker and several pharmaceutical subsidiaries to reduce its debt. The family has also made the businesses more transparent. When it recently tried to inject several privately held companies into the CP Group's listed companies at dubious valuations, the family listened to complaints by minority shareholders and is now negotiating with them. "They're torn between allegiance to the family and to the shareholders," said Mark Mobius, whose Templeton fund held a 7% stake in the CP Group.

The Singapore government has taken significant steps to curb the potential evils of family-controlled management that include unrelated conglomerate diversification. For example, Singapore banks must dispose of the bulk of their non-core holdings by July 2004 to comply with new regulations. However, recent developments at UOB, an extremely well-managed family company, demonstrate that families have a way of maintaining that control. Founded by a group of Overseas Chinese businessmen in 1935, UOB is one of the bigger Asian banks, and owns one of the biggest stock-brokerage operations in Singapore. It stands out as one of the few large family-run companies in Singapore. Wee Cho Yaw, the current chairman and CEO, succeeded his father, the founder and first chairman, Wee Kheng Chiang. The next generation of Wee sons appears well trained to run various parts of their corporate empire. To comply with the new regulations, in 2002, UOB sold a stake in Haw Par, a property and health-product company that makes Tiger Balm ointment, by distributing most of the shares it owns to UOB's stockholders. The company thereby set the stage for Haw Par to emerge as a holding company for UOB's other non-core assets. After July 2004, the bank cannot own more than 10% of a non-financial company or have property holdings exceeding 20% of the bank's capital funds. Salomon Smith Barney estimated that UOB's equity stakes in various hotel and property companies amount to S$1.3 billion. Sin Mui Tan, head of research at Merrill Lynch, expected the family to inject the bank's other holdings, which include stakes of 45% in both property and hotel groups, United Overseas Land and Overseas Union Enterprise, into Haw Par as well.

Analysts expected the Wee family, which controls both UOB and Haw Par, to increase its stake in Haw Par and to make a partial or full takeover of the company. The Wee family's stake in UOB was diluted in 2001 when the bank acquired a smaller rival, Overseas Union Bank, and currently stands at 11.1%. By increasing the stake in Haw Par, which owns a 4% stake in UOB, the Wee family could increase its effective stake in UOB. If the proposed share distribution goes ahead, the Wee family will increase its stake in Haw Par to about 18.5% from 15 %[24].

Issues of corporate governance specifically contribute to the weakness of Chinese companies. PRC Chinese companies, for instance, have astonishingly complicated ownership structures. Zhang Ruimin, Haier's CEO, described his company as a "collective" rather than state-owned. In fact, the company has publicly owned units, other government-owned units, and still other upper-management controlled units. These complex structures have an impact on managerial incentives and decision-making and have implications for investors who often cannot understand reporting relationships. The Haier group's finances are something of a black box and many investors have failed to comprehend how the company plans to pay for its expanding product lines and geographical forays. The Haier group comprises dozens of companies, but only one has a listing on Shanghai's Stock Exchange. That listed unit — refrigerator and air-conditioner maker Quingdao Haier — faces stiff pressure from domestic competitors. In July 2002, it reported that net profits in the six months through June fell 45%, to US$26 million.

▲ Lack of institutional memory

Many Chinese companies lack an institutional memory. Because of their concentrated, often family-controlled, structures, most Chinese and Overseas Chinese companies depend heavily on the personal experiences of their owners and long-time key executives. Highly centralized, often top-down, decision-making permeates these companies. If the owners or key executives die or, more unlikely, defect, companies lose their base of market knowledge. This loss of key personnel can cause much greater short-term damage to Chinese companies than to most Western companies, which tend to nurture institutional memory through professionalization and codification of data. Their managers use dispersed decision-making that minimizes the damage caused by the demise or defection of key executives.

SOME STRATEGIES THAT WORK

Eastern planning displays several strengths abroad (offensive strategies) and at home (defensive strategies).

▲ Tactical speed

Abroad, tactical speed, stemming from the managers' decision-making styles, can provide success when Chinese managers have experiential data from similar markets and understand the potential effectiveness of strategies. On first-time investments, Chinese and Overseas Chinese managers generally invest relatively small amounts of money that they can afford to lose. They conduct subjective evaluations of opportunities using their prior experience, inputs from trusted associates, and readily available data. The managers fill in strategic gaps as they gain first-hand knowledge of their new products and markets.

"We like to work fast," said Michael Jemal, president and CEO of Haier America Trading. (So fast, in fact, that Jemal expected US sales to hit US\$1 billion by 2005, just 10 years after Haier entered the market.[25]) Haier has aimed to compete not just on price, but also on market-share through user-friendly design, innovative features and top service for a wide range of appliances and consumer electronics. The company's long-term plans have included persuading US consumers to associate its brand name with those of the highest quality Japanese companies, including Toyota and Sony. But, while these Japanese companies took years to reach pre-eminence in the US, Haier has seemed to want it all done yesterday. Zhang Ruimin, Haier's CEO, took an ailing Chinese SOE that was selling shoddy refrigerators and, by stressing quality, transformed it into a company with US$5 billion in sales worldwide and a stranglehold on the Chinese market. Indeed, Haier has quietly become the world's sixth-largest appliance maker.

To achieve growth, Zhang adopted a structure that seems designed to provide maximum nimbleness. Many successful Japanese companies in the US typically work through wholly-owned subsidiaries headed by managers from headquarters. Conversely, Haier American Trading is a JV formed in 1999 between the parent company that holds a majority stake, and a small group of US investors led by Jemal. More importantly, Jemal, with two decades of experience in the US appliance market, has run US operations, not the Chinese parent. Jemal and other US managers have insisted they have great autonomy to promote their brands and to scour for new accounts.

Haier has enjoyed its biggest success to date in compact refrigerators, typically used in college dormitories and offices. In 2003, the company claimed to have 40% of the market, but released no accounting or profit figures for its US subsidiary. Although Haier has competed mostly on price, it also sells an upper-end wine cooler. The company worked hard to give the wine cooler a classy look: it features a smoked-glass door, slightly curved body, soft interior lighting and slide-out chrome racks. "We've associated ourselves with a product that is attractive to high-end consumers," Jemal explained. The wine cooler, which sells for US$400, made the cover of the International Wine Accessories catalogue in Spring 2001. The product also provides an example of Haier America's spotting an opportunity and moving quickly to capitalize on it. Haier introduced its first model in July 2000, less than a year after a US-based team conceived and designed it. The Chinese company sold 100,000 units in 2001, and had a dozen models available in 2002. Popular retailers such as PC Richards and Best Buy liked the product and displayed it prominently in their New York and Los Angeles stores.[26]

MOLTECH POWER SYSTEMS[27]: CHINA'S CHARGE INTO US BATTERIES

In October 2002, the Chinese government made a groundbreaking move into US manufacturing by acquiring Moltech Power Systems, a bankrupt battery-maker from Gainesville, Florida. The Shanghai Huyai Group, a Chinese state-owned chemical company, paid US$20 million to acquire the US battery manufacturer. In 2001, Moltech filed for bankruptcy because of competition from Chinese producers of rechargeable batteries. The Moltech deal marks the first time that the Chinese government has moved to acquire and to operate a company in the US. Previously, it had bought large numbers of overseas assets since 1999, but had moved them back to China so that it or local companies could run them.

The negotiations between Moltech and Huyai were as unconventional as the deal itself. Christopher Higgins, a 14-year-old schoolboy and son of Marty Higgins, Moltech's president, played a major part in the negotiations. "Christopher is studying Mandarin in school," Marty Higgins explained. "He is very bright, a straight-A student, and I don't speak the language. He knows enough to say 'My dad needs a higher price.'"[28]

The Chinese government's goals in acquiring Moltech include gaining technology, know-how, equipment, management and a solid customer base in the US, Higgins surmised.[29] Moltech manufactures a lightweight, high-drain battery with a technological edge over batteries that local Chinese companies currently manufacture. Electric bikes, which are gaining popularity in China, incorporate Moltech's batteries.

While Huyai planned to move some of Moltech's equipment to a new plant in Shanghai, Moltech's management will remain in Florida, in Newcastle-under-Lyme (in the UK) and in Mexico to run the business. Unusually for a takeover in manufacturing, Moltech will lose no jobs. Instead, the number of employees in Florida will likely double to more than 200 in 2003. The Chinese government also hopes to enjoy more influence on Capital Hill as it employs US workers and, in this instance, Chinese interests also directly involve US jobs.

▲ Learning

At home, Chinese companies have demonstrated an astounding ability to learn from their competitors and collaborators and to transfer this knowledge to the Chinese market. Their successful learning strategies appear to stem from their ability to fuse both hard and soft data, and to cross-validate their market information through subjective and objective means. The IT sector provides many examples of this learning. The Chinese government has targeted the IT industry as one in which to acquire technology, and insists that foreign companies share technology with their mainland partners. This strategic approach is paying dividends. Chinese companies are learning to make some fairly sophisticated products via JVs with Western and Japanese manufacturers, and are often beating them in the Chinese market with their products. For example, China's Capitel Group has a JV with Nokia China to produce mobile phones but has also branched out on its own, designing and making middle-market wireless phones. "Capitel is a partner, but also a competitor," said Chijin Liu, vice-president of Nokia China. "We extend our help so that they can learn how to build and promote a local brand. This is inevitable."[30] Nokia is also helping a domestic competitor to become a global competitor in a much shorter period of time than Capitel would have been able to do on its own.

▲ Distributional dominance

Joe O'Leary of the Polaroid Corporation believed that "distribution in China is one of the biggest challenges that Western companies face".[31] At home, Chinese companies work hard to exploit their networks and *guanxi* to gain control of distribution. Chinese companies such as TCL in mobile-phone handsets (which it started making in 1999) and Legend in computers (which it started making in 1990), effectively wielded their local distribution networks that reach deep into the countryside. In 2003, TCL held third place and Legend first place in their respective markets.

Chinese regulations generally treat distribution as a distinct sector, rather than an inherent element of manufacturing. Consequently, the central government has to approve any foreign participation in distribution. Provincial and local governments control market access to an even greater degree than the central government. Foreign companies have to gain local licenses to operate and generally have to compromise. Local governments control distribution channels to allocate and to manage market share, to protect favored industries from competition and to shape investment patterns. The power of local governments ranges from influencing the export ratios of foreign companies, to approving labor contracts for JVs that seek to shed pre-existing distribution staff, to designating local manufacturers who qualify for distribution rights.

Other circumstances provide considerable leeway for local companies to leverage their *guanxi*:[32]

- Regulations on distribution incorporate considerable ambiguities leading to both legitimate differences in interpretation and considerable legal efforts to find loopholes.
- Central and local governments routinely use this ambiguity to confer privileges on favored companies or industries, and to withhold normal rights from companies or industries as a form of protectionism.
- Administrative guidance from various and competing sources can override the basic laws or regulations, either explicitly or unofficially.

- Provincial or local governments may interfere with the national limits on distribution by their generosity (to lure investment or to meet local goals) or restrictions (to protect local interests)

Guanxi with local army officials assumes particular importance for distribution. Some estimates suggest that the People's Liberation Army (PLA) controls distribution of goods for up to about 80% of the Chinese population. Its control over manufacturing facilities also makes the PLA China's largest and most diversified manufacturer of industrial and consumer goods. Any company that competes with the PLA in China must maintain good relationships with the military leadership.

Both Western and Chinese companies know that distribution critically affects financial collections (most notably, accounts receivable), marketing and service. Companies have to know their customers to get paid in China and this knowledge requires intimate participation in distribution. When restrictions on distribution insulate foreign or Chinese companies from their customers, they also cannot undertake direct market research and have to rely on less-sophisticated surrogates. For example, interns at General Motors (GM) in Beijing have scoured the streets of the capital to find out who is buying their cars after the middlemen get them, so that GM can build *guanxi* with the buyers.

To a lesser extent, Overseas Chinese companies also control distribution in Southeast Asia. In the mid 1990s, the American discount retailer K-Mart discovered that relationships between the distribution channels and Singapore's own low-end retailers curtailed K-Mart's success. K-Mart had to rely on its US suppliers, and could not develop local sources for its products. With its higher costs, K-Mart could not compete effectively on price at the low end of the market; its discount-store position in the market also prevented it from raising prices for profitability. K-Mart opened two stores in Singapore, and closed its doors within two years following significant losses.

SOME STRATEGIES THAT FAIL

Eastern planning also displays several weaknesses abroad (offensive strategies) and at home (defensive strategies).

▲ The limits of *guanxi*

Guanxi involves navigating complex relations between networks of power, prestige and influence. Even the most seasoned and successful wielders of *guanxi* can fall prey to its minefields, especially when discrete or overlapping networks clash, as Yang Bin's experiences reveal.

In Chapter 6, we highlighted entrepreneur Yang Bin's extraordinary rise as China's Tulip King. Several attributed his rise to his strong, provincial political connections and *guanxi*. However, Yang Bin appears to have reached the limits of his *guanxi*. On September 24th, 2002, Kim Jong Il, the North Korean dictator announced that the Chinese businessman would have unfettered administrative control over a new free-trade zone in Sinuiju, a bleak backwater near the Chinese border. Besides his political connections, Yang had achieved fame for his quixotic project to transform a gritty corner of China into a replica of old Europe. A Chinese Foreign Ministry spokesperson officially welcomed the Sinuiju zone. However, on October 4th, as Yang was preparing to leave for North Korea, the Beijing government arrested him for suspected tax evasion, falsifying company reports and violating land-use laws. "China is my motherland and I will always love her," said Yang as the police arrested him. "Of course, the mother can sometimes misunderstand the child, and the child does not always obey."[33] On July 15th, 2003, in a closed-door hearing, a Shenyang judge convicted Yang of fraud and bribery and sentenced him to 18 years in prison.

By arresting and sentencing Yang, Beijing sent a signal to its one-time Communist ally, North Korea, that it should consult more about its radical plans to create a Hong Kong-style economic and political zone directly across the Yalu River from the Chinese military. Yang confirmed that North Korea had not informed China in advance of the September 24th announcement, and this probably accounted in part for Beijing's pique.

Yang's political patrons included Bo Xilai, the governor of Liaoning Province that includes Shenyang, where Yang planned his ambitious theme park, Holland Village; and Deputy Prime Minister Li Lanqing. Yang appears to have received very special treatment in that deal: for example, he skirted normal procedures to secure the 544-acre parcel of land that the local government had zoned for agricultural use. However, some of Yang's key political patrons had fallen before him. Amid a major corruption scandal in 2000, Beijing executed Shenyang's vice-mayor and sentenced its terminally ill mayor to life in prison, where he later died.[34]

▲ Poor governance

Some Chinese companies have faced increasing pressures from minority shareholders and outside investors for increased disclosure, transparency and accountability. Generally, these Chinese companies have managed relations with their investors poorly and fanned concerns over transparency. Debacles due to poor governance in 2002 include Yang Bin's Euro-Asia Agricultural Holdings, Beauforte Investor's Corp and Paul Y-ITC.[35] Indeed, in 2004, a crisis of credibility surrounds mainland Chinese companies started by new entrepreneurs who nevertheless follow secretive, traditional, Chinese management practices and seem extremely vulnerable to shifting government networks

Some Chinese companies have launched belated strategies in response to this crisis of credibility. For example, in 2002, New World tried unsuccessfully to respond to pressures for increased disclosure through restructuring. However, the company released too little information on its debts and cash flows and continued to trade at an 84% discount to its net value. Similarly, Hang Lung Group, listed on the Hang Seng Index, included for the first time in its annual report a section on corporate governance, detailing the structure of its boards and committees, accountability and internal audit policies, and corporate codes of conduct. Chaoda Modern Agricultural Holdings also said it would report quarterly to improve transparency and to restore confidence in the mainland's firms. Unfortunately, Chaoda looked too much like Euro-Asia: privately owned, in the agricultural business, and with abnormally high profit margins and exponential growth rates in revenues and profits. Chaoda's auditor refused to sign off on its results.

▲ Failure against high-end competitors

Speed without some prior understanding of markets is not a strength. Without prior knowledge, either through direct or lateral transfers of experience across industries, Chinese strategies falter abroad. Indeed, 70% of China's exports consist of labor-intensive products such as garments, toys, shoes and furniture. By contrast, the country's companies are increasingly producing capital-intensive products such as computers, cars or semiconductors, but they are not exporting them. These companies are also not attacking foreign companies in their home markets. Legend Group, for instance, produces China's biggest computer brand and is a stunning success in its domestic market. But its CEO, Yang Yuanqing, conceded that it would be years before he would even think about going head-to-head with IBM in the USA. In cars, all the JVs between foreign and Chinese companies (with the exception of Honda in Guangzhou) sell only to the domestic market. Shanghai's semiconductor plants, too, aim at the booming demand for simple commodity chips inside China.

Even the best-run Chinese companies have trouble fighting Western companies on their own terrain and Acer provides such an example. In the 1980s, Stan Shih built the Acer Group into one of Taiwan's greatest success stories. By the mid 1990s, Acer had become one of the few high-profile non-Japanese Asian brands. Now, just 27 years after its birth, Acer has hit a mid-life crisis. Most of the US$9 billion conglomerate, which produces everything from LCD monitors to cell-phones, is still thriving; but Acer Inc., its flagship company (and the one closest to Shih's heart), is not. In 2001, sales dropped to US$3.2 billion, from a peak of US$5.8 billion in 1999, and profits sank to US$30 million, down from US$232 million two years earlier. Acer's share of the global PC market slipped from 4% in 1996 to 2.9%. (Dell had the largest market share with 14%.) The problem: Acer suffered a knockout against PC industry heavyweights in the USA during the 1990s, losing tens of millions of dollars in the world's largest and most cut-throat PC market.

In 2000, the brilliant and indomitable Shih unveiled a sweeping strategy to return Acer Inc. to health. He decided to pull out of the USA and focus on China's huge and fast-growing market. Shih wanted to transform Acer Inc. from a top-ten global PC manufacturer into a marketing and services powerhouse, selling its own PCs and IT expertise to Greater China and then to the rest of the world. "The higher value-added," said Shih, "is in R&D, intellectual-property creation, and marketing" — not in making things on the cheap.[36]

However, according to Kitty Fok, IDC's Hong Kong-based research director for PCs, Acer's market share in China hovered around 3% in 2001, compared with 31% for Legend. Also, since entering China in 1998, Dell has attained a 4% market share, the second highest among foreign companies, after IBM's 5%. Like Acer, Dell is eyeing the consumer market. In July 2001, Dell rolled out a budget desktop called the SmartPC, which sells for about US$600. Richard Ward, who heads Dell's consumer business in Asia, said the company offers "international quality at a local price".[37] Acer, makes the identical pitch with its marketing slogan in China: "Global brand at a local price." However, Chinese consumers know of Acer as a Taiwanese company and may see it as something neither foreign (which carries cachet) nor local (which Chinese see as inexpensive). Nevertheless, for its future, Acer has to compete in China against US companies at the high end. J.T. Wang, Acer Inc.'s president, said he had only one guideline in this mighty war: "Don't do business with losses."[38]

WEBS ANCHORED ON GREASE

Asian economies, especially China's, are undergoing enormous changes in the form of advancements in technology, increases in market size and wealth, and the advent of fierce new foreign competitors for local markets. China's growth and exports depend on Western investments and, to the Chinese government's amazement, Western multinational corporations, with their enormous contributions to the country's growth and exports, have become surprising stakeholders in Chinese policies and plans. These changes have exposed the old weaknesses of Chinese planning, and have created new weaknesses, especially in crisis management, where methods of control and command no longer seem to apply. Chinese planning is at a cross-roads in the global economy, as the government's handling of Severe Acute Respiratory Syndrome (SARS) revealed.

▲ Sickness and subterfuge

According to the World Bank, SARS, which originated in China's Guangdong province, in mid November 2002, has propelled East Asia into an economic period "as troubled and uncertain as any since the 1997–98 financial crisis". SARS has threatened China's credibility, and forced the central government to admit that it misrepresented and suppressed key data on the spread of the virus. Table 7.1 provides a timeline for this epidemic.

Even before the real numbers of SARS cases began to surface, organizers were canceling international events in Beijing as foreigners and foreign tour-groups were staying away. Dependants of foreigners living in Beijing were beginning to leave. On April 23rd, the World Health Organization (WHO) advised travelers not to go to Beijing.

In late April 2003, China's leaders moved to address their credibility problem. The government removed two senior officials from their party posts; health minister Zhang Wenkang and Beijing mayor Meng Xuenong. However, neither of these officials had ordered the news blackout on the development of

SARS as it spread across Guangdong in February and reached Beijing in March, and they may have been made to serve as scapegoats.

To rescue its credibility, the central government also cancelled the week-long May Day holiday — normally a time when millions travel in crowded trains and buses. It ordered transport operators to screen out passengers showing signs of SARS, such as fever and persistent coughing. It advised citizens to avoid crowded areas and warned of quarantines if citizens had contact with SARS patients. It ordered Beijing's schools to close for two weeks.

This about-face does not appear to have emerged solely from a concern for public health. For example, the central government is dawdling on the far bigger problem of HIV/AIDS, which, according to a Centre for Strategic and International Studies' (CSIS) report, may infect between 10 and 20 million Chinese within seven years. The leaders appear to have reacted more to the damage to China's image abroad, and the realization that disseminating timely information may create less economic damage than controlling it.

Concerns over image had prevented earlier disclosure. For example, the Chinese leadership did not want the parliament's two-week annual session, which began on March 5th, to be marred by panic over a disease. The Party controls the media through secret directives issued by its propaganda department, which is overseen by a member of the Politburo's Standing Committee. The Standing Committee, headed by the president and party chief, would have known about the decisions to suppress news coverage of SARS and to avoid taking preventive measures in Beijing that might alert the public to the problem.

On April 2nd, China's cabinet, headed by prime minister Wen Jiabao, held its first meeting to discuss the SARS problem. The cabinet appointed the health minister, Zhang Wenkang, to take charge of SARS prevention. In justification of the government's actions, Zhang told a news conference the next day that "the ordinary people of the mainland are not like the ordinary people of Hong Kong. Their education level is lower. If we released information like they did in Hong Kong, there would be chaos." Zhang would not have made such a remark if Wen had instructed complete honesty on the epidemic.

Jiang Zemin, President Hu Jintao's predecessor, remains China's most powerful man as commander-in-chief of the armed forces. Jiang played no role in handling the SARS crisis. Of Beijing's 175 hospitals, the armed forces controls 16 and none had any obligation until mid April to report SARS cases to the city's authorities (even though, with their often superior facilities, they served both military and civilian patients). The Ministry of Health said that it knew of no deliberate cover-ups, but a daring official newspaper has suggested otherwise. The *China Business Times* has accused Beijing's officials of "making false reports" and provincial governments of giving tardy, incomplete and falsified figures to avoid blemishing officials' careers. Falsifying data appears endemic in China's bureaucracy, partly because officials at all levels fear that their superiors may use mishaps reported in their jurisdiction to overlook them for possible promotion or to dismiss them.

The *China Business Times* also highlighted the disparity between the government's decision in late April to scrap the May Day holiday and a statement by a senior tourism official in early April that China should use the movement of millions of holidaymakers around May Day to demonstrate that China is "the safest tourist destination". Again, the official was presumably speaking in the knowledge that the prime minister would fully agree with him.

The WHO has also stated that local authorities strenuously resisted its investigation teams in Guangdong province and Beijing. Initially, too, vice-premier Wu Yi's intercession had also failed to change the government's attitude. Wu finally sent her own teams to Shanxi province to obtain accurate reports. Government bureaucracies that resisted efforts to coordinate activities further complicated this tug of war between the capital and the provinces.

On April 22nd, the Chinese government appointed veteran troubleshooter Wang Qishan as acting mayor of Beijing. The mayor has assured panicked residents that food supplies remain plentiful; has met with nervous heads of multinational corporations; has instituted daily reporting of SARS cases; has implemented a public-education program about the virus; and has provided the WHO with an office adjacent to his own. However, one Western banker expressed doubts about Wang, whom he sees as a consummate CCP operator: "Coming clean may not be one of Wang's reflexes...in many ways he is from the old school."[36]

Despite Wang's efforts, the WHO remained concerned about the slow pace of sharing key data. Its official spokesperson, Mangai Balasegram, indicated that Beijing's records of SARS are seriously flawed: the information does not show how half the city's patients caught the virus.[39] The data also failed to reveal who is getting the virus and when they contracted it. "We need to know more in order to be helpful," the WHO's China representative, Henk Bekedam, said.[40]

TABLE 7.1[41]: TIMELINE OF THE FIRST EPIDEMIC OF THE NEW MILLENNIUM

November 16, 2002
First known case of atypical pneumonia occurs in the city of Foshan, Guangdong province.

December 2002
Cases appear in cities around Guangzhou.

January 2003
Food handlers and chefs comprise an unusually high 5% of all infected cases. The Chinese government keeps the outbreaks a secret.

February 10, 2003
Two rumors reach the WHO's Beijing office: An e-mail reports that a "strange contagious disease" has killed more than 100 in Guangdong; and a phone call from the US Embassy relays an American citizen's account of "a strange disease that causes bleeding, with many deaths, in Guangzhou".

February 11, 2003
The Chinese Ministry of Health reports the outbreak of acute respiratory syndrome to the WHO, but plays down the concerns.

February 12, 2003
Officials in Guangdong report 305 cases of the disease and five deaths since November 16, 2002

February 21, 2003
An infected doctor from Guangzhou stays at Hong Kong's Metropole Hotel. Eventually 12 other guests are infected, nine of whom travel around the world.

March 5, 2003
A 78-year old woman, a guest of the Metropole, dies in Toronto — Canada's first case.

March 12, 2003
The WHO declares a global alert for the first time in its history and cautions against travel to countries with outbreaks of SARS.

March 26, 2003
The Chinese government revises the number of cases in Guangdong through February to 792. The epidemic begins to have major economic consequences for Asia.

March 31, 2003
A Hong Kong apartment complex is quarantined as the government is faulted for not doing enough.

April 2, 2003
The Chinese government announces 384 new SARS cases, bringing Guangdong's total to 1,190.

April 3, 2003
A WHO team heads to Guangdong. The Chinese Minister of Health says that SARS is under "effective control".

April 16, 2003
After inspecting city hospitals, the WHO's experts say that Beijing is significantly underreporting numbers of SARS cases.

April 20, 2003
The Chinese government admits to a national total of 1,807 cases. The central government dismisses two senior officials.

May 5, 2003
The Chinese government admits that the SARS epidemic has not reached its peak. So far, SARS has infected nearly 4,280 people in China and killed about 206. Globally, it has infected more than 7,000 people in 30 countries, killing more than 461. Hong Kong scientists say the virus is mutating. The WHO renews its advice that travelers avoid infected parts of China while the virus rages out of control.

June 17, 2003
The WHO lifts its travel advisory against Taiwan but retains Beijing on its alert list. SARS appears "under effective control". The latest statistics indicate a global total of 8,460 SARS cases and 799 deaths due to the virus. China has emerged as the worst-affected country, with 5,300 people infected and 346 deaths.

June 24, 2003
The WHO lifts its travel advisory against Beijing but urges caution against future outbreaks.

endnotes

1. *The Economist*, "The best and the rest".
2. Prahalad, C.K., and G. Hamel, "The Core Competence of the Corporation".
3. Rosen, D. H., *Behind the Open Door*.
4. Haley, G. T., C. T. Tan and U. C. V. Haley, *New Asian Emperors: The Overseas Chinese, their Strategies and Competitive Advantages*.
5. Chu, T. C., and T. MacMurray, "The Road Ahead for Asia's Leading Conglomerates".
6. Redding, S. G., "Entrepreneurship in Asia,"; and Haley, G. T., and C. T. Tan, "The Black Hole of Southeast Asia: Strategic Decision-Making in an Informational Void."
7. Haley et al, op.cit.
8. A. Gary Shilling, "Broken China,", p.156.
9. Balazs, E., *Chinese Civilization and Bureaucracy*.
10. Eckholm, E., "Order Yields to Lawlessness as Maoism Recedes in China".
11. Compiled from Yoon, S-k., "Telecoms — Cheap Talk in China", and Zerega, B., "A tough call".
12. *The Economist*, "The communist entrepreneur".
13. Ibid.
14. *The Economist*, "Bush telegraph".
15. Gilley, B., "Henderson Land — The pitfalls of property".
16. Cheng, A. and H. Vriens, "Superman vs. China".
17. Fukuyama, F., *Trust: The Social Virtues and the Creation of Prosperity*.
18. Ghosh, B. C., and C. O. Chan, "A Study of Strategic Planning Behavior Among Emergent Businesses in Singapore and Malaysia".
19. *Business Times*, October 17, 1997.
20. Yeo Hiap Seng, a family-owned company, appeared paralyzed through an intense family feud.
21. Kahn, J., "The Pinch of Piracy Wakes China Up on Copyright Issues".
22. Haley et al, op.cit.

23. *The Economist*, "The best and the rest".
24. Webb, S., "Heard in Asia".
25. Biers, D., "A Taste of China in Camden".
26. Sprague, J., "China's manufacturing beachhead".
27. Compiled from Doran, J., "China to own and operate US company", p. 4; Kahn, J., "Chinese company to buy and run a bankrupt US battery maker", p. 2; and Allen, J. T., "China charges into Florida", p.48.
28. Compiled from Doran, op.cit.
29. Allen, op.cit.
30. Lawrence, S. V., "Formula for Disaster"; and Haley, U. C. V., "Here There be Dragons: Opportunities and Risks for Foreign Multinational Corporations in China".
31. Rosen, op.cit.
32. Ibid.
33. Kahn, J., "China hold capitalist chief of North Korea Trade Zone".
34. Ibid; and Lynch, D. J., "Chinese success story has plot twist".
35. *South China Morning Post*, "Corporate credibility crunch".
36. Lee, C. S., "Acer's last stand".
37. Ibid.
38. Roberts, D., and M. L. Clifford, "Beijing Calls in Troubleshooter".
39. Associated Press, "Beijing's SARS records are flawed, WHO says".
40. Roberts and Clifford, op.cit.
41. Compiled from Rosenthal, E. (2003), "From China's Provinces, a Crafty Germ Breaks Out"; Wonacott, P., C. Hutzler and K. Chen (2003), "In SARS Shake-up, China Shows its not alone in the World"; Associated Press, op.cit.; and Roberts and Clifford, op.cit.

8

STRATEGICALLY
EVALUATING WESTERN
STRATEGY

"Without stirring abroad
One can know the whole world;
Without looking out of the window
One can see the way of heaven.
The further one goes
The less one knows."

Tao Te Ching

Book 2, Chapter 47, Stanza 106

INTRODUCTION

The above verse from the *Tao Te Ching* reflects classical Western approaches to strategic planning. China's financial sector demonstrates some of the difficulties that Western planners confront in this market. The numbers for China look enticing. It has over US$1 trillion in household savings and almost all of it lies unused in four huge and dysfunctional state banks. Less than US$16 billion of the savings lies in mutual funds. If the Chinese introduce funded pension schemes in 2004, their savings in mutual funds could grow to US$400 billion by 2010. Yet, despite well-thought-out strategies, Western financial companies have failed to penetrate this huge market.

Reluctantly, several Western companies have formed JVs with local partners in the financial sector. For example, in 2003, ABN-Amro formed a JV with Xiangcai Hefeng, one of China's two-dozen fund-management companies, to launch the country's first three foreign mutual funds. The previous year, despite convoluted negotiations, ABN-Amro had failed to reach a similar agreement with another Chinese fund-management company. Simultaneously in 2003, J.P. Morgan Chase admitted that it had abandoned a potential deal with Huaan, China's most respected fund-management company. Control and strategic philosophies were the sources of disagreement in these JVs and attempted JVs. Western asset managers avoid JVs, even in sophisticated markets. Many, such as Fidelity, the world's largest retail-fund company, rule out JVs on principle, believing that the exchanges involved are often unequal: Fidelity's managers could donate valuable technology and talent but have no decision-making authority over investments, marketing strategy and regulatory compliance. American banks, still lurching from scandals on Wall Street, place particular emphasis on regulatory compliance. Besides financial risk, the companies fear tarnished reputations and potential penalties if their Chinese partners are caught engaging in securities-related violations (as many Chinese securities companies do). Western banks have an additional reason to avoid JVs in China: state or local governments run all Chinese banks — directly or indirectly — and interfere in managerial appointments and lending. Market-driven, meritocratic Chinese banks do not exist, and, without control, Western banks fear they cannot steer most of them towards profitability. Even the People's Bank of China Governor Zhou Xiaochuan has lamented the role of family and personal "connections" in the state-run banking sector, which has contributed to the high level of bad loans:

The Chinese, however, have no intention of yielding control. When China joined the WTO in December 2001, it agreed to open up its financial sector gradually. In fund management, Western companies have to form JVs with local companies, and must remain minority partners, with a maximum stake of 33% now and 49% from 2005. In banking, Western companies cannot hold more than 20% in domestic banks, with a cap of 25% on total foreign holdings. Until 2006, they cannot conduct local-currency business with Chinese citizens. Consequently, despite their philosophical and strategic misgivings, Western companies can access China's lucrative financial sector only through investing in Chinese banks.

Some Western companies have been buying stakes in the handful of publicly listed, state-controlled Chinese banks. For example, in January 2003, Citibank bought 5% of Shanghai Pudong Development Bank, a listed bank.[1] Issues of transparency and good governance loomed large. In March 2004, Newbridge Capital (a JV between Texas Pacific Group and San Francisco-based Blum Capital) bought a 4.82% stake in China Minsheng Bank, after the International Financial Corporation, the World Bank's private lending arm, showed confidence by obtaining a 1.2% stake. Yet, at the time of writing, Minsheng, a supposed poster child for good corporate governance in China, had just disclosed that it faked a shareholders' meeting four years ago. Minsheng's rush to come clean on the eve of its Initial Public Offering (IPO) in Hong Kong probably reflected concerns about its image to potential foreign investors rather than domestic-market participants. Earlier, Newbridge Capital, had also devised a shrewd strategy to control Shenzhen Development Bank (SDB) and to create an environment where it could employ Western strategies and processes. Guided by an experienced Chinese negotiator, Weijian Shan, Newbridge chose SDB because it was the only Chinese bank with a large proportion (72%) of its shares in public hands. Thus, even a small stake could yield practical voting control andNewbridge obtained permission for a 20% stake. A separate contract gave Newbridge's management control of SDB and took effect in October 2002. The issue of control proved contentious. SDB's local shareholders, many of whom are also its borrowers, questioned whether they could still make lending decisions. In mid-May 2003, SDB renounced the contract authorizing Newbridge to manage the bank. Simultaneously, China's top regulator, the Chinese Banking Regulatory Commission's chairman Liu Mingkang, affirmed Beijing's approval of the deal. Newbridge considered legal actions against both the Shenzhen government and SDB for breach of a legally-binding agreement, but hoped to avoid direct confrontation. In October 2003, SDB said Newbridge was seeking an international arbitrator to intervene between it and the Chinese bank's biggest shareholders on the issue of control. Other Western companies have pushed for the most they can get, short of control. ABN-Amro abandoned its first potential JV when its Chinese counterpart refused to give the Dutch company more than 20%. Its new partner, Xiangcai Hefeng, has agreed to the maximum in the fund-management sector. Several of Xiangcai Hefeng's managers had worked abroad, were used to the legalistic Western business culture, and agreed to put all commitments in writing, including vetoes for ABN-Amro in such areas as portfolio and risk management, and compliance. Thus, ABN-Amro identified key areas in which to exert Western strategic practices, then identified a potential partner with an appropriately experienced management team, and obtained its desired strategic practices through contractual controls.

Western banks and fund managers that have succeeded in obtaining a toehold in China are those that have taken a leap of faith; currently, European companies appear more comfortable than the Americans in doing so. J.P. Morgan Chase's failed relationship with Huaan provides such an example of cultural comfort zones when setting negotiating priorities. Huaan began negotiating with a team that came mostly from Jardine Fleming Asset Management, a British company with long experience in Asia. However, Jardine Fleming had just been bought by Chase Manhattan, which in turn merged with J.P. Morgan. As these mergers evolved, and negotiating teams changed, so did negotiating priorities. As the *Tao* indicates, the new American managers may have sought to "know the world" without ever having "stirred abroad". For example, one European manager we spoke to expressed the view that, "The Americans think that China is just America in the East. They make absurd requirements on compliance, process and control." This caution, though, may indicate wisdom. As the *Tao* states, "The further one goes, The less one knows." Five years ago, Wejijian Shan, Newbridge Capital's director of Asian operations who grew up in the PRC, cautioned the company that even the best-laid plans fail. "In China there is a lack of respect for private property. If you combine that mentality with the attitude that to be rich is glorious, you can understand what the problems are for foreign investors in China."

The next section covers some of the assumptions underlying Western strategic planning and implementation. The ensuing sections explore some strengths and weaknesses, as well as successful and unsuccessful strategies, of Western companies. The final section explains why sometimes Western companies may propose plans that China rejects.

POURING FOUNDATIONS

Several strategic-management textbooks cover the basic model of Western strategic planning outlined in Table 8.1. The model provides a clear indication of the complexity and the linear analytical approach that serves as the ideal of Western planning. For example, corporations should have "a strategic planning staff charged with supporting both top management and the business units in the strategic planning process".[2] The staff's primary responsibilities should be to identify and to analyze company-wide strategic issues, and to suggest corporate strategic alternatives to top management; and to work as facilitators with business units to guide them through strategic planning.

TABLE 8.1:[3] THE WESTERN STRATEGIC MANAGEMENT MODEL

Basic Elements	First Breakdown	Second Breakdown	Third Breakdown
ENVIRONMENTAL SCANNING	External	Societal Environment	General Forces
		Task Environment	Industry Analysis
	Internal	Structure Culture	Chain of Command Beliefs, Expectations Values
		Resources Competencies,	Assets, Skills, Knowledge
STRATEGY FORMULATION	Mission	Reason for Existence	
	Objectives	What Results & When	
	Strategies Policies	Plan Broad Guidelines for Decisions	
STRATEGY IMPLEMENTATION	Programs	Activities Needed to Accomplish Plan	

	Budgets	Cost of Programs	
	Procedures	Sequence of Steps Needed to do Job	
EVALUATION & CONTROL	Performance	Process to Monitor Performance & Correct if Needed	

Thus, strategic planning at most Western corporations centers on the activities of staff who have been trained in using the planning technologies currently in vogue. Yet few of these staff have had substantial experience in line management or in the corporation's operational functions. Consequently, Robert Kuok, the Asian sugar, property, hotel and media tycoon said, "When I hear somebody's got an MBA, I have a feeling of dread, because normally they come to me with an over-pompous sense of their own importance. And no way are you going to prick that bubble, with the result one day there will be a cave-in in their department. So, they learn painful lessons at my expense"[3].

Additionally, line managers, and personnel who deal with day-to-day problems of generating corporate profits, do not have primary responsibility for planning and may actually be the last to know of corporate plans.

Western strategic-planning technologies reflect the environments in which they originated and in which they have been used. These technologies incorporate abundant, easily available data on companies, industries, markets, and environments; and significant investments in staff to collect, to collate and to analyze that data. The staff then interprets the information and recommends alternative strategies for senior managers to accept, to reject or to modify for implementation by line managers.

Western strategic planning methods differ from those employed in Asia in the amounts of hard data that planners require and the intensity of involvement of staff and line managers. First, Western planners generally require an information-rich environment. When they cannot obtain reliable, hard data or information (as in China), they must make use of alternatives, including experience, their line managers' strength. Hence, the type of information companies use in decision-making should range from the hard data that staff analysts require to the subjective data that line managers develop through experience. Second, Western planning generally utilizes a staff-intensive approach to analysis and decision-making. The personnel involved may have expertise in various technologies of data analysis and manipulation that transform raw data into usable information. However, as a result of their duties, they rarely develop the intimate contact and knowledge of corporate operations, products and markets that line managers have. Similarly, line managers generally lack the time to develop and to maintain specialized knowledge of analytical technologies. Yet, effective strategic planning, especially in volatile environments, requires drawing on both data and experience, on both staff and line managers. Table 8.2 highlights these strategic-planning constructs through the research of six strategy theorists: Charles Hofer and Dan Schendel; Michael Porter; C. K. Prahalad and Gary Hamel; and Henry Mintzberg.

TABLE 8.2:[5] CHARACTERISTICS OF STRATEGIC PLANNING

Strategic Theorists	Staff/Line-Dependent	Data/Experience-Dependent
Hofer & Schendel	Staff	Data
Porter	Staff	Data
Prahalad & Hamel	Staff/Line	Data/Experience
Mintzberg	Staff/Line	Data/Experience

▲ Planning, classically

Charles Hofer and Dan Schendel[4] have contributed to the more influential concepts of classical Western strategic planning. Michael Porter's approach shares many characteristics with these theorists. As Table 8.2 indicates, all present strategic planning as being staff- and data-dependent. Their preferred styles of strategic planning and decision-making demand the particularistic, straight-line, analytical rationalism that Nisbett and his colleagues[5] found comes naturally to Westerners. Yet analytical rationalism appears best suited to relatively stable, information-rich situations where managers can collect, analyze and interpret data sequentially to generate the information upon which they base decisions. Classical strategic planning assumes that the greater the amount of objective, high-quality, hard data managers obtain, the better, more accurate results they can generate with high-quality analyses, and thereby reach even higher-quality decisions. These assumptions, while intuitively compelling, depend on accurate explanatory models of how measured variables interact to create reality.

Research has challenged the assumptions underlying classical strategic planning. For example, John Sterman[6] found that as situations became more complex, decision-makers became less responsive to inherently crucial variables and more vulnerable to forecasting errors. In more chaotic, rapidly evolving situations, classical strategic planning tends to disintegrate. Thomas Stewart[7] reported on a 1995 experiment to test the decision-making paradigms underlying official Marine Corps doctrines. In the first part of the experiment, marines in leadership and combat-development programs went to the New York Mercantile Exchange to compete (on simulators) against its traders; not surprisingly, the traders trounced the marines. The second part of the experiment saw the traders take on the marines in simulated war games; the traders once again trounced the marines, much to the shock of their hosts. The traders had used their characteristic, intuitive, decision-making processes in both instances and proven that, in the chaotic, rapidly evolving situations found in the battlefield, on the trading floor, or in the global business environment, intuition usually beats straight-line rationality. The results of the experiment prompted the Marine Corps to rewrite its doctrine. Stewart quotes the new Marine Corps' doctrine as reading:

"The intuitive approach is more appropriate for the vast majority of ... decisions made in the fluid, rapidly changing conditions of war when time and uncertainty are critical factors, and creativity is a desirable trait."

Classical planning assumes that several distinct, objective variables identify corporate environments, and that generally statistically-based models reveal important links between these variables. Capable managers using classical planning can generate accurate models with freely available, relatively unbiased data, and when corporate employees and their customers share relatively homogenous cultural outlooks. However, several problems can confound the assumptions of classical planning; planners can err by using straight-line logical rules similar to those that the marines used against the traders.

First, though managers may obtain objective data on some processes such as production-line efficiencies and quality control, they rarely obtain objective data on strategic environments. Realities clash especially hard when personnel collecting field data and personnel analyzing the data at headquarters have different cultural or experiential perspectives, as in international-business situations. In these situations, personnel often differ markedly in how they interpret and report the phenomena they observe, as Nisbett et al noted.[8] When significant errors infest managers' understandings of important variables, their measurement or relationships, managers fail to develop effective strategies.

In addition, as summarized in Table 8.2, classical strategic planning depends heavily on substantial staff input: the staff collects, collates and analyzes large amounts of data to understand business environments and decision situations, and then generates strategic recommendations for senior managers. Frequently, planning staff has little or no line-management or operational experience. Often, their understanding of business situations derives from analytical techniques and their collection and interpretation of data; they have little knowledge of the nuances of corporate operations, their companies' relationships with the value chain and other stakeholders, or any direct familiarity with and understanding of markets. These planning processes, taught in premier MBA programs, separate what Mintzberg[9] labeled the companies' minds and hands; the planning usually lacks the heart, guts and instinct that Asian managers rate so highly.

Finally, as Sterman[10] found, more complex situations lead to less accurate analyses and forecasts. Strategic planning becomes more complex in foreign markets because of additional critical variables originating in host markets, and the effects of interaction between the markets and cultures of the home and host countries.

▲ Developing core competencies

C. K. Prahalad and Gary Hamel,[11] in their seminal 1990 article, argued for an internal focus to companies' strategic planning. They contended that companies must exploit their core competencies to achieve the greatest possible success. Core competencies comprise skills that companies refine and hone over the years through their various business activities and that provide them with opportunities to succeed.

Core competencies do not guarantee success, however, as more than one set of skills can contribute to core competencies in given industries or markets. Thus, competitors can seek to develop and to possess different core competencies. The relative competitive value of different core competencies changes over time with changes in operating environments — competitive, regulatory, and technological, changes in customers' preferences, or changes in the company's mission or strategic focus. As the requirements for success in product markets change, companies may seek to develop new core competencies, and even discard old ones. For a skill to become a core competency, it must:

- provide potential access to various markets;
- make important contributions to the perceived benefits companies provide their customers; and
- prove difficult to imitate.

Prahalad and Hamel did not provide a blueprint for planning, nor did they prescribe specific investments in staff or infrastructure; rather, they argued for bringing a strategic perspective to strategy formulation. Consequently, their dictates on building competitiveness transcend Western companies and apply equally to Chinese or other Asian companies with different strengths and opportunities, as we identified in Chapter 7.

▲ Crafting strategies

Using the compelling metaphor of a potter crafting her product, Henry Mintzberg[12] postulated that skilled individuals and companies craft effective strategies using both their minds and their hands. The potter planned with her mind. She selected the correct amount and type of clay for her current project and went to work with her pottery wheel. However, Mintzberg noticed that sometimes she did not produce the figure she had planned. He questioned her about the discrepancy. She responded that as she worked, she often found that miscalculations, insights, instincts or even whims made her produce something different from what she had intended for her market. In Mintzberg's perspective, her planning of the mind had failed, yet her hands had saved the day. Her instinctive reactions seemed to flow directly from her hands. Her hands represented the profound, ingrained and intimate knowledge of her craft and her customers, and triggered her ability to innovate and to offset the failures of her mind. The resultant product incorporated the purposeful reaction on the part of her hands to unexpected developments or intuited changes in market preferences. Companies plan with their minds when they engage in classical strategic planning; they plan with their hands when line management adapts corporate plans to meet specific challenges. Mintzberg[13] argued that strategic planning without either the mind or the hands remains incomplete and usually sub-optimal.

Planning of the mind requires heavy investments in data acquisition, intense data mining, and analytical interpretations of the resulting information. Staff dominate planning of the mind: this mode of planning does not necessarily require line-management experience, intimate knowledge of managing production lines and sales forces, experience with the company's markets, customers and suppliers, or an understanding of the company's operations. Planning of the mind does require intimate knowledge of analytical and planning models and the data that they use. Those responsible for planning of the mind have no direct responsibility for generating corporate profits. The primary value of staff analysts stems from their expertise in the analytical tools they employ.

Just as the mind represents staff, the hands represent line managers. Line managers develop significantly different expertise from staff. They direct the functional activities of the company's value chain. They are the worker ants of the business world — striving to accomplish company goals as efficiently and effectively as possible. In their daily activities, line managers encounter all the excellent, adequate and inadequate elements of the company's strategic plans. Generally, the line managers follow those elements of strategic plans that provide solutions for problems and direction for activities. Often, drawing on their instinctive understanding of their particular industry and market, they adapt on the spot the inadequate elements of the strategic plan. Without similar exposure to the variety and complexity of day-to-day business problems, staff managers cannot develop the deep, rich and textured understanding of the requirements for success that line managers have. Indeed, staff managers, through their scientific, economic and statistical models, strive to develop less-complex depictions of the real world — a Real-World Lite. These models help to generate important insights and understanding, but lack the nuances of the real world. Line managers understand and live within those nuances.

Mintzberg[14] postulated that strategic planning consists of minds and hands performing the following four activities:
- detecting discontinuities;
- knowing the business;
- managing patterns; and
- reconciling change and continuity.

First, Mintzberg argued that companies earn profits primarily during periods of stability. One of the primary functions of managers is to detect discontinuities as early as possible and adapt their company's strategies to meet those discontinuities rapidly and successfully. When dealing with minor discontinuities, managers should make minimal changes to historically successful strategies and minimize disruption to the smooth functioning of the company. Line managers who react to minor difficulties on the spot, without seeking approval from senior managers, are undertaking planning of the hands. In doing so, they strive to stay within the spirit and general direction of the established strategic plan. They undertake this responsibility as too much time taken to resolve minor problems would create significant disruptions to the smooth operations of the company. Major discontinuities call for more formal planning of the mind, but managers should also seek to return quickly to stability and to maximize profits once again.

THE PROJECTED ECONOMIC IMPACT OF SARS:[15] DISCONTINUITIES IN STRATEGIC PLANNING

In May 2003, the Asian Development Bank (ADB) calculated the likely effect of the SARS epidemic under different scenarios. It forecast losses mounting to US$28.4 billion in the four most vulnerable economies — China, Hong Kong, South Korea and Taiwan. According to the ADB, SARS would have the worst effect on Hong Kong's economy, reducing its economic growth by four percentage points in 2003, and thereby taking it down to negative territory. The bank assumed that the affected countries would contain the outbreak by July 2003, but projected the gloomier figures on the epidemic remaining unchecked for a further six months.

Generally, the ADB predicted that the Asian economies would feel the economic impact of SARS disproportionately. Tourism accounts for at least 10% of GDP in most of the affected Asian countries. Additionally, countries such as Hong Kong and Singapore depend almost completely on service industries that demand regular and varied human contact that customers wish to avoid during the epidemic. "When SARS hits an economy, it causes uncertainty generated by fear and this has direct and indirect effects like a loss of consumer confidence; tourism suffers, investment drops and government revenue also drops," said the ADB's chief economist Ifzal Ali.

In May, many companies had temporarily closed down their Asian operations, and visitors to some destinations had fallen by half or more. Some of the economic damage could have been moderated with more accurate and timely information on the disease, the ADB said. "A lack of information creates difficulties for individuals to accurately evaluate the consequences of a particular event," the bank said. More open borders, and the interconnected global economy, can contribute to the spread of the disease. The ADB said that regional governments should cooperate more fully to contain this and future outbreaks, and that state spending on healthcare may have to rise as a result. Table 8.3 covers some the economic impact of SARS.

TABLE 8.3:[16] THE ECONOMIC IMPACT OF SARS

ECONOMIES	Estimated 2003 GDP Growth before SARS (percentage points)	Estimated 2003 GDP Growth if SARS lasted 2 Quarters (percentage points)	Estimated Reduction in Annual GDP levels if SARS lasted 2 quarters (US$ billions)
East Asia	5.6	4.7	20.7
PRC	7.3	7.0	5.8
Hong Kong	2.0	-1.4	6.6
South Korea	4.0	3.5	3.0
Taiwan	3.7	1.8	5.3
Southeast Asia	4.0	2.5	7.7
Indonesia	3.4	2.3	2.0
Malaysia	4.3	2.9	1.3
Philippines	4.0	3.2	0.6
Singapore	2.3	0.7	2.0
Thailand	5.0	3.4	1.8

Second, Mintzberg contended that planning and implementation of plans become most effective when managers thoroughly understand their company's business. Some research findings confirm that the best-performing companies recruit their CEOs internally — even when their boards are seeking transformational change.[17] Specifically, line managers learn the nuances, potential problems and synergies that can arise when a company's different functions coincide and interact with those of their suppliers and customers. Their knowledge of the hands arises from the day-to-day actions the managers take to accomplish company goals and to generate profits. For managers to "know the business", both the mind and the hands must recognize the value of the other's contributions.

Third, Mintzberg proposed that managers steer through periods of stability most profitably by recognizing environmental patterns and developing effective behavioral patterns in response. For maximum effectiveness, these behavioral patterns must manipulate the company's controllable variables efficiently. Thus, effective managers must collectively manage the two sets of patterns to interact and to mesh optimally.

Finally, Mintzberg suggested that managers should not manage change, but rather quickly work through discontinuities to re-establish stability. During periods of rapid change or discontinuities, profits become uncertain and highly variable — conditions not conducive to optimizing shareholder value. Managers should strive to re-establish stability, where profits are more certain and optimal shareholder value becomes achievable.

▲ Planning: Emergent vs. deliberate

In another seminal article, Henry Mintzberg and James Waters[18] elaborated on strategic plans, categorizing them as either deliberate or emergent. Deliberate strategic plans emerged from accepted classical strategic planning, primarily through planning of the mind. Emergent strategic plans coalesced through the collective behavioral patterns of employees[19] reacting to environmental stimuli, primarily through planning of the hands. Mintzberg and his colleagues[20] argued that the most effective realized strategic plans combine both deliberate and emergent elements.

Emergent strategic plans represent the collective experiences of a company's managers and the company's learned business behaviors. In Mintzberg's terminology, these plans "bubble up" from lower- to higher-level managers. Line managers, reacting to day-to-day problems that their company's plans either ignore or cannot solve, create rudimentary plans that percolate through to senior managers. Senior managers and staff can then expand and elaborate on the company's deliberate plans by incorporating aspects of some of these emergent plans.

Senior managers can generally choose from multiple emergent plans: different line managers encountering similar problems in their daily activities will rarely develop identical solutions. These local adaptations tend to maintain the company's profitability without requiring the attention of senior managers. However, over time, minor discontinuities collectively can create major discontinuities and line managers' adaptations no longer suffice to maintain optimal profitability. In well-managed companies, bubbling-up can have long-term competitive implications and provide much-needed company-wide solutions: The local adaptations feed into the company's new deliberate plans to regain stable business environments. Consequently, the best managers will facilitate this process.

CORPORATE PLANNING AROUND SARS:[21] EMERGENT AND DELIBERATE STRATEGIES

In late May 2003, the Japanese electronics company Matsushita Electric Industries discovered that some workers at its two Beijing plants were running a high fever. Later, doctors confirmed that five workers had contracted SARS. Matsushita immediately sent 5,600 workers home, the majority from its biggest and oldest factory in China making color-television parts. Then it brought in city-health workers to scrub the plant with disinfectant and announced a 10-day shutdown at the plant, to cover the SARS incubation period. Subsequently, Matsushita shifted some production to Mexico.

For foreign companies, SARS demonstrated that low cost does not mean low risk, as managers pondered the impact of shutdowns and stalled business deals. Some companies relied on technology, such as videoconferencing, to display products to customers in and from China, and used the Internet to speed transactions. However, many managers worried that if the crisis dragged on, the quality of the products they were sourcing in China could deteriorate because of the lack of face-to-face contact. The reluctance of managers to move to China could also become a choke point for further expansion. Tony Brown, Ford Motor Company's vice president for purchasing, said that managers had been unable to move from Beijing to Ford's purchasing office in Shanghai because of SARS.

At the Beijing headquarters of Motorola Inc, the US telecommunications company, 100 employees worked from their office on alternate days only in order to reduce crowds and to inhibit transmission of the disease in crowded places such as elevators. On April 29th, Motorola shut down its Chinese headquarters for more than a week after one of its employees contracted SARS. As of June 2003, Motorola had postponed non-essential travel of its employees within China, which delayed the launch of products and hamstrung efforts to reach customers in smaller cities.

Some analysts believe that SARS and similar epidemics will increase pressure on companies to localize the top management of their Chinese operations if the health risks of operating there remain high. Some US companies seem to be becoming more cautious about expanding operations in China and of maintaining too large a presence there. If this is the case, countries like Mexico, Thailand and Malaysia will probably benefit.

Short-term, SARS increased manufacturing costs for companies which had become accustomed to just-in-time deliveries. In May 2003, Lite-On Technology, a Taiwanese company that makes printers, PC components and mobile phones for Sony, Hewlett-Packard and Dell at a massive plant in Guangzhou, was stocking two weeks of extra inventory for some products and asking its Chinese suppliers to do the same. Asimco Components Group in Anhui province, which makes rubber seals and other auto components for several US companies, was following a similar strategy. The company had spent US$20,000 on SARS prevention, including increasing inventories by two weeks (in case imports of raw material were delayed by SARS checkpoints at ports and on highways), hiring a hospital to disinfect the factory before the morning shift each day, and distributing Chinese medicine to the workers. The factory remained SARS-free, but as foreign managers were unable to visit to introduce new products, SARS caused financial troubles for the company.

Japanese technology companies especially are urgently debating whether to disperse or to concentrate production bases. For the past several years, Japanese companies have shifted their production to China, amid fierce global competition. As the SARS epidemic forced them to close local plants, they were under pressure to determine whether to seek operational efficiency or to avoid the risk of suspending production. Although most leading Japanese manufacturers operate several bases elsewhere in Asia, one Japanese manager emphasized that "production lines represent a great concentration of know-how and expertise. It is not easy to quickly transfer them elsewhere."[22]

In April 2003, Oki Electric Industry decided to postpone transferring its production of monochrome printers to China from Thailand. The major electronics manufacturer produces automated teller machines at factories in Honjo in Saitama Prefecture (Japan) and Shenzhen in Guangdong Province, and printers in Fukushima (Japan), Thailand and Shenzhen. To make operations more efficient, the company had previously decided to integrate production of lower-level models into the Shenzhen plant. However, later, Oki feared that even if one worker fell ill with SARS, the entire plant would have to close for two to 10 days, resulting in a temporary suspension of output.

THE STRENGTHS OF WESTERN COMPANIES

Just as Asia's business environment bolstered Asian companies, the Western industrial democracies nurtured Western companies through unprecedented market and financial transparency. This transparency provides Western companies with confidence in the system's legitimacy and relative stability, and frees them to engage in long-term investments in innovation, brand equity and personnel. For Western companies, trust remains important for the efficient operation of commerce, but occurs more at the systemic than the individual level.[23][24] Economists have termed the strengths of Western multinational companies, spawned by their business environments, as intangible assets which give them advantages over local companies.[25] These intangible assets translate into the strategic strengths of proprietary capabilities, institutional memory, marketing capabilities and growth.

▲ Proprietary capabilities

Proprietary capabilities include the ability to appropriate product and process technologies. Over the past four decades, product and technology life cycles have become increasingly compressed as innovations have poured into the market in an increasingly furious torrent. The semi-conductor industry provides a vivid example of this trend. Indeed, Gordon Moore, Intel's co-founder, made his famous observation in 1965, just four years after the invention of the first planar-integrated circuit. The press dubbed it "Moore's Law" and the name stuck. In his original paper, Moore observed an exponential growth in the number of transistors per integrated circuit.[26] This exponential growth coupled with ever-shrinking transistor size would result in increased performance and decreased cost. Moore predicted that this trend would continue for the near future. In subsequent years, the pace slowed down, but data density has doubled approximately every 18 months, the current definition of Moore's Law, to which Moore has given his blessing. Most experts, including Moore, expect Moore's Law to hold for at least another two decades.

The West's capacity for technological innovation dominates that of non-Japanese Asia, or any other geographic region. Currently, only Taiwan's Acer Computers, out of all computer companies headquartered outside the US and Japan, has ever sold hardware technology to Japanese or US companies. Western markets and strategic planners shape decisions on technology and product development. The markets fund start-ups to exploit new technologies when large companies move too slowly. The markets also help to spawn new technologies through various value chains to create new, commercially viable products and industries. Clay Dunn, director of strategic development at Dow

Chemical Pacific, identified this creation and appropriation of technology as a significant strength for his company vis-à-vis Chinese companies, which seemed to sometimes confuse value creation with using the latest or most-fancy equipment.

▲ Institutional memory

Professionalized Western strategic planning contributes to company-wide institutional memory that transcends individual managers. In well-managed Western companies, analysts study, dissect and measure both surprising mistakes and surprising successes. In the best-managed companies, the analysts also catalog and codify their results for future reference and re-analysis. The public can inspect much, though not all, of a public company's business data. Conversely, in Asia's more personalized strategic management systems, only strong managers can vigorously dissect errors and disseminate these results to other stakeholders. Consequently, in Asia, most stakeholders, including other managers, never fully comprehend mistakes or successes nor incorporate their understandings into future decisions. Without the Western emphasis on the comprehensive acquisition and analysis of data, the record of success and failure, and the reasons behind them, often dissipate after individual managers retire.

▲ Marketing capabilities

As Stan Shih has pointed out, "Branding is natural to an American company". While he referred only to US companies, his statement applies generally to Western and Japanese companies. Western strategic planners have special skills in measuring brand equity and this measurement whets further investments in brands. Historically, Chinese and East Asian companies have tried to ensure demand for their products by controlling distribution channels and offering preferential access to favored products. However, the strengths of Western companies derive not from their control of distribution channels but from investments in brand characteristics, advertising and cultivation of perceptions of distinctiveness. Major Western companies have developed brand names such as Coke, Jaguar or Perrier that provide enormous brand equity and global recognition. Consequently, the companies incur negligible initial costs to build awareness when entering new markets or developing new products.

▲ Growth

Through relying on quantitative data to model interactions with markets, Western strategic planning can extend enormously the reach of controlling family members or managers. The largest privately held Overseas Chinese companies are equivalent in size to medium-sized enterprises in the West; the largest privately held PRC companies seem even smaller. Yet, Western family-controlled companies, such as Ford Motor Company, tower over their respective industries. In Asia, companies grow until trusted family members or associates can no longer control or understand assets. But Western strategic planning needs only data of sufficient quantity and quality to support decision-making models. This assumption provides strength in some industries such as autos, pharmaceuticals or chemicals where size provides the concentration of capital and the economies of scale necessary to compete. Consequently, Philip Ng, executive director and CEO of Far East Organization, specifically identified size as a competitive disadvantage for Chinese companies vis-à-vis their Western competitors.

Western professionalization also minimizes the mistakes of inexperience, and maximizes the benefits of training. Companies can hire managers globally assuming that their training has generally prepared them for their positions; more specific training programs can socialize new employees into a company's ways of doing things. Processes, technologies and decision rules based on relatively objective data aid the new managers in their strategic decision-making.

Many large Western companies also have immense capital resources and easy access to additional capital to fuel growth.

Because analysts view most large Western companies as excellent credit risks, managers can acquire capital in financial markets around the world at substantial discounts over local companies. Because of additional capital, Western companies can make substantially greater investments than their local competitors in emerging markets, and also incur lower costs.

THE WEAKNESSES OF WESTERN COMPANIES

The weaknesses of Western companies also emanate from their strengths and include data blinders, project orientations and tactical lags.

▲ Data blinders

Generally, data fuel Western strategic planning. Over-reliance on specified, high-quality, formatted data can blind many companies to threats and opportunities when the data prove non-existent, unreliable or slow to obtain. As we saw in Chapter 6, the French company Cerestar blundered in China because it refused initially to collect the data it would have in France and chose to rely on its JV partner. Its managers also had little knowledge of the data and analysis that they could obtain readily in China. As Clay Dunn of Dow told us, "It seems to me that the trick [of good decision-making in China] is to ensure enough analysis has gone into the details that you can make a 'data-based' decision. But, also extract yourself from the details and ensure you have a realistic big picture that holds water."

▲ Project orientations

Western companies tend towards exclusively project-oriented, tactical strategies in marketing without viewing investments as future options.[27] The Japanese companies have emphasized the fusion of operational (tactical) and strategic concerns. Yet, Western companies often fail to justify investments in market research or in infrastructure against the consequences of not undertaking those investments in knowledge and capability. Timely market research might avoid comprehensive failures in present projects, or might enhance speed of action and potential for future successes in the markets; consequently, Western companies should base estimated rates of return on more than present projects. Especially in markets such as China, which is characterized by a dearth of timely, high-quality information, managers should view investments in market research, data acquisition and company infrastructure primarily through the lens of strategic investments, and only secondarily through the lens of operations or tactical investments. Information-gathering that transcends specific projects provides the necessary base of data, market knowledge and market experience to create a solid understanding of the new markets. This holistic information-gathering would also enable Western managers to understand when to show flexibility in strategic planning as they would then have a better understanding of what they do not know.

▲ Tactical lags

Tactical speed includes capabilities to implement decisions quickly and to respond adroitly to market changes. When compared with privately owned Chinese and other Asian companies, Western companies appear slow and plodding in day-to-day actions. Western planning systems greatly contribute to companies becoming tactical laggards, as managers have to collect, to check for accuracy, to refine and to analyze large amounts of data to reach sound strategic decisions. Indeed, as Billy Ho, manager for corporate quality, marketing & public affairs for 3M Hong Kong, succinctly identified, despite his company's emphasis on speed, the greater the risk, the slower the decision. In Asia, additional circumstances that slow managers include:

- limitations on the quantity and quality of data;
- fewer accepted crosschecks on suspect data;
- rapidly evolving and growing markets which contribute to the obsolescence of data;
- inconsistently enforced government policies on markets; and
- changing government policies that roil markets and the quality of data.

SOME STRATEGIES THAT WORK

Western planning displays several strengths abroad (offensive strategies) and at home (defensive strategies).

▲ Maintaining product quality

Abroad, quality provides a significant strength. Dr. Elmar Stachels, chairman and general manager of Bayer China Co., Ltd. (Hong Kong) and Bayer (China) Ltd. (Beijing), stressed the importance of product quality in Bayer's strategy when he told us, "In China you must show flexibility to succeed, but you must never compromise on two things; you must never compromise on your objectives and you must never compromise on quality. Product quality must meet world standards at the very least." He recognized that Bayer had to maintain the perception that its products enjoyed world-class quality — anything less and Bayer's brand name would cease to sell products. Every sales call would then become a cold call; Bayer would then have to work much harder for its revenues and profits.

▲ Creating manufacturing efficiencies

Abroad, manufacturing efficiencies allow Western companies to compete with the significant advantages in labor costs enjoyed by their emerging-market competitors. Yet, many have risked advantages in process technologies by exposing their most advanced technologies to foreign markets. Thomas Lee Boam, a US commercial attaché in Beijing, stressed that if Western companies did not have intellectual-property protection as part of their Chinese business plans, they faced serious trouble.[28] Despite the tremendous risks, Western companies can fight piracy in China, where counterfeiters can reverse-engineer almost everything. For example, Coca-Cola makes its product so well and distributes it so cheaply that counterfeiters find no margin. Budweiser makes its beer cans with fluted edges that counterfeiters cannot duplicate either cheaply or easily. Chinese counterfeiters can brew beer and call it Budweiser — but they cannot put it in cans that look authentic.

▲ Erecting barriers to market entry

Asian companies have great difficulty competing with Western companies in Western markets. The large, complex markets, intense competition and myriad offerings of established, high-quality, brand-name products erect enormous barriers to entry. Costs for Asian companies include those associated with advertising and promotion, product distribution and logistical flows, as well as development of required and expected levels of after-sales service in consumer and business markets. Relationships matter in Western markets, as they do in Asian, and the building of necessary relationships extracts costs from foreign competitors. The maturity of Western markets also contributes to making them extremely unforgiving. In mature markets, unknown or foreign brands have to snatch sales and market share from established brand names and companies — expensive and often-chancy goals as competition on price also becomes important.

▲ Harvesting information

The wealth of readily available information in Western markets removes the advantage many established emerging-market companies enjoy in their home markets — the exclusive control of vital market information. Strategic information in Western markets also requires a trained, and preferably experienced, corps of staff to acquire and to analyze market data and to convert it into usable information for senior managers. Asian companies often have difficulty adjusting to this relative parity of information. As Chinese and Overseas Chinese companies now recruit from the best Western universities, this strategy has less success for Western companies. However, as Clay Dunn of Dow explained, "One common problem that still exists is [that] many Chinese people have poor analytical skills...they are excellent in math, but they are usually poor in applications. My Chinese colleagues attribute that to the traditional lack of emphasis on developing systematic analytical skills in the Chinese educational system."

SOME STRATEGIES THAT FAIL

Western planning also displays several weaknesses abroad and at home.

▲ Rotating managers

Many Western companies rotate their managers and key personnel regularly to maintain corporate cultures, standards and practices. Yet, in Confucian societies, loyalties have primarily personal dimensions. Virtually all the Chinese managers we interviewed stated that having a reputation for good relationships and good introductions offers tremendous advantages to foreigners (or indeed to locals) to get through doors. Billy Ho, of 3M Hong Kong, concluded, "Until you build up trust, it matters, but it is changing by generation — the younger generation especially. You also see that in China they try never to go so far as to destroy a relationship and any chance of renegotiating and doing business in the future." Hence, when companies transfer managers out of Greater China and other Asian countries after a term of three years (the most common long-term assignment), they have to go through the whole process of "building up trust" once again. To avoid this problem, many companies hire locals. Western companies should permit their home-country nationals who are thriving in China or other Asian business environments, and performing up to or beyond expectations, to stay there if they desire.

▲ Enforcing standard operating procedures

Phillip Spanninger, vice president, International TRW Overseas, identified flexible, experienced, diverse managerial cadres that operate with high levels of support from headquarters as being key to success in China. Flexibility and adaptability contribute to good, long-term management. Allowing subordinates to operate by local standards overseas can prove a difficult policy for senior managers to follow, but sometimes becomes necessary. When the required data and data quality do not exist, to insist that managers follow the same planning procedures overseas as at home ensures garbage-in/garbage-out (GIGO). Yet many Western companies display bureaucratic rigidity. Instead, well-run Western companies should relax standard operating procedures when their enforcement is ineffective, or detrimental to local operations.

FOUNDATIONS LAID ON SHIFTING SANDS

Despite the best-laid plans, according to Wang Zhile, a professor at the Chinese Academy of International Trade and Economic Cooperation, only about one-third of the 354,000 foreign companies operating in China in 2001 turned a profit.[29] Yet a 1999 survey by the American Chamber of Commerce in China showed that, while 58% of its member companies had lower profit margins there than in other global operations, 88% had plans to expand. Deloitte & Touche's survey in 2002 confirmed that 90% of foreign-owned companies in China planned to expand their operations within the next three years. In 2003, about 424,196 foreign companies, big and small, operated in China (according to MOFTEC). Michael Furst, executive director of the American Chamber of Commerce in Beijing, informed us that about two-thirds of its member companies were making some profits but not up to anticipated levels, while about one-third were making losses. When their foundations appear to be laid on shifting sands, many foreign companies desperately attempt to placate the influential Chinese government, rather than to abandon the potentially lucrative market. This section explores one such strategy, which we call kowtowing.

▲ The kowtow and its consequences

In Imperial China, inferiors made an act of supplication to their superiors by kneeling and knocking their heads on the floors. This kowtow, or prostration, ceremony was performed most commonly in religious worship by commoners who came to make requests of the local district magistrates and by foreign envoys that came into the emperor's presence. By the Ming period (1368–1644), the ritual, especially as made to the emperors by foreign envoys, involved "three kneelings and nine prostrations". To foreign envoys seeking trade and relations with China, kowtowing signified their country's acknowledgment of the Chinese emperor as the "son of heaven" (*t'ien-tzu*) and China as the Central Kingdom (*Chung-kuo*) in the world. As such, in the late 18th century, foreign envoys increasingly resisted kowtowing. Despite kowtowing, harmony between the Chinese emperor and foreign envoys or barbarians could only continue when the latter followed the emperor's "Way" (*gui-shun*).

When belligerence and litigation fail (as they often do in China), faltering Western companies try to recover by kowtowing, especially in high-technology areas that the Chinese government has designated as strategically important. The Chinese government has officially announced its "Way" in this area: that of acquiring Western technology, especially in software manufacturing and design where China remains weak. This way often clashes with the profit goals of Western companies, as Microsoft's perils demonstrate.[30]

Microsoft first entered the PRC in 1992, three years after it had entered Taiwan. At first, Microsoft battled the piracy that was rampant in the software industry by suing Chinese computer makers that loaded pirated Microsoft operating systems on their computers; and by suing Chinese companies that used the pirated Microsoft software. Microsoft won none of the litigation in the Chinese courts and came to be viewed by the Chinese government and people as a US giant bullying tiny Chinese companies.

In 1999, Microsoft China's general manager, Juliet Wu, resigned and wrote a book accusing the company of arrogance and selfishness. She identified the US company as an enemy of Chinese consumers because it would not slash prices. (Microsoft generally garners a gross profit margin of 85% on its most popular software.) Shortly after, most Chinese government officials and ministries blacklisted Microsoft's software in favor of the free Linux.

Confrontation as a strategy had failed Microsoft in China and it decided to reverse course. By 2001, Microsoft's operating system had become the most popular in China with 60% of the market; however, 90% of Microsoft's software available in China was pirated. A pirated version of Windows XP sells for US$5.50 on Chinese streets, as compared with US$245 for a legitimate copy from a store. In late 2001, Microsoft decided to kowtow. The company will commit US$750 million over three years through the Beijing government's state-planning department to promote research and training in China. This is over and above the US$1 billion it already spends annually on its business and research in China. This effort amounts to one of the most expensive kowtows a foreigner has ever offered China. Microsoft is helping to build a software industry from scratch, forming JVs with indigenous companies that Beijing picks, promoting basic research at Chinese universities, and training students and entrepreneurs (that it knows constitute future competitors) in its own state-of-the-art development methods.

Microsoft's local partners are making profits in China. One partner, a Beijing-based company, Vimicro, founded by the Ministry of Information Industry, and only one of five worldwide that Microsoft has authorized to use Windows XP for digital-imaging chips, has already earned several million dollars in profits. Microsoft's bottom line has changed little and the company appears no closer to profitability. Its revenues from China totaled only US$85 million in 2002 — yet it should have taken in nearly US$400 million for its share of software in brand-new computers alone. Chinese ministries and departments, including the Post Office, the Ministry of Information Industry, the National Statistics Bureau and the Chinese Academy of Sciences, have re-endorsed their earlier decision to support Linux systems. In 2002, the Chinese Post Office issued contracts with IBM to use Linux at 1,200 post offices. Craig Mundie, Microsoft's senior vice-president and chief China strategist, expressed the hope that the company would make some money over the next two decades. As in ancient times, despite kowtowing, harmony between the Chinese government and Microsoft appears likely only when the latter follows the government's way. In the next section, we propose a map for effective strategies by Western and Chinese companies.

endnotes

1. *The Economist*, "Strings Attached".
2. Ibid, pp.37—38
3. Tanzer, A., "The Amazing Mr. Kuok."
4. Adapted from Wheelen, T.L & J. D. Hunger, *Strategic Management and Business Policy* , p.9.
4. Hofer, C. W., and D. Schendel, *Strategy Formulation: Analytical Concepts*.
5. Nisbett, R. E., K. Peng, I. Choi, and A. Norenzayan (2001), "Culture and Systems of Thought: Holistic Versus Analytic Cognition"; Peng, K., and R. E. Nisbett, "Culture, Dialectics and Reasoning About Contradiction."
6. Sterman, J. D., *Business Dynamics: Systems Thinking and Modeling for a Complex World*.
7. Stewart, T. A., "How to Think with Your Gut".
8. Nisbett et al, op.cit.
9. Mintzberg, H., "Crafting Strategy"; Mintzberg, H., "The Fall and Rise of Strategic Planning"; and Mintzberg, H., and J. Waters, "Of Strategies, Deliberate and Emergent".
10. Sterman, op.cit.
11. Prahalad, C. K. and G. Hamel, "The Core Competence of the Corporation".
12. See note 9.
13. Ibid.
14. Mintzberg, H., "Crafting Strategy".
15. Asian Development Bank, News Release No. 076/03; BBC News "SARS could cost Asia $28bn".
16. Asian Development Bank, News Release No. 065/03.
17. Collins, J., *Good To Great*.
17. Mintzberg and Waters, op.cit.
19. Mintzberg, "Crafting Strategy" and "The Fall and Rise of Strategic Planning".
20. Ibid; and Mintzberg and Waters, op.cit.

21. Compiled from Leggett K., D. Bilefsky and T. Zaun, "Foreign firms face setbacks as SARS cases mount in China"; Konrad, R., "Silicon Valley pushes technology to cope with SARS"; *Nikkei Weekly*, "Firms mull future of China operations"; Hung, F., "As virus worsens, Asia looks to West for options"; *Nikkei Report*, "Foreign firms mull changes in Chinese Investments: Survey".

22. *Nikkei Weekly*, op.cit.

23. Fukuyama, F., *Trust: The Social Virtues and the Creation of Prosperity*.

24. When betrayals of trust occur (see the recent financial and accounting scandals involving WorldCom, Martha Stewart Inc., etc.), trust in the economy generally continues until investors seriously question the transparency of financial markets and perceive systemic failure. See Feder, B. J., "WorldCom enabled huge fraud, investigations find".

25. For a more complete academic discussion of these intangible assets, see Haley, U. C. V., 2001, *Multinational corporations in political environments: Ethics, values and strategies*.

26. Moore, G. E., "Cramming more components onto integrated circuits".

27. Haley, U. C. V., "Assessing Business Risks in China".

28. Meredith, R., "The Counterfeit Economy".

29. Haley, U. C. V., "Here There be Dragons: Opportunities and Risks for Foreign Multinational Corporations in China".

30. Meredith, R., "Microsoft's Long March".

Part IV

TRAVELLING
TOWARDS
STRATEGIC
CONVERGENCE

A UNIFIED MODEL OF STRATEGIC PLANNING

Thus Something and Nothing produce each other;
The difficult and the easy complement each other;
The long and the short off-set each other;
The high and the low incline towards each other;
Note and sound harmonize with each other;
Before and after follow each other.

Tao Te Ching

Book 1, Chapter 2, Stanza 5

INTRODUCTION

The *Tao* views the world as a collection of complementary, interdependent opposites. Drawing on Taoism, managers and companies actively influence their world.

A well-spent life includes an active search for balance and harmony, while success in life can help attain balance and harmony. Thus far in the book we have compared and contrasted Chinese and Western strategic planning to promote greater understanding of their characteristics and interdependencies. In this chapter, we discuss a convergence between the two for increased effectiveness in the new global economy. The unified planning system we propose incorporates the strengths of both Chinese and Western companies, while compensating in part for their weaknesses. First, we synthesize our previous discussions on differences between Eastern and Western cognitive styles. Next, we discuss circumstances that are driving managerial convergence in general and Chinese-Western convergence in particular. Finally, we draw on the metaphors of the Silk Road, and on the teachings of the *Tao*, to introduce our strategic model of managerial convergence.

COGNITIVE STYLES AND STRATEGIC DECISION-MAKING

In Chapter 1, we highlighted some research findings contrasting Eastern and Western cognitive styles. Table 9.1 summarizes some of these findings and explores their implications for strategic decision-making in China.

First, when processing information, the Chinese generally tend to employ holistic perspectives, while Westerners employ particularistic perspectives. The Chinese also emphasize interdependent relationships between different variables. Their managers look for the relationships surrounding problems to generate possible solutions. Western managers, by contrast, isolate the problem from its surroundings to generate possible solutions. Validities deal with the measurement and acceptance of realities and truths. Chinese managers often accept multiple realities and truths, while Western managers generally

TABLE 9.1: EASTERN VS. WESTERN COGNITIVE STYLES

Characteristic	East Asian	Western
Processing	Holistic	Particularistic
Focus	Relational	Differentiation
Validities	Multiple	Single
Analytical Preference	Experience/ empirical	Formal explanatory models
Decision-making preference	Reasoning-based	Rule-based
Solution preference	Unique	Universal
Locus of control	Situational	Individual

concentrate on one or two. In so doing, Western managers often limit their strategic options. In contrast, the Chinese rarely discard plausible realities completely; less-favorable investment choices, for instance, often linger as plausible options as their determining characteristics have fluidity.

Second, effective Chinese managers often emphasize their experience and empirical evidence over the formal explanatory models that Western managers prefer. These analytical preferences lead to reasoning-based decisions and offer uniquely tailored solutions for the problems that the Chinese managers encounter. Through their use of explanatory models, Western managers can develop rigorous decision rules to aid their strategic decision-making. However, these rules tend to generate universal solutions that the managers then have to fit to whatever problems arise, irrespective of their appropriateness to the specific case.

Finally, Chinese managers tend to deny their ability to control situations (though not necessarily their ability to influence them). Culturally, managerial insistence on control over situations where data and variables often interact in ways that can't be predicted comes across as empty boasting. Managers could lose face if they lost control after such boasts. This predilection sometimes leads to unfortunate circumstances where managers deny that problems exist until they can either control the problems completely, or the problems disappear. In the West, managers would lose face if they did not claim control of situations and incipient problems; loss of control, though not desirable, does not carry the same stigma as it does in China.

When Chinese or Western managers confront alien and unfavorable data environments, their traditional cognitive styles may fail them. However, Western companies must improve their information-processing capabilities to compete more effectively in high-potential, data-poor markets such as China, and with competitors from these markets. Figure 9.1 highlights market-research expenditures per capita: while the industrialized countries dominate on market-research expenditures, the Asian countries, including Japan, incur miniscule expenditures per capita, indicating a deliberate attempt on their part to maintain information scarcity as a strategic tool. In 2001, China spent 15¢ per capita on market research, compared to US$22 and US$28 per capita for the USA and the UK, respectively, indicating the astounding information gaps that companies from these countries have to bridge.

Applying standard operating procedures derived from headquarters overseas have rarely served Western companies well in China. On the other hand, Chinese companies seeking success in overseas markets must cultivate their strategic long-term perspectives, especially investments in brand-names, and in technological and institutional capacities, to compete more effectively against Western and Japanese companies in mature, information-rich markets. In Western markets, Chinese companies lose the government networks, experience, and insider information that give them an edge at home.

FIGURE 9.1: MARKET RESEARCH EXPENDITURES PER CAPITA IN 2001[1]

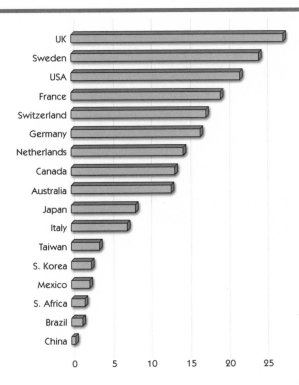

Figure 9.2 covers advertising expenditures per capita, which indicate efforts to build and to maintain brand recognition. Industrialized countries, including Japan, dominate on advertising expenditures per capita. Asian countries, including China, incur miniscule advertising expenditures per capita, indicating little effort to build brand recognition as a strategic tool. In 2001, China spent US$4 per capita on advertising, compared to US$355 and US$456 for Switzerland and the USA, respectively. Advertising expenditures per capita in the USA exceed those of any other country. In the new interdependent, global economy, the disparate Chinese and Western management styles must converge to create an effective, more comprehensive and adaptable strategic-management system.

FIGURE 9.2:[2] ADVERTISING EXPENDITURES PER CAPITA IN 2001

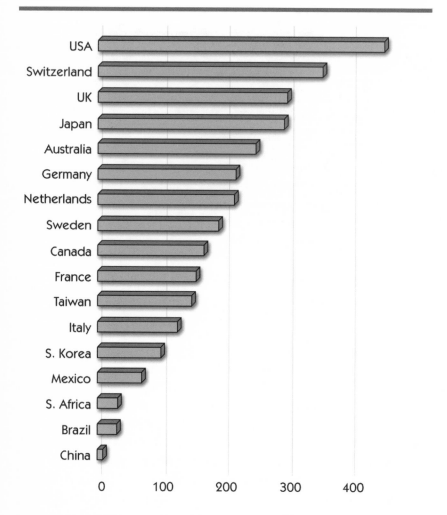

MANAGERIAL CONVERGENCE

We argue that managerial convergence occurs when the underlying managerial philosophies of two or more business cultures clash in competition; while each culture shows significant strengths in particular situations, one displays general superiority. In managerial convergence, companies from the weaker business cultures adopt and adapt the perceived strengths of the stronger cultures to strengthen their competitive positions. With successful adaptations, the weaker companies will show resurgence. Consequently, alternating periods of advantage will ensue between the two business cultures, as was apparent in the case of the US and Japanese business cultures. As we shall see later, companies such as Legend demonstrate that managerial convergence has already begun between Chinese and Western companies.

Convergence has often occurred when managers focused on serving foreign markets after building strength and expertise in their home markets. It is often the newer business cultures that took the first steps towards convergence (for example, the USA vis-à-vis Europe, or Japan vis-à-vis the West). Here, the newer culture's companies adopted certain business practices and technologies from the established culture, adapting and refining them to become global players. Usha Haley's[3] research on the behavior of multinational corporations in foreign markets offers one reason for such convergence. Through her research on 322 US companies spanning a decade, Haley determined that the companies behave as chameleons that adapt to local environments in host countries, rather than as catalysts that change them.

TWO HISTORIC CONVERGENCES: THE CLASH OF THE TITANS

The most significant influences on US management originated in the UK, from which its early elite largely originated. Until the early 20th century, when the USA became an economic and military power, US elites looked to the UK in particular, and Europe in general, for ideologies. In the late 19th and early 20th century, and in response to increasing demands for trained managers, US managers and universities founded new business schools that offered the MBA degree. The world's first mass-production, Ford-Model-T economy developed mass-produced professionals to lead its companies in a global economy. At first, Europe's elites and business cultures recoiled from the new US management systems; for example, Servan-Schreiber's[4] *The American Challenge* decried the coming Americanization of Europe. Later, Europe responded with its own business schools. The Europeans adopted and adapted the best US practices for a managerial convergence.

In rebuilding after World War II, Japanese companies had adopted and adapted from US companies, but most especially from the largely ignored US thinkers Edward Deming and J. M. Juran. The Japanese success changed global competition. In the 1970s, American companies sought to adopt those characteristics of Japanese management, such as just-in-time inventory management, lean manufacturing and quality-control systems that managers perceived as contributing to Japanese success. Japanese companies came to depend on Western markets for their profits, and their Western competitors became more resilient. Consequently, the Japanese once again adopted the best practices of Western companies, such as their profitability horizons. American and Japanese management influenced each other through quality circles, total-quality management and continuous improvement. New US business philosophies, such as re-engineering and Six Sigma, emerged. As the convergence continues, all parties are continuing to evolve.

Managerial convergence embodies several characteristics. First, adaptations reflect the environmental influences from whence the companies originate. For example, European managers adapted US strategic management to reflect Europe's unions, hierarchical societies and social-democratic movements; and US managers adapted Japanese management to reflect the more arms-length US relationships between managers, labor and governments, and the greater power of US shareholders. Companies nevertheless maintain many cultural and economic characteristics, despite converging.

Second, for convergence to occur, companies must seek to serve each other's markets, rather than simply rationalizing production costs while maintaining their traditional markets. The managers who seek convergence must also perceive weaknesses vis-à-vis their foreign competitors that they can mitigate or eliminate through adopting foreign business practices. For example, only after competing with Overseas Chinese and Chinese companies in East Asia and China did Western companies perceive tactical lags as a problem and tactical speed as a requirement for success. Several Western companies that we researched are adopting structures and practices that enhance their tactical speed in China against local competitors.

Third, convergence generally occurs in competitive markets, when companies feel threats to their domestic markets. Hypercompetitive Chinese markets with razor-thin margins are forcing Chinese companies to go abroad as well as to adopt Western best practices to compete effectively at home and abroad.

Fourth, successful convergence places a premium on adaptability. For example, Japan Inc.'s inability to adapt has led to a long-term economic crisis that has lasted for over a decade. Though some Japanese companies, such as Sony, Toyota, Honda and Nissan, have continuously adapted and maintained their competitiveness, the bulk of Japanese managements and bureaucracies have resisted changing their business and government cultures. Consequently, government policies and strategic-management systems are failing Japan Inc. In this regard, Hiroshi Okuda,[5] president of Toyota Motors, believes that Japan must change again. "It is 30 or 40 years[6] so we must adjust again," he said. "Maybe we can try and come back in another 50 years ... It will take 50 years for the Japanese to gain [these skills]; the Japanese people will not change in 10 years or 20 years ... On a mid-term and long-term basis we have to change the [Japanese] system, but until there are changes, which is a transitional period, we can make use of the resources, the human resources, from abroad." He speculated that during Japan's transitional period, companies would have to hire foreigners who introduce new skills, seed these skills, and depart.

Historically, convergence generally occurred between companies originating from relatively stable, mature economies, with established accounting and business-information systems. Yet, Chinese companies originate from emerging markets. In the next section, we indicate why managerial convergence will nevertheless occur between Chinese and Western companies.

LEGEND MEETS THE WEST:[7] DÉJÀ VU ALL OVER AGAIN

Legend Group, founded in 1984, is China's largest desktop-PC maker, with a 28% market share in 2002. After enjoying years of astounding growth, the company now faces the same problems as Western computer manufacturers: slowing growth, heightening price competition and narrowing margins.

"Our earliest and best teacher was Hewlett-Packard (HP)," said Liu Chuanzhi, Legend's chairman.[8] For more than a decade, Legend served as HP's distributor in China. Liu studied and adapted HP's way for China's market. In the 1990s, Legend introduced its own brand of PCs.

While Legend had lower costs than Western companies, its biggest advantage lay in its distribution network. The Chinese government owns 65% of the company And Liu used his government network to sell computers to SOEs. He could not match Western companies in R&D spending, but adapted for the local market. For example, Legend introduced a new keyboard for Chinese characters. In 1997, it beat Western companies to become China's top-selling brand by offering lower prices and comparable quality that the company tailored for the Chinese market.

However, by 2003, price wars were raging at the high end of the Chinese PC market, an echo of the battles that started in the West in the late 1990s. In late May 2003, Legend reported a 2% drop in profits and a disappointing 5% rise in revenues. To recapture growth, Legend has moved into new markets in China, such as notebook computers, servers, mobile phones, MP3 music players and digital cameras. It is laying the ground for further new products, including IT services and network products. It is also turning out a new line of application-based desktop computers. Most ambitiously, like HP and Dell before it, Legend has longer-term plans to take its business overseas to recapture growth. In April, the company changed its English brand name to the sleeker "Lenovo".

In the new competitive environment, Liu said he worried more about Western companies, especially Dell, than domestic competitors. "There's a lot we can learn from Dell," he said. He thinks Dell's management of functions such as logistics, procurement and inventory is "astounding" and acknowledged that "while our cost control is very similar, to be honest with you, Dell is a little bit better."[9]

Legend will cede its major strengths — distribution and *guanxi* — when it goes overseas, where it does not have established sales, service and distribution networks. Mary Ma, chief financial officer and senior vice-president of Legend's publicly traded unit in Hong Kong, recognized that in the USA individual customers reward brand awareness, while corporate customers value suppliers that can provide entire computer systems, including services. Computer-related services constituted just 6% of China's IT market, compared to 40% in the USA. However, in preparation, Legend planned to offer more services as well as to increase spending on R&D to about 3—5% of revenue, from 1.8% in 2003. It also "hoped to use other people's distribution channels, or partnerships."[10]

Legend offers a story of convergence. The company began by learning distribution from Western companies, and then using that knowledge to dominate its home market. Legend plans to use the same learning strategy as the keystone to building its overseas distribution networks. Legend has won the first battle against Western competitors at home; whether it can win the international wars will depend on its ability to learn, to adapt to and to prosper in the global competitive environments that it has helped to create.

CHINESE-WESTERN CONVERGENCE

Unlike past managerial convergences, the convergence between Greater China and the industrialized West includes, primarily, developing economies with advantages in population and potential market size, with established economic powers. The potential size and growth rates of China's markets serve as powerful magnets drawing Western companies to its economic promise. However, to establish strong, profitable market positions in China, Western companies will have to adopt strategic-planning systems that have proven effective in these information-scarce markets. As Figure 9.1 indicated, several Asian countries, including the more established economies of Taiwan, Japan and South Korea, have what many Western managers would consider to be informational-void economies rather than established, mature markets. Yet many Western companies enter China without a coherent and appropriate business plan, and with disastrous results. As we saw earlier, according to the American Chamber of Commerce in Beijing, one-third of US companies in China are losing money. Lack of adequate information for strategic planning, and faulty assumptions about the quality of available information, are the obstacles on which most of these Western companies stumble. Mark Helman, the China manager for a major US retailer, confessed that for his company "prior planning was basically limited to surfing the Internet to get a few facts about our industry in China". The retailer closed down its Chinese operations within three years.[11] In Chapter 7, we also noted how Chinese companies suffer when they lose their home-turf advantages and use of traditional strategies, including control of distribution channels. Indeed, Figure 9.2 indicated the enormous discrepancy in investment between Western and Chinese strategies to create brand recognition through advertising, which creates enormous barriers to entry for the Western markets. Researchers and analysts have presented Chinese and Western managerial systems as being mutually exclusive; yet evidence suggests interdependence and mutual influence. Studies of Overseas Chinese and Chinese companies,[12] and of Asian subsidiaries of Western companies, have shown that managers can successfully incorporate and adapt elements of their competitors' planning strategies. Our research among CEOs of Chinese and Overseas Chinese companies and senior managers of Western companies found substantial evidence of an informal acceptance of managerial convergence; and an explicit recognition that flexibility and adaptation enhance success.

CHAMELEON-LIKE, ARTESYN MEETS THE EAST

Artesyn, a US multinational with headquarters in Florida, possesses highly successful Chinese operations. The company has succeeded through playing the part of a chameleon. In managing its Chinese operations, Artesyn has metamorphosed into an Overseas Chinese company using largely Western controls and taking a largely Western strategic perspective. Indeed, the four-step investment guidelines that its managers described to us mirror those of the Overseas Chinese. Artesyn's investment guidelines for information-scarce China include:

1) Investing small amounts initially — Artesyn launches small subsidiaries until it gains confidence in its decisions and in its knowledge of the new products and markets.

2) Investing in known environments — Artesyn invests where it either already knows the local authorities or where it can determine through research that the local authorities have a pro-FDI track record and display honesty in their dealings with investors.

3) Investing with history on their side — Artesyn invests where the local economy has a vibrant private sector and does not tailor its business practices to those of SOEs.

4) Investing in locals — Artesyn works hard to find and to train good, entrepreneurial local managers. The company, however, prefers competent foreign managers to locals who fail to show initiative.

Artesyn has two goals with its Chinese investments. First, it does not measure success by the profitability of individual investments, but by the contributions made by those investments to overall corporate profitability; and second, it ascertains how the investments optimize and rationalize overall corporate-cost structures.

Thus, Artesyn has undertaken managerial convergence in China by adapting Western planning models to fit local, uncontrollable, situations. For its Chinese strategy, Artesyn's managers follow the same planning procedures as US headquarters. However, they use personal judgment, subjective data and information from reliable sources to fill in the gaps in their objective data.

The first steps to convergence have been taken. As Legend's managers indicated earlier, major Sino-Asian companies are building Western skills and adapting their managerial practices for perceived benefit. Until recently, former Chinese prime minister Zhu Rongji served as dean of China's most prestigious business school, Tsinghua University's Business School, and significant factions within the government endorse Western management systems and practices. Other trends indicate further convergence:

- Top Western business schools have provided training for many of the PRC's first-generation and Greater China's second- and third-generation business leaders.
- Many of these business leaders also have significant experience working in Western companies.
- Local economic and political elites have invested heavily in founding and building their own top business schools, which are now increasingly comparable to the best in the West.[13]
- Overseas Chinese and PRC Chinese companies are making successful forays into Western markets and will continue to expand their Western subsidiaries and investments.
- Pressure from stakeholders for better governance, increased disclosure and transparency from Chinese companies is mounting.[14]

- China's WTO membership, and the international trade it fosters, should contribute to closer contact and competition between different managerial cultures.

In addition, globalization and rates of environmental, social and technological change will contribute to increased managerial convergence between Chinese and Western companies.

▲ Globalization

In Chapter 6, we discussed how fierce price competition in China is contributing to global deflation across key industrial sectors. In Chapters 7 and 8, we tracked how SARS in China has affected the global economy. Both discussions highlight facets of globalization — increasing interdependence and increasing complexities.

Western companies investing in Asia have historically developed a network of production facilities to serve their home markets in Europe, Japan and North America.[15] Now, companies such as Dell and Walmart are also developing value chains throughout China and Asia to serve Asian and, especially, Chinese markets. Because they have environments that differ significantly from those in the West, Asian markets require different skills that companies have to adopt if their local operations are to be successful.

▲ Rates of environmental change

Business and social environments in Asia are changing at a phenomenal rate, especially in China. Today, China's political environment provides a limited local democracy in many regions. Its social environment is providing greater support and encouragement to private entrepreneurs than at any time in its long history.[16] The first generation of the urban elite, the product of the one-child policy, is voicing its views. The central government is promulgating and attempting to enforce codes of law that affect business environments, such as those on copyright protection. Inflexible companies and business cultures, or those with unbending company-wide standard operating procedures, will probably not survive the coming storms. To succeed, Western companies and managers should adopt the more flexible and adaptive strategic styles found in Asia and other emerging markets.

▲ Rates of technological change

The China Internet Network Information Center has announced that China is close to overtaking Japan as the world's second-largest online Internet population: the number of Chinese with Internet access increased by 75% in 2002, to reach 59.1 million. Sweeping technological changes over only the past decade include, for example, a period when a million new mobile-phone customers joined every month. Technological changes that have significantly altered business environments and opportunities in China include Internet and e-mail access; widespread computerization; nationwide notification of business opportunities to subscribers through China's wireless Internet system; access to world-class products and services in the more economically developed regions of China; and greater availability of credit and debit cards.

▲ Rates of social change

Kwek Leng Joo, managing director of City Developments, Ltd., emphasized the rate of social change in China when he commented that, since 1992, "China [has] opened up — the kind of changes that have taken place in the society, not just the economy, but the impact on society, is pretty strong. This I would say is the first generation to be exposed to a new sort of culture, a new kind of social orderliness." Technological change has contributed to social change. For example, the China Internet Network Information Center revealed that 40% of Internet users in China are 24 years of age or under. For these young users, the Internet and Internet cafés provide avenues for freer expression. While the government appreciates the Internet as an important facet of technological progress, it wants to retain control over the technology as a medium of political expression. Migrant labor portrays another facet of the social changes bubbling in China. The country's manufacturing prowess draws on its severely skewed economic growth: migrant workers from the interior have fed the coastal, export-oriented industries, keeping wages low. Government statistics on unemployment do not account for these migrant workers, a potential source of social unrest. Kwek also spoke of a growing "network of Chinese who have gone to the US or Europe to study and returned. To work in China now is huge. They are going to pose a very significant workforce that will lead China into the future. I think they are moving in. Their time is not here yet; the number in relation to the working population is still not significant, but I can see that it has become a trend."

▲ Systemic failures

Both Chinese and Western planning appears sub-optimal for the business environments that are evolving. Western managers over-manage, while Chinese managers under-manage. As discussed in Chapter 8, the West's over-management can create strategic torpidity, tactical slowness and an inability to adapt to rapidly changing situations, especially in the absence of high-quality information. As discussed in Chapter 7, the Chinese companies' under-management can lead to rigidity, and limit competitiveness in foreign environments with which managers are unfamiliar or have no experiential data on which to rely. To compete effectively, companies must develop capabilities to manage effectively in both information-rich and information-void environments.

THE SILK ROAD TO MANAGERIAL CONVERGENCE

Just as the *Tao* indicated the importance of "the Way" to achieve spiritual wealth through balance, the legendary Silk Road pointed the way to material wealth through commerce. The Silk Road provided a conduit between the ancient empires of Rome, Egypt and China. The Roman Emperor Tiberius, commenting on Rome's trade deficit with China and India, complained, "The ladies and their baubles are transferring our money to foreigners." [17]

FIGURE 9.3: MAPPING THE SILK ROAD

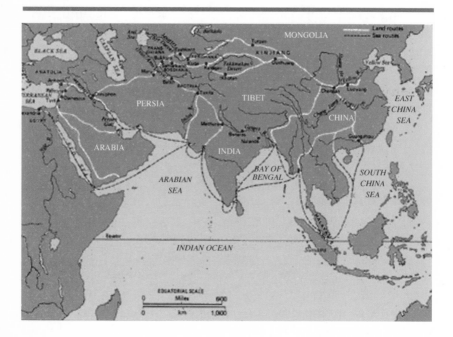

As Figure 9.3 shows, the Silk Road was not a single road or way. Numerous major and minor roads emerged, including land and maritime roads; no right or single road provided unchallenged access to commerce. Second, the Silk Road enhanced commerce in general, not just trade in silk, through drawing on country-specific assets and skills. Caravans to China carried gold and other precious metals, ivory, gems and glass (which China did not manufacture till the 5th century AD). Caravans from China carried furs, ceramics, jade, bronze objects and lacquer. Barter existed along the Silk Road and objects changed hands several times. But it was ideas, especially religion that came to form the single most important commodity that traveled the Silk Road. Buddhism came from India to China along the Silk Road. The Eastern Han Emperor Mingdi sent a representative to India to discover more about this new religion. Future missions returned bringing scriptures and Indian priests. The new religion, carried by missionaries, priests, pilgrims and merchants, spread slowly eastwards along the Silk Road, adapting to local cultures and beliefs along the way. Merchants also spread Christianity through the Silk Road. Believers consecrated the first Nestorian church in Changan in 638 AD and the sect lasted till the 14th century. At its apogee under the T'ang Dynasty, Changan, one of the Silk Road's starting points and the dynasty's capital city, had a population of two million. The census of 754 showed that more than 5,000 foreigners — merchants, missionaries and pilgrims[18] — including Turks, Iranians, Indians, Japanese, Koreans and Malays, lived in the city.

In homage to the Silk Road, and to echo our emphasis on the need for adaptability, we introduce in the next and final chapter our strategic-planning model: the Adaptive-Action Road Map (ARM). The ARM draws on our experiences in Asia and other emerging markets such as South Africa and Mexico, to chart the Silk Road for success in these information-poor markets as well as those of China in the global economy. Like the *Tao* and the Silk Road, the ARM presents a series of paths to strategic success through the convergence of the Sino-Asian and Western strategic-planning cultures. In particular, the ARM incorporates the West's particularistic processing approach, along with the East's holistic approach, to provide flexibility in analytical techniques. Indeed, the ARM will function most effectively when managers use quantitative, qualitative and experience-based data for strategic decision-making.

endnotes

1. Compiled from Jones, M. C., "And our survey said", and US Census Department 2001 population estimates.

2. Ibid.

3. Haley, U. C. V., *Multinational Corporations in Political Environments: Ethics, Values and Strategies.*

4. Servan-Schreiber, J. J., *The American Challenge.*

5. Clark, Tanya, "Reinventing Japan, Inc.".

6. Okuda views Japanese Prime Minister Hayato Ikeda's era, from 1960–64, as the period which sowed both Japan's earlier successes and present malaise.

7. Compiled from *The Economist*, "Legend in the Making"; Buckman, R., B. Dolvenin and S. V. Lawrence, "The chips are down for China's computer Legend"; and Bradsher, K., "Chinese Computer Maker Plans a Push Overseas".

8. *The Economist*, "Legend in the Making".

9. Buckman et al, op.cit.

10. Bradsher, op.cit.

11. Kurlantzick, J., "Making it in China".

12. Haley, G. T., C. T. Tan and U. C. V. Haley, *New Asian Emperors: The Overseas Chinese, their Strategies and Competitive Advantages.*

13. For example, in September 2002, Li Ka-shing and his Hutchinson-Whampoa group donated S$19.5 million to the Singapore Management University, the largest donation to a Singaporean university. The Singapore government will donate an additional S$58.5 million to the business school as part of a matching-grant program.

14. For example, the International Monetary Fund has insisted that Asian countries adopt standards of transparency in accounting rules, investment regulations and managerial processes.

15. Haley et al, op.cit.

16. For example, President Jiang Zemin invited private entrepreneurs to join the CCP.

17. Wilford, J. N., "Under Centuries of Sand, a Trading Hub".

18. For an excellent discussion of the Silk Road and its importance to commerce and religion, see Oliver Wild's The Silk Road at http://www.ess.uci.edu/~oliver/silk.html.

10

THE SILK ROAD OF STRATEGIC PLANNING

"Lay plans for the accomplishment of the difficult
before it becomes difficult;
make something big
by starting with it when small."
Tao Te Ching
Book 2, Chapter 63, Stanza 149

INTRODUCTION

Li & Fung, Hong Kong's largest export-trading company, serves as a global innovator in the development of supply-chain management. Founded in 1906 by the present chairman's grandfather, and drawing on traditional Chinese management practices, Li & Fung looks like the traditional Overseas Chinese company on steroids. On behalf of its customers, primarily European and US companies, the company works with an ever-expanding network of thousands of suppliers around the world, especially in Asia's emerging economies, sourcing clothing and consumer goods ranging from toys to fashion accessories to luggage. Rather than owning any production facilities, Li & Fung coordinates numerous quality-conscious, cost-effective producers who can deliver on deadlines for its customers. In 2003, the company enjoyed an annual turnover of US$4.2 billion and employed about 5,000 people worldwide. Yet this company is beginning to rethink its planning, its strengths and weaknesses.

Victor Fung, chairman of Li & Fung, provided some insights into the planning process that guides his company's change. Fung felt the conflicting needs to plan as well as to act opportunistically; to systematize and to professionalize as well as to nurture hands-on experience. While his grandfather had to leverage one or two very influential relationships, he has to manage systems of relationships to add value. Li & Fung uses state-of-the art distribution and logistics systems and managers have to make a great many small decisions every day. Therefore, Fung told us, "You need structure, hierarchy and process." In effect, Li & Fung consists not of one supply chain but tens of thousands — every product has a supply chain. He acknowledged that one of the company's biggest problems is "to administer. How do we pool our knowledge and share? We don't think we can replace the human being with a machine. We [still operate] on a kind of gut feel ... our managers use rough heuristics. You may be able to program some of these heuristics in your machine, but you are exploring the limits of artificial intelligence."

In line with the *Tao*'s advice, Victor Fung started transforming his traditional company before any of his competitors, and before change became a necessity. In the 1980s, while his competitors concentrated on supplier partnerships to improve cost and quality; he focused on innovation, flexibility and speed by breaking the traditional value chain. In addition, Fung implemented his changes in small, incremental steps. His company's structure epitomizes Fung's focus and his acceptance of change. Unlike other trading companies that organized geographically, with countries as profit centers, Fung organized his company along divisions that serve individual customers (such as the Gap, Gymboree or Espirit) — across geographical areas. Li & Fung grew or fell with its major customers across the world, not with economic regions. Before any one else, Fung had anticipated the need for some simple and adaptable strategic rules for the new global economy.

Drawing on the truths propounded by the *Tao*, and the strengths and weaknesses of Western and Asian managers, this chapter proposes a system of adaptable strategic rules for success. We call these rules for effective strategizing our Adaptive-action Road Map (ARM). The next sections provide topographical and in-depth plots of the ARM.

ARMING MANAGERS FOR SUCCESS

The ARM synthesizes our research and proposals for international strategic success. It draws on both the responses of the managers we interviewed formally for this book (see Appendix A) and on feedback from several thousand European, Latin American, US and Asian managers that we have taught, worked with and consulted for over two decades.

The ARM hinges on flexibility and adaptability to rapid change. The Chinese character for change, *Yi*, began as a pictograph for a chameleon — a lizard that adapts to its environment by changing color as the light and environment change. Indeed, the *Tao Te Ching* tutors: "The hard and the strong are the comrades of death; the supple and the weak are the comrades of life."[1] The *Tao* thus emphasizes the adaptable nature of life and the importance of flexibility as the way to live, to thrive and to succeed. Successful businesspeople must perforce incorporate adaptability into their strategies. The incredibly adroit Robert Kuok, CEO of the Kerry Group and Shangri-La Hotels, reinforced this view: "I adapt like a chameleon to the particular society where I am operating at the moment."[2] His competitors echoed that sentiment: Robert Riley, managing director of the competing Mandarin Oriental Hotel Group, said of Kuok, "He's a local everywhere he goes."[3] The ARM's strengths emerge in rapidly changing, volatile and emerging markets; it has greatest applicability in emerging growth markets such as China, Southeast and South Asia and Latin America. These emerging markets represent about two-thirds of the world's population and, over the last 40 years, have become the fastest-growing economic regions in the world. Unlike Europe and Japan, Asia and Latin America have young populations: over 50% of the populations of many Asian and Latin American countries are 15 years old or younger, which indicates the potential for even greater market changes. Table 10.1 presents the 20 largest countries in the world by population and GDP. Bold type distinguishes emerging from developed economies.

TABLE 10.1: THE WORLD'S LARGEST MARKETS IN 2002

Rank	Population[4]	Gross Domestic Product[5]
1.	**China**	United States
2.	**India**	**China**
3.	United States	Japan
4.	**Indonesia**	**India**
5.	**Brazil**	Germany
6.	**Pakistan**	France
7.	**Russia**[+]	United Kingdom
8.	**Bangladesh**	Italy
9.	**Nigeria**	**Brazil**
10.	Japan	**Russia**[6]

11.	**Mexico**	**Mexico**
12.	**Philippines**	Canada
13.	Germany	**South Korea**
14.	**Vietnam**	Spain
15.	**Egypt**	**Indonesia**
16.	**Ethiopia**	Australia
17.	**Turkey**	**Argentina**
18.	**Iran**	**Turkey**
19.	**Thailand**	**Iran**
20.	United Kingdom	Netherlands

Table 10.1 highlights that two emerging markets rank among the five largest economies; indeed, emerging economies constitute 16 of the 20 most populous countries and 10 of the 20 countries with the largest GDPs. Successful managers must know how to strategize for success in these emerging markets and to translate their plans for stakeholders of developed markets.

For companies whose operations straddle both emerging and developed economies, the abilities to assimilate, to co-ordinate and to wield different kinds and textures of information form crucial components of success. Victor Fung vividly captured the need for successful global managers to traverse two hemispheres. He saw his company as an information node:

"I have a picture in my mind of the ideal trader for today's world. The trader is an executive wearing a pith helmet and a safari jacket. But in one hand is a machete and in the other a very high-tech personal computer and communication device. From one side, you are getting reports from suppliers in newly emerging countries, where the quality of information may be poor. From the other side, you might have highly accurate point-of-sale information from the [US] that allows you to replenish automatically. In other words, you're maneuvering between areas that have a lot of catching up to do — you're fighting through the underbrush, so to speak — and areas that are already clearly focused on the [next] century."[7]

FIGURE 10.1: THE ADAPTIVE-ACTION ROAD MAP (ARM)

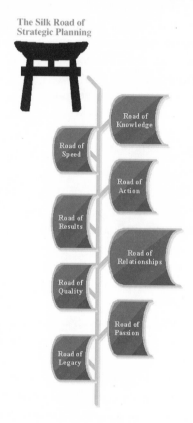

The next sections describe these roads in more detail.

The ARM charts a successful course along the Silk Road for executives carrying machetes and high-tech communication devices. Figure 10.1 graphs the ARM. Managers today must recognize that no company stands alone. To succeed, companies must interact effectively with other companies — both cooperatively and competitively — with suppliers, government and supra-government agencies, employees, facilitating agencies, special-interest groups, shareholders and, most importantly, with customers. These interactions form networks of interdependencies that determine a company's success. In the global economy, these networks assume more importance. The

ARM indicates eight strategic roads that managers must travel to succeed in the global economy. Fusing best practices from Eastern and Western strategic approaches that we have highlighted, the ARM identifies:

* **The Road of Knowledge** — Experiential, qualitative and quantitative knowledge coalesces into a necessary whole for managers. The Road of Knowledge emphasizes that knowledge is a strategic investment for companies. To take timely and necessary tactical and strategic actions, management must dedicate itself to acquiring and disseminating holistic knowledge.

* **The Road of Speed** — Both strategic and tactical decision-makers should use their knowledge of their company's businesses and markets to get their products to market before their competitors. For tactics, speed assumes paramount importance. Speed requires that line managers at decision points have the authority to choose quickly from various options and to beat competitors to the draw.

* **The Road of Action** — The rapidity of change in emerging markets compounds difficulties in making product-market decisions. Uncertainty can slow actions to a crawl. Most efforts to reduce uncertainty before taking action merely disguise uncertainty, not reduce it. The Road of Action irrevocably reduces uncertainty and allows managers to use market activities to learn more about product markets.

* **The Road of Results** — Capital, time, effort and personnel must flow towards success. The preliminary returns trickling in from various investments provide data on their success. Managers should use these preliminary data to decide on further investments. Counter-intuitively, short-term measures often provide better indicators of success than long-term measures.

❖ **The Road of Relationships** — People provide the key to success; successful companies encapsulate and focus the collective actions of their staff to create prosperity and value for their customers. Companies create value through formal and informal relationship networks. The Road of Relationships fuses relationship marketing and employee empowerment beyond commonly accepted views in the East and the West: while Easterners generally apply the concepts only to long-time, close business associates, customers and employees, Westerners generally see the concepts as distinct and unrelated.

❖ **The Road of Quality** — Growing globalization and efficiencies are driving down costs; competitiveness will focus on quality and should know few limits. Because of this intense global competition, companies will need both brand image and market presence, backed by quality, to outdo competitors.

❖ **The Road of Passion** — Managers should work as if their life depended on it; it does. The Road of Passion reflects the Eastern belief that executives should derive passionate joy from the industries in which they work; the Western belief that companies should passionately commit to the markets they serve; and the universal belief that executives should passionately dedicate themselves to their own and their company's success.

❖ **The Road of Legacy** —It is the management of companies that shapes perceptions and eventually their legacies. Managers should display a commitment to leaving society and the world a better place than they found it, to bringing something special into the world. Companies that act responsibly while generating profits will also reap long-term success.

THE ROAD OF KNOWLEDGE

The Road of Knowledge indicates that managers must treat knowledge as a strategic investment. An ancient Chinese proverb warns, "The person who does not worry about the future will shortly have worries about the present." Yet market research almost always focuses exclusively on present, not future, worries, and develops static pictures of markets at specific points in time. For effectiveness, market research should transcend specific projects and incorporate quantitative data that have long-term strategic ramifications, as well as experiential and qualitative data.

Frank Martin, president of the American Chamber of Commerce in Hong Kong, highlighted the traps of relying on traditional market research in Asia: "The numbers work very well until you get to the end of the day; then you find out they don't add up." To make strategic decisions in volatile markets, managers must have steady streams of usable data flowing into their knowledge bases — especially when operating in new markets. Understanding market trends, their positions in the past, present and future, especially bolsters strategic decisions. Michael Furst, executive director of the American Chamber of Commerce in Beijing, emphasized this point when he said, "What kind of numbers do you want? Look at the trends. Even when the exact data are wrong, the trends are usually right." Only permanent, strategically directed and longitudinal market research enables managers to develop accurate perceptions of market trends.

Experiential and qualitative data also complement quantitative data. Experience provides managers with interpretive lenses to translate quantitative data into useful business information. Managers also need first-hand experience to maximize their flexibility and to minimize their response times to environmental opportunities and challenges. Consequently, for effectiveness, companies must incorporate the experience of their managers into their knowledge bases. Complementing longitudinal market research with qualitative data and managerial experience enhances the company's capacity to seize market initiatives and to influence the environments in which they operate.

Finally, to enable lateral transfers of knowledge across industries and markets, companies must codify and disseminate knowledge gained through market research and managerial experience. Many Western companies concentrate on information systems that rely on staff-generated knowledge. Without intimate experience, staff analysts cannot transcend individual projects or see connections between projects. On the other hand, line managers make such lateral transfers as a matter of routine. As we discussed in earlier chapters, Chinese and Asian strategic planning draws on these lateral transfers, which require an understanding of entire markets and industries, not just specific projects.

In global economies, IT provides a major tool to codify and to disseminate knowledge across a company's operations. While other trading companies are either in bankruptcy or teetering on the edge of it, Hong Kong's Li & Fung used IT successfully as part of the Road to Knowledge. Victor Fung explained how IT helped his company: "When people talk about supply chains, they're thinking of a very stable system that is competitive. We are able to give each order a customer places its own customized supply chain. And it changes; one day you're getting a fabric from here, the next you're switching to there. But the customer gets the same result. In fact, we have tens of thousands of supply chains running through our company, all through our IT systems."

Li & Fung rode the Internet revolution and views IT as a series of investments in knowledge. Fung, in particular, saw IT as an evolving tool for disseminating knowledge: "Now all this talk about revolutionary technology is OK. There's a lot of new technology that we have bought and we like to be fairly fast about it. But I am sure that ten years from now there will be another revolutionary new technology. This is not going to end." Li & Fung has prospered through investing heavily in the Road of Knowledge necessary for its customers' success, and then through providing that knowledge to its customers.

In sum, the Road of Knowledge requires that companies

- use traditional Western market-research, data-collection and data-analysis.
- use traditional Asian, subjective, data-gathering and processing.
- value subjective and objective data-acquisition strategies.
- build a broad-based, deeply intuitive understanding of their markets.
- build a broad-based, deeply intuitive understanding of their strategic directions and postures.
- build an in-depth core of experience of markets among managers.
- build understanding and communication between staff and line managers.
- see strategic situations from holistic and particularistic perspectives.
- incorporate diverse sources of knowledge into strategic and tactical decision-making.

THE ROAD OF SPEED

The Road of Speed involves decisions about getting to markets with products before competitors. The Road of Speed becomes especially important in tactical decisions. The line managers must already have traveled down the Road of Knowledge — that is, they must have knowledge that comes from personal experience and qualitative data, as well as access to quantitative, longitudinal market research. The line managers must also communicate pertinent business-unit and market-specific data to their superiors and colleagues. Stan Shih of Acer highlighted this communication between line and staff when he said that he and his executive council often made decisions based upon a collective "gut feel" and that success - was "all in the implementation".[8] This communication helped Acer to achieve the best tactical speed of any major computer company.

As Shih highlighted, implementation becomes key in the Road of Speed. For tactical speed, line managers in the field must have freedom to adapt strategic plans, within the company's overall strategic postures, to confront specific business problems and to respond to competition. For this to be effective, the managers must also understand the company's internal and external business patterns and how they relate. These patterns provide line managers with forewarnings of future requirements, and of the best ways to meet those requirements. A company's core competencies, for example, stem from internal patterns of behavior that provide customers with significant benefits. These core competencies also reflect well-honed skills. Line managers using these competencies would deploy strategies more quickly and more effectively than those relying on different sets of skills.

The Road of Speed is even more important in tactical decision-making. Yet long-term perspectives should not contribute to losses and strategic lethargy. Managers and planning staff should remember one of General George S. Patton's strategic dictums: "A good plan today is better than a perfect plan tomorrow."[9]

Haier's experience with its Access Plus freezer provides a quick glimpse into the Road of Speed. Michael Jemal, Haier's head of US sales, generated the concept for the product in early 2001. On a trip to China, Jemal floated the idea to Haier's CEO, Zhang Ruimin. The following day, Zhang rushed Jemal from his hotel back to Haier's headquarters and into a conference room to reveal a working model of the freezer. Ten months later, on November 9, 2001, Haier introduced the Access Plus into US markets at an unveiling in New York.[10] The company has used the Road of Speed often in the USA. Since hitting US shores in the 1990s, Haier has dominated some market niches, such as compact refrigerators for dorms and offices, and created the market for stand-alone wine coolers. Haier has shown that the Road of Speed can provide avenues for success in both mature and emerging markets. Since opening its manufacturing plant in Camden, South Carolina, in 2000, Haier's sales have grown to US$200 million, and may reach US$1 billion by 2005. Only two years after breaking ground on its first US manufacturing facility, Haier has reported profits on its US operations.[11]

The Road of Speed requires that senior managers:

- endorse strongly the Road of Knowledge and incorporate it in strategic planning and implementation.
- commit firmly to train middle and lower managers in the use of the Road of Knowledge.
- invest in communication capabilities.
- advise line managers of broad strategic directions and perspectives.
- provide line managers with latitude to adapt strategic decisions for their markets.

THE ROAD OF ACTION

The Road of Action shows how managers can use market activities to learn about uncertain product markets. As Pierre Wack noted, "The future is no longer stable; it has become a moving target. No single right projection can be deduced from past behavior."[12] Financial analysts ignore uncertainty through using point estimates, few of which take the error ranges of market forecasts into consideration. Yet high levels of uncertainty invalidate financial techniques that use net-present-value theory in their projections.[13] Generally, forecasting techniques become less reliable as uncertainty increases, paralyzing tactical and strategic decisions. "In China," as Robert Shi, Chief Representative, European Financial Group, noted, "one year is a long time, things can change dramatically and the data are often wrong."

Several techniques attempt to dispel uncertainty, but significant caveats attend them. For example, market researchers try to dispel uncertainty through relying on standard-error estimates; yet the validities of these estimates rest on the validities of researchers' understanding of the markets. Mis-projections of product markets in developed countries include Coca-Cola's introduction of New Coke into the USA in 1985. Coke's managers and researchers failed to understand Coke's true hold on the American psyche. More serious mis-projections attend product markets in volatile emerging markets. In the extremely rapid changes that characterize China and other emerging markets, data rapidly become obsolete, as we saw earlier with Cerestar's experiences. Market research also yields unreliable results in these volatile markets because of the time that elapses before research yields results, the inability of researchers to understand their changing markets, and miscommunications between researchers and populations under study. Especially in business-to-business markets, and through their regular contacts with customers, line managers often have more up-to-date information on product markets and potential than market researchers.

The Road of Action would seem to contradict popular management philosophies such as Six Sigma, which advise that managers should never proceed beyond the limits of their data and analysis.[14] However, this contradiction occurs only when the complete and high-quality data that Six Sigma requires for managing processes do not exist. Consequently, managers' insistence on generating these data can slow tactical strategies considerably. As Clayton Christensen has pointed out,[15] "By the time data shows that market share is eroding, it's often too late to fix the problem ... To make accurate predictions about where business is going, managers have to go on gut. When innovations are looming, what's worked in the past is a dangerous guide."[16] When managing operations in emerging markets, managers often have "to go on gut".

Managers can reduce uncertainty in product markets by maintaining relatively short payback periods, just as companies in rapidly evolving high-tech industries have done traditionally.[17] Our research indicates that the Overseas Chinese reduce uncertainty by undertaking initial investments that do not risk their company's survival. They probe new product markets through relatively small initial investments that promote learning about the markets' characteristics. The companies also maintain high levels of liquidity to fund products and tactical adaptations. Over time, if the managers discover that the businesses promise profits and fit into their company's strategic posture, they expand and adapt their initial investments and strategies. Conversely, if the managers discover that the businesses do not have high potential, they cut their ties before suffering significant financial losses or loss of face.

Some successful Western companies in China have also gone down the Road of Action. Elmar Stachels, chairman and managing director of Bayer China, told us how his company made decisions about product markets: "When we decide to invest ... we start with a moderate step-by-step approach. We decide on our locales through business contacts and due diligence investigations. As confidence evolves, we go for win-win situations."

In the mid 1990s, the Wuthelam Group, an Overseas Chinese company, made its foray into the New Zealand property-development markets down the Road of Action.[18] While holidaying in New Zealand, one of the company's senior managers in property operations ran across an advertisement for a property in receivership. The property piqued his interest and he visited the site. He liked what he saw — a seaside property with a marina and an additional NZ$10 million in improvements. The asking price also seemed reasonable. The receiver valued the property at NZ$25 million, but seemed willing to negotiate on a purchase price. The manager immediately opened negotiations and Wuthelam purchased the property for NZ$17 million. Despite scanty data, Wuthelam's manager did not view this initial investment in New Zealand as either uncertain or risky: The company paid NZ$8 million below valuation and NZ$7 million above the value of improvements. A loss of the entire investment would represent less than 2% of Wuthelam's annual revenues and would not endanger the company. Because of this initial success, the company has expanded investments in New Zealand's property markets; it has also adapted its strategy as it learned more about the markets.

THE ROAD OF RESULTS

The Road of Results indicates that in emerging and turbulent markets in particular, short-term performance serves as the best yardstick of a market's strategic value. As described earlier, companies such as PepsiCo and Microsoft have never made a profit in China, despite their attempts to do so for over a decade. Their managers have viewed China as a long-term strategic market and their investments have aimed at building sustainable long-term positions without any short-term or perceivable benefits. We argue that these strategies are unproductive and futile.

In emerging markets such as China, managers have great difficulty in obtaining market information, including feedback on potential long-term successes. In such circumstances, short-term underperformance signals that a company's strategies or tactics are failing and may not contribute to long-term success. As we have described in this book, several factors contribute to these failures, including poor understanding of market characteristics, overcapacity, poor infrastructure and lack of government support. Our research has revealed that in China both Western and Chinese companies have attained success through a series of successful short-term moves that they leveraged for further successes — rather than through long-term investments with no discernable payback. Indeed, in information-void markets such as China, throwing good money after bad may indicate a cognitive bias to which managers succumb — escalating commitment to a losing course of action.[19] Li Ka-shing of Hutchison Whampoa told us that one of the keys to his success was never forming strong attachments to specific projects, and knowing when to cut losses.

The workings of a dike offer useful insights into the Road of Results. Once cracks appear in the dike, floodwaters begin to seep through. But, when one crack expands and gives way, water bursts onto the surrounding lands. Simultaneously, the water pressure on the other weak points is relieved. In our analogy, the flow of water represents the investment traveling down the Road of Results. The growing breach in the dike of the successful leak represents the growing profits of the successful project. The companies' further investments should flow rapidly towards those initial investments that show the greatest short-term profitability.

Putting the emphasis on short-term performance does not imply that managers should not strive very hard to sustain profitability and competitive advantages over the long term. Coca-Cola entered China in 1981, one year earlier than PepsiCo. Initially, like PepsiCo, it argued for a long-term perspective. Eventually, it discovered the Road of Results to attain sustainable profitability.[20] In the 1980s, the company found that Coke was selling poorly in China, as consumers thought it tasted like herbal medicine. Consumers preferred orange- and lime-flavored drinks. The company therefore invested in Sprite and Fanta and sold more of these brands while building Coke's brand image through advertising. In the 1990s, consumers began to accept Coke and sales eventually overtook sales of Sprite. Meanwhile, Coca-Cola also focused on taking as much control as possible of JVs, moving quickly to establish majority control. It sought partners such as China International Trust and Investment Corporation (CITIC), an SOE with Western-style management and tremendous *guanxi*; and Robert Kuok's Kerry Group, which also had tremendous *guanxi* and access to top-level government leaders. These strategic partnerships allowed Coca-Cola to position itself for the longer term, while acquiring a greater understanding of short-term dynamics. The company reduced its investment risks by pouring its capital into concentrate plants, leaving the more capital-intensive bottling plants to its partners. It also leveraged the political influence it obtained through its JV partners to obtain government approval for new bottling plants. The company finally made a profit, a decade after entering China. It has retained equity majority ownership in its JVs to exercise managerial control. As discussed in Chapter 6, Pepsi has never sought control of its JVs, with disastrous results.

Kathleen Eisenhardt and Donald Sull described the successful traversing of the Road of Results by Yahoo! when they argued that the company's managers "know that the greatest opportunities for competitive advantage lie in market confusion, so they jump into chaotic markets, probe for opportunities, build on successful forays, and shift flexibly among opportunities as circumstances dictate".[21] With small, quickly initiated investments, large and medium-sized companies can initiate many different investments worldwide. Managers should evaluate the preliminary returns from these investments, along with available data on industries and competitors, against criteria they developed previously. This managerial evaluation should then prompt the go/no-go decisions on further investments, as General Electric (GE) did in China.

LIGHTS ON THE ROAD OF RESULTS: GE IN CHINA

In 1992, on a visit to China shortly after the investment frenzy began, GE's CEO, Jack Welsh, expressed his determination to invest US$1 billion in Chinese factories. More than a decade later, GE has barely made half that investment and most of GE's deals have failed to materialize. Part of the reason for this stems from GE's stringent requirements for a minimum rate of return, which most of the Chinese projects could not meet. However, by adhering to the Road of Results, GE has achieved and sustained profitability in China.

GE entered China in 1994 by investing US$60 million in a JV with China's biggest light-bulb manufacturer, Shanghai Jiabao. The JV, however, failed to meet expectations. Managers set prices too high, creating space for low-cost Chinese manufacturers. Simultaneously, they underestimated their chief foreign competition, Philips, whose well-established brand drove GE's to a distant second place. GE's China chief, David Wang admitted, "We bought a local company and had to fix a lot. We underestimated the amount of time necessary for internal restructuring and so lost sight of the market."[22]

Seeing the problems with its first JV, Welch rejected GE Appliance's second proposal to set up a US$300 million refrigerator factory in Tianjin with Korean and Chinese partners. This would have constituted GE's biggest investment. It would also have furthered a cherished strategic goal of carrying GE's brand to Chinese consumers. But, unlike other CEOs, who sacrificed financial returns for supposed strategic advantage, Welch recognized that this JV faced the same pitfalls as the light-bulb factory. He killed the project and GE avoided the fate of other foreign consumer-durable companies, such as Whirlpool, that saw losses mount in China.

Meanwhile, a few of GE's businesses found profitable niches. The Beijing CT-scan factory has become the world's biggest, with sales of over US$400 million in 2000, two-thirds of which were in China. In the early 1990s, protected by import quotas and without serious domestic competition, the factory made huge profits from supplying China's ill-equipped hospitals. After the Chinese government lifted import quotas in 1995, GE cleverly shifted course. The factory beat off internal competition from GE factories in three other countries to become a global production center. The resulting export orders gave the factory the economies of scale necessary to keep local prices competitive.

Aircraft leasing is GE's most lucrative business in China. This business grew in the early 1990s as newly created regional airlines competed to expand their fleets. GE Capital financed 40% of outstanding airplane leases in China, and became the single largest contributor to the parent company's US$1.5 billion revenues from China in 2000. Even here, GE chose selectively. GE Capital refused to enter related businesses, such as railcar leasing, that have left Japanese finance companies with huge losses. Similarly, after the Asian financial crisis, the US company bought billions of dollars in cheap assets in India, Thailand and Japan, while studiously avoiding any expansion of its portfolio in China.[23]

THE ROAD OF RELATIONSHIPS

The Road of Relationships indicates that companies create value by nurturing formal and informal relationship networks with internal and external stakeholders. It is through its relationships with employees that a company builds roads of communication, exchange and transport to customers through distribution and communication channels. To succeed, managers must build mutually beneficial relationships with employees, suppliers, government and facilitating agencies to create value for their customers. Philip Spanninger, vice-president, international, for TRW Overseas, Inc., highlighted the special importance of mutually beneficial relationships in Asia when he said, "In China, Korea, actually in all of Asia, relationships are extremely important. They have long memories here and pay attention to relationships and how they evolve over one's career." Mutually beneficial relationships can also provide paths to success for companies beyond Asia.

Though he is delegating more business control to his sons in 2004, Robert Kuok still epitomizes success through the Road of Relationships. He saw himself "as the little string that ties the rings together". Kuok focused on strategy and building relationships across his myriad businesses, which include the *South China Morning Post*, Citic Pacific, food, luxury and middle-market hotels, real estate, sugar and oil plantations and newspapers, and which span Indonesia, Hong Kong, the PRC, Australia, Malaysia, Singapore, the Philippines and Thailand. His relationships incorporate partners, governments, consumers and employees and have given him an enormous edge over competitors. In 1993, when the Coca-Cola Company was contemplating changing strategy in China, it chose Kuok as a perceptive local partner who could implement strategies quickly and would not force it to compromise on its core values. Speaking of his company's choice of partner, Coca-Cola president John Farrell said that, "What could take us 10 to 24 months, [Kuok] could do in two months. His whole life has been built around building networks with the Overseas Chinese and in China. [His] ability to do things fast is incredible."[24] Yet Kuok left day-to-day management of the businesses to 35 trusted senior executives, including half-a-dozen relatives, who reported directly to him and networked among themselves.

While Western companies have generally viewed relationship marketing and employee empowerment as being separate and distinct from each other, Eastern companies have generally viewed these concepts as being interdependent —though they applied them primarily to long-time employees, long-time customers and close associates. The Road of Relationships in the ARM both unifies and transcends these different approaches. The Road of Relationships argues for companies creating value for their entire value chain — not just for customers, but also for suppliers, distributors, facilitating agencies, employees and, sometimes, for government agencies. Clay Dunn, director of strategic development at Dow Chemical Pacific, Ltd., argued for creating value through relationships when he told us, "*Guanxi* is developed through working together with the department or person over a long period of time — to create win-win situations, to gain confidence and to get to know each other." For companies, success emanates from creating trust and through building networks of win-win situations within value chains.

Without incorporating human relationships, value chains become archipelagos of autonomous units pulling in different directions for their own benefit. Fukuyama[25] argued for the economic importance of trust in commercial relationships; indeed, as we highlighted in Chapters 6 and 7, trust cements the Chinese networks and provides participants with enormous economic opportunities, often giving them an edge over Western competitors.

Effective and efficient communication between diverse internal and external stakeholders requires high-capacity and flexible information/communications systems. To use the Road of Relationships effectively in a global economy, companies must build their information systems and invest in IT to continue to enhance their value chains. Victor Fung accepted the central role that IT played for Li & Fung on the Road of Relationships:

> "Frankly, I am not unhappy that the business will be more dependent on IT…As the global supply network becomes larger and more far-flung, managing it will require scale. As a pure intermediary, our margins were squeezed. But as the number of supply chain options expands, we add value for our customers by using information and relationships to manage the network. We help companies communicate through a world of expanded choice. And the expanding power of IT helps us to do that.
>
> "Li & Fung uses IT to create narrow and deep relationships, to achieve customer intimacy, to link … For one of our global customers, Seibok, we created a proprietary webpage that they use to link all their global buying. The locals may understand each other, but they don't talk to each other; they do talk to us. We are set up in all the different countries, and so we can consolidate [Seibok's] buying. So we achieve customer intimacy on a global basis."[26]

As Li & Fung has shown, orchestrating information from a wide spectrum of companies and personnel within their value chain enhances their influence and increases value for their customers and other participants; it also helps to build the strongest, most profitable relationships.

PRINTING MONEY: IDG IN CHINA

The Road of Relationships enhances a company's ability to minimize external opposition from stakeholders and the general public to its actions, goals and objectives. International Data Group (IDG), the US-based technical-publishing company, provides such an example of how to traverse this road successfully. The company's chairman, Patrick McGovern, made his first trip to China in 1980. His relationship with the Fourth Ministry of the Machine Building Industry resulted in China's first tech magazine, *China Computerworld*. Since then, he has made more than 70 trips to forge close personal relationships with several senior government officials. These relationships have helped him to amass a stable of 22 magazines and 30 Internet sites, at a rate of almost one new title per year. This astonishing rate of development has taken place despite a ban on FDI in the publishing industry and the sentencing to death for corruption of one of IDG's Chinese JV partners. In 2003, China was IDG's second-largest market after the USA and, unlike many foreign companies, IDG makes profits in China. In 2000, the company's Chinese operations produced US$150 million in revenues.

IDG follows a simple formula in China: the company signs a contract with a government agency, puts in a little cash,[27] and gives the local marketing team a lot of marketing advice and leeway. Because of its strong relationships with the government, IDG was able to skirt the prohibition on FDI in publishing. McGovern elaborated on his company's approach: "We rely upon our Chinese partner, which is typically a government organization, to make sure we're complying with whatever government regulations there are, either corporate or press laws."[28]

Employing local staff helps IDG to cultivate support from the public as well as to maintain low wage costs. The local distribution network also keeps costs low and helps to cement relationships with important public figures. Following Chinese practice, the post office — rather than an in-house department — handles the circulation of magazines. For each publication, the company spends 4¢ of every dollar on circulation, as opposed to 22¢ in the US. On the downside, IDG does not know its subscribers, as the post office keeps the lists, but the huge cost savings make this trade-off acceptable. IDG has also used its relationships to diversify its publishing activities. For example, in 1998, it signed a deal with Hearst Corporation to publish *Cosmopolitan*, *Esquire*, *Modern Bride* and *Good Housekeeping* in China.

IDG has built its business in China on the basis of win-win relationships — relationships that provide wins for the Chinese government, Chinese people, business associates, employees, customers, shareholders and managers.[29]

THE ROAD OF QUALITY

The Road of Quality emphasizes that as global hyper-competition increases, product quality, brand-image quality and service quality become increasingly important factors for success. Elmar Stachels of Bayer highlighted this road when he told us, "Quality is one thing that you can never compromise on."

In Chapter 6, we discussed how China has become a global deflationary force, contributing to sliding prices across myriad industrial sectors; success built on price competition alone is ephemeral, even in China. In a recent interview, Terry T. M. Gou, founder and CEO of Taiwan's out-sourcing powerhouse Hon Hai Precision Industry Co., emphasized this point. Hon Hai is Taiwan's largest investor in China. Yet Gou underscored that for success in China, "It's not all about costs. It's about quality … If you want to make your quality good, this comes from the culture. We took 20 years to build this culture."

Although lower labor and material costs provide emerging markets with their competitive advantages as production centers, commitment to the Road of Quality provides sustainable profitability. Acer's Stan Shih alluded to the sustained advantage provided by this road when he told us, "It is very difficult to set up a name brand. But if you don't take this road, you will always work for others."

As China's largest appliance-maker, Haier has a substantial brand image. However, deflationary pressures have lowered sales growth year on year since 1999. Zhang Ruimin, Haier's CEO, has long known the importance of quality in maintaining brand image and brand share. In 1985, the government appointed him to run the lackluster SOE (which was to become the Haier Group Co) that manufactured refrigerators. "The real problem was that workers had no faith in the company and didn't care," Zhang recalled. "Quality didn't even enter into anybody's mind."[31] After a customer complained about the quality of its products, Zhang arranged a vivid demonstration of what he expected. He lined up 76 defective models of the 400 on the factory floor. He picked up a sledgehammer and told those responsible for their production to smash them. He also smashed some himself. "The message got through that there's no A, B, C, and D quality," he said. "There's only acceptable and unacceptable."[32]

Another example of how following the Road of Quality brings success is provided by the experience of the Toyota Motor Corporation. Just 12 years after it launched its brand in the USA, Lexus vaulted to the top of a very competitive field. Kousuke Shiramizu, Toyota's quality guru, explained the company's approach to product quality:[33]

> "In building the Lexus, our operating principle has been to cut the margin for error in half. Everything was fair game, such as reducing the small space between body panels. This helps reduce wind noise when the car is being driven. We also went to extremes to rethink the way we made cars — everything from the casting of the stamping dies used to form the car's metal parts to the exterior finish. Previously, our mainstay cars had gaps [between the front and rear doors] of about seven millimeters. Our goal for the LS 400 was to cut that average in half, to 4 millimeters."

The product quality, as well as Toyota's brand image and consistently high service, attracted new buyers away from competing Cadillac, Jaguar and Mercedes-Benz products.

THE ROAD OF PASSION

The Road of Passion reflects the Eastern belief that executives should derive passionate joy from the industries in which they work; the Western belief that companies should passionately commit to the markets they serve; and the universal belief that executives should passionately dedicate their efforts to their own and their company's success.

When traversing the Road of Passion, managers often act instinctively and intuitively as athletes do when "in the zone". When in the zone, athletes are able to act in calm concentration, shutting out extraneous prattle and dipping seamlessly into their experience and knowledge to arrive at perfect results. Managers traversing the Road of Passion display similarly perfect concentration and timing. Goh Hup Jin, the chairman of Nipsea Holdings and a director of Wuthelum Holdings, told us that industries in which managers display excellent timing are those for which they entertain high degrees of emotional and psychic involvement. He described these industries as "labors of love".

When telling us why a senior manager acted on gut feeling in New Zealand to arrive at an excellent strategic decision based on little quantitative data, he elaborated:

> "Would I have gone to New Zealand and made the same decision? No. But not because I would never decide that way. It is because I do not like the property industry. Some industries are labors of love [for managers]. To make a decision in that fashion, it must be in an industry, which is a labor of love. If I had gone to New Zealand and encountered a similar situation in an industry I love, yes, I would make a decision in very much the same way."

Dan Bricklin, the creator of the first electronic spreadsheet, VisiCalc, indicated that the Road of Passion contributed to his success as an entrepreneur: "I do know that unless you find your true calling and love your craft, the risks may outweigh the rewards. Sure, training, talent and that most elusive component, good timing, are essential. But they are not enough. You need to have a true passion for what you are doing."[34]

This passion leads to the Yogic stance of *ekagrata*, which derives from the Sanskrit word for "one-pointedness", where all senses engage in determined and fixed concentration on a single goal — in this case, a single-minded managerial focus on relating the company's core competencies to their markets.

Bill Gates, the CEO and founder of Microsoft, observed how his friend, legendary investor Warren Buffet, CEO of Berkshire Hathaway, traveled the Road of Passion:

"When you are with Warren, you can tell how much he loves his work. It comes across in many ways. When he explains stuff, it's never 'Hey, I'm smart about this and I'm going to impress you'. It's more like, 'This is so interesting and it's actually very simple. I'll just explain it to you and you'll realize how dumb it was that it took me a long time to figure it out.' And when he shares it with you, using his keen sense of humor to help make the point, it does seem simple."[35]

Yet, for effective management, the Road of Passion should not become an addiction. Hinduism, Buddhism and Taoism have long advocated passion, but also advocate a detached involvement as a method of effective management. In detached involvement one perceives not just the "labor of love", but also its relationships, including one's involvement with the labor. Jagdish Parikh, managing director of the Lemuir Group of Companies, elaborated on detached involvement when he said: "Consider the way you hold the steering wheel of a car while driving ... As a learner you must have held onto the wheel tightly — an illusion of control! But once you had been driving for some time, how would you hold the wheel? Much more lightly, with mastery — a balanced 'detached-involved' relation with the wheel."[36] Li Ka-shing of Hutchison Whampoa reflected this understanding when he argued that intense love of a specific company or business unit, without understanding of context, could lead to foolhardy business decisions. Effective managers know when to quit, despite their love of their work and their business. When companies, business units or products can no longer serve markets profitably, or can no longer compete effectively, managers cannot let their commitment interfere with an economically viable decision to cut their losses.

THE ROAD OF LEGACY

The Road of Legacy recognizes that top managers shape stakeholders' perceptions and expectations, and eventually their legacies. Through their strategic decisions, managers should commit to leaving their societies and the world a better place than they found it, to bring something special into the world. The Road of Legacy does not specify what decisions and actions managers should take; but it does specify the lens through which managers should view their day-to-day business decisions. This road indicates that the most successful strategies over the long term will seek to create value for society and posterity. Companies that act responsibly while generating profits will also reap long-term success. Clay Dunn, director of strategic development at Dow Chemical Pacific, spoke of the Road of Legacy when he told us that companies must view their effect on history and long-term benefits for stakeholders, and not just their immediate profits:

> "The court of world public opinion provides our license to operate. Multinational companies have significant resources and in that way have some power. It will become increasingly important [that] these companies use that power in a way that is seen as just and to some degree for the greater good. Otherwise, like any other power in history that lost the endorsement of the people, they will be overthrown. This is why diversity programs and localization of foreign sites is so critical. Over time they will become global companies, and not just multinationals, if they survive long term."

David Finn[37] argued that managers who ignored posterity in their decision-making were shortchanging themselves, their companies and their societies. He differentiated between managing to achieve greatness and managing to achieve fame. True greatness does not always bring fame with it. Finn stated that, "to sense the potential of posterity in one's daily business life, one has to feel deeply about some aspect of one's work. One has to be committed to do or to create something that will accomplish some good in the world ... The key ingredients are dedication to a profound idea and the determination to carry it out."[38]

Charles Coffin, who followed founder Thomas Edison as CEO of GE, left such a legacy of greatness, though not of fame. Coffin never outshone Edison, who held patents on the electric light, the phonograph, the motion picture, the alkaline battery and the dissemination of electricity. Coffin, however, oversaw two groundbreaking social inventions that cemented his company's legacy — the research laboratory and systematic management development. Jim Collins elaborated on Coffin's contribution this way: "While Edison was essentially a genius with a thousand helpers, Coffin created a system of genius that did not depend on him."[39] Indeed, as a nod to Coffin's legacy, his era (1892–1912) became the "Steinmetz era", in homage to the brilliant GE electrical engineer Charles P. Steinmetz. Coffin had built the stage on which geniuses played for GE and the world and then stepped away from the limelight.

The Road of Legacy reflects the Asian emphasis on duty to the community, but imposes a wider Western definition on what constitutes that community. Companies must act responsibly while generating profits. In short, companies and managers must act with an eye focused on the legacy that their decisions, made today, will build for the future. Managers of successful companies have come to understand that it behooves their companies to adopt policies that seek to maximize the sustainability of business activities. Markets will punish companies that damage environments or societies, increase the costs of externalities, or undertake activities that erode stakeholders' trust.

Indeed, an Ernst & Young 2002 survey indicated that managers of the largest companies recognize that corporate social responsibility (CSR) molds corporate longevity and profitability.[40] Ernst and Young's researchers found that:

- 72% of company directors have a commitment to CSR;
- 94% perceived CSR as delivering real business benefits;
- 39% believed CSR led to improved business performance; and,
- 79% believed CSR will increase in importance over the next five years.

The Road of Legacy also reminds us that our profits today must also leave room for profits tomorrow. To prosper tomorrow, companies need to retain the social, economic, political, physical and ecological environments necessary to maintain an acceptable standard of living, to ensure the sustainability of the business and of the economies in which they reside. George Merck II, founder and CEO of Merck and Co., understood this aspect of the Road of Legacy. In *Time* magazine in 1952, Merck stated that "Medicine is for people, not for profits". His company undertook several philanthropic causes, including dispensing streptomycin to Japanese children after World War II. Yet Merck did not wear rose-tinted glasses or see himself as a naïve do-gooder with no eye on profits. Austere and patrician, he believed that a company should do something useful and do it very well. "And if we have remembered that, the profits have never failed to appear. The better we remembered, the larger they have been." Following this axiom, his company encouraged its employees to seek useful applications for their inventions, with immediate social and ultimate corporate benefits. In 1978, researcher William Campbell, while testing a new compound to battle parasites in animals, thought it might prove effective against another parasite in humans that causes horrific itching and blindness. The potential customers, tribal people in remote locations, had no money to buy it. Undaunted, Campbell penned a memo to his employer to pursue the idea. Today, 30 million people a year receive Mectizan, the drug inspired by his observation, largely free of charge.[41]

LI KA-SHING: THE ROAD LESS TRAVELED

Many consider Li Ka-shing, CEO of Hutchison Whampoa, to be the most successful Chinese entrepreneur in the world. The son of a teacher, Li was born in Chiuchow, China, during the late 1920s and, in his words, "lost his childhood to the war". His father fled with his family to the British colony of Hong Kong after the Japanese bombed and attacked Chiuchow. As World War II gained momentum, the family split up for the children's safety: Li's mother and younger siblings went into safer regions in China; Li and his father stayed in Hong Kong to support their family monetarily. From the age of 12, Li started working at odd jobs to help out. Not long after, with Hong Kong in Japanese hands, his father succumbed to tuberculosis. Li's dreams of getting a formal education and becoming a doctor died also. He now assumed responsibility for his mother and younger brother and sister.

Li redoubled his work efforts and turned to self-education. He used any spare income to buy used textbooks to study, and then traded them for others. His dedication paid off and his jobs improved. In 1950, at the age of 22, he used his job as a top plastics salesman as a springboard to start his own plastics company, Cheung Kong. He came to dominate the market for plastic flowers, and when Hong Kong's manufacturing sector began to falter, Li quickly moved into property development, and then into services. Cheung Kong made history on September 25, 1979 as the first Chinese company to assume control of one of the old-line British colonial trading companies, Hutchison-Whampoa, which was the second-largest British-owned Hong Kong company at the time. Cheung Kong Holdings, Li's holding company, and its associated companies have a current value of US$48.3 billion and employ more than 70,000 people.

When pressed for his secret to success, Li emphasized, "I relied on hard work — hard work and the ability to make money ... You must be hardworking, frugal, steadfast, willing to learn and to build up a creditable name ... It is very important to devote yourself to work. You need to be interested in your business. If you are interested in your business you are bound to do well." His contemporaries and former associates, such as Simon Murray, a former executive director of Hutchison-Whampoa, attributed his success to "his willingness to listen, his timing in the market, and the speed with which he acts — good deals don't stay on the table very long".

Li has also traveled on the Road of Legacy. Unable to obtain a formal education or to realize his dream of becoming a doctor, he has made major contributions of time and money to educational and medical institutions around the world. He helped to found

Shantou University in 1981, paying 70% of its annual HK$120,000,000 budget. Over the years, he has supported it to the sum of HK$1.2 billion. He also meets regularly with the University's Board, Faculty Council and students to listen to their concerns and to determine what he can do next. These discussions have included brainstorming sessions on recruiting better faculty, developing programs and exploring how the University can serve the community better. He has lobbied officials in the Ministry of Education in Beijing on behalf of the University's programs and goals. He has identified his personal goals as transforming Shantou University into one of China's key universities and using it to benefit the local community and China. Li says, "My time will pass, but this [the University] will remain." Li has attempted to ensure that his personal stretch of the road less traveled, the Road of Legacy, becomes a well-worn highway.

A TRAVELER'S OBSERVATIONS

In this book, we have attempted to identify a Road Map for succeeding in a global economy. Anchored in the ancient *Tao*, our ARM bridges both Chinese and Western philosophies to indicate avenues to success for companies in the interconnected societies and economies in which we live.

When recounting his travels to China in the 13th century, the Venetian merchant Marco Polo did not mention the Great Wall, but spoke eloquently of a fascinating bridge. Indeed, this bridge served as the only architectural wonder in China that Marco identified. Some have questioned the authenticity of his tale based on these descriptions; but at that time, the Great Wall to keep out barbarians had fallen into disarray. The rivers, though, flowed bountifully and bridges perhaps captured an epiphany for this traveler, as they do for us.

First built in 1192, the Luguo Qiao Bridge lies a dusty 16 kilometers outside Beijing. Today, the Yongding River that ran below it for 800 years has run dry as city planners have diverted water to Beijing. Still hauntingly beautiful, Luguo Qiao evokes wonder, and inspires poetry and prose across cultures. Our parting hope is that the ARM provides the Road Map to individual bridges over bountiful rivers for the companies and managers that use it.

FIGURE 10.2: MARCO POLO'S BRIDGE

"Upon leaving the capital and traveling 10 miles, you come to a river named Pulisangan, which discharges itself into the ocean, and is navigated by many vessels entering from thence, with considerable quantities of merchandise. Over this river there is a very handsome bridge of stone, perhaps unequalled by any other in the world. Its length is 300 paces, and its width eight paces; so that 10 mounted men can, without inconvenience, ride abreast. It has 24 arches, supported by 25 piers erected in the water, all of serpentine stone, and built with great skill.

On each side, and from one extremity to the other, there is a handsome parapet, formed of marble slabs and pillars arranged in a masterly style. At the beginning of the ascent the bridge is something wider than at the summit, but from the part where the ascent terminates, the sides run in straight lines and parallel to each other. Upon the upper level there is a massive and lofty column, resting upon a tortoise of marble, and having near its base a large figure of a lion, with a lion also on the top. Towards the slope of the bridge there is another handsome column or pillar, with its lion, at the distance of a pace and a half from the former; and all the spaces between one pillar and another, throughout the whole length of the bridge, are filled up with slabs of marble, curiously sculptured, and mortised into the next adjoining pillars, forming altogether a beautiful spectacle. These parapets serve to prevent accidents that might otherwise happen to passengers."

The Travels of Marco Polo[42]

endnotes

1. Lau, D. C., *Lao Tzu: Tao Te Ching*, Book 2, Chapter 76, Stanza 182
2. Tanzer, A., "The Amazing Mr. Kuok", p.90.
3. Ibid.
4. Bureau of the Census, US Department of Commerce, 2002.
5. United States Central Intelligence Agency, *World Factbook, 2002*.
6. We classify Russia as an emerging economy because of its per-capita income, which is roughly 85% of Mexico's.
7. Magretta, J., "Fast, global and entrepreneurial: Supply Chain Management, Hong Kong style".
8. Haley, G. T., C. T. Tan and U. C. V. Haley, *New Asian Emperors: The Overseas Chinese, their Strategies and Competitive Advantages*.
9. Patton, R., "When a Dash Becomes a Siege".
10. Sprague, J., "Haier Reaches Higher".
11. Ibid.
12. Wack, P., "Scenarios: Shooting the Rapids", p.73.
13. Haley, G. T., and S. M. Goldberg, "Net Present Value Techniques and Their Effects on New Product Research".
14. Pande, P. S., R. P. Neuman and R. R. Cavanagh, *The Six Sigma Way: How GE, Motorola and Other Top Companies are Honing Their Performance*.
15. Business 2.0, "What Makes a Great Leader?"
16. Ibid, pp.72–73.
17. Haley and Goldberg, op.cit.
18. Haley et al, op.cit.
19. Haley, U. C. V., and S. A. Stumpf, "Cognitive Trails in Strategic Decision-Making: Linking Theories of Personalities and Cognitions".
20. Yan, R., "Short-Term Results: The Litmus Test for Success in China".
21. Eisenhardt, K. M., and D. Sull (2001), "Strategy as Simple Rules".
22. *China Economic Quarterly* (2001), "The Best Multinationals in China".
23. Ibid.
24. Tanzer, op.cit.

25. Fukuyama, F., *Trust: The Social Virtues and the Creation of Prosperity.*

26. Magretta, op.cit.

27. China's top tech magazine, *China Computerworld*, with 170,000 paid subscribers and 10,000 pages of advertising, began with $200,000.

28. *China Economic Quarterly*, "The Best Multinationals in China".

29. Kroeber, A. R., "The Best Multinationals in China: Five Companies that Made It".

30. *Business Week*, "The Stars of Asia".

31. *Business Week*, "Zhang Ruimin, CEO, Haier Group, China".

32. Ibid.

33. *Business Week*, "Q&A: From the Nexus of Lexus."

34. Bricklin, D., "Natural-born entrepreneur", p.4.

35. Gates, B., "What I learned from Warren Buffet", *Harvard Business Review*, p.6.

36. Parikh, J., *Managing Relationships: Making a Life While Making a Living.*

37. Finn, D., "The Price of Ignoring Posterity".

38. Ibid.

39. Collins, J., "The Ten Greatest CEOs of All Time". p.68.

40. Grant, et al., *Corporate Social Responsibility: A Survey of Global Companies.*

41. Collins, op.cit., p.64.

41. *The Travels of Marco Polo*, Chapter 35, "Of the Interior of Cathay, The River Named Pulisangan and the Bridge Over It", p.149.

LIST OF
INTERVIEWEES[1]

---

1 Surnames are underlined;
job titles were those held at the
time of the interview

1. Mr Steven <u>Chan</u>
   Executive Chairman, Superior Multi-Packaging, Ltd.
2. Mr <u>Chen</u> Jiulin
   Director of China Aviation Oil (Singapore) Corp, Ltd.
3. Director, External Affairs, Asia Pacific for a major media and entertainment conglomerate (This executive requested that both his name and his company's name be kept private.).
4. Mr Clay <u>Dunn</u>
   Director of Strategic Development, Dow Chemical Pacific, Ltd.
5. Dr Victor <u>Fung</u>
   Chairman, Prudential Asia Investment, Ltd., and Li & Fung
6. Mr Michael <u>Furst</u>
   Executive Director, The American Chamber of Commerce People's Republic of China.
7. Mr <u>Goh</u> Hup Jin
   Chairman, Nipsea Holdings International, Ltd., and Director, Wuthelum Holdings Pte. Ltd.
8. Mr Billy T. <u>Ho</u>
   Manager Corporate Quality, Corporate Marketing & Public Affairs, 3M.
9. Mr H. Y. <u>Ho</u>
   Director of Manufacturing, Artesyn Technologies Asia-Pacific, Ltd.
10. Mr Austin C. T. <u>Hu</u>
    Deputy Chief of Mission, The World Bank Office, Beijing.
11. Mr <u>Kuok</u> Khoon Ean
    Executive Chairman, Kuok (Singapore), Ltd.

12. Mr <u>Kwek</u> Leng Joo
    Managing Director, City Developments, Ltd., and President Singapore Chinese Chamber of Commerce and Industry.
13. Mr <u>Li</u> Ka-shing
    Chairman of the Board, Huchison Whampoa, Founder and Chief Executive Officer, Tom.Com.
14. Ms Rita <u>Liaw</u>
    Executive Director, Hong Kong Ethics Development Centre.

15. Dr <u>Lo</u> Wai Kwok
    Managing Director, Artesyn Technologies Asia-Pacific, Ltd.
16. Mr <u>Lu</u> Qun
    Director of Product Engineering, Beijing Jeep Corporation, Ltd.
17. Mr Frank <u>Martin</u>
    President, American Chamber of Commerce in Hong Kong.
18. Mr Philip <u>Ng</u>
    Executive Director and Chief Executive Officer, Far East
    Organization, Singapore.
17. Mr <u>Pan</u> Shi Yi
    Founder and Chief Executive Officer, Redstone Development,
    founder and Chief Executive Officer, SOHO Development.
18. Mr Robert Y. H. <u>Shi</u>
    Chief Representative, European Financial Group,
    Beijing Representative Office.
19. Mr Stan <u>Shih</u>
    Founder and Chief Executive Officer, Acer Computers.
20. Dr Philip <u>Spanninger</u>
    Vice President, International, TRW Overseas, Inc.
21. Dr Elmar <u>Stachels</u>
    Managing Director, Bayer China Company, Ltd., and
    Chairman and General Manager, Bayer (China) Ltd.
22. Mr <u>Wah</u> Chu
    Business Unit General Manager, Pepsico-Hong Kong/China.
23. Mr <u>Wee</u> Ee Cheong
    Deputy Chairman and President, United Overseas Bank, Ltd.
24. Mr Y Y <u>Wong</u>
    Chairman, WyWy Group.
25. Mr Henry <u>Yu</u>
    President, Beijing McMahan Investment Consultation Co.
26. Dr <u>Yan</u> Lan
    Chief Litigator, Gide Loyrette Nouel.
27. Dr Edward <u>Zeng</u> – Founder and Chief Executive Officer,
    Sparkice.com.

appendix **B**

BIBLIOGRAPHY

AFX News (2002), "Focus. China Airline Industry restructuring seen easing competition", October 14.

Allen, J. T. (2002), "China charges into Florida", *US News & World Report*, November 4, p.48.

Asian Development Bank (2003), News Releases No. 065/03 and No. 076/03, May 9.

Asian Wall Street Journal (2002), "Hainan Airlines Posts Higher Net", August 20, p.M8; and "China Attracts more Investments from Foreigners", September 17.

Associated Press (2003), "Beijing's SARS records are flawed, WHO says", May 10.

Aviation Daily (2002), "China limits foreign investment by single company to 25 percent", August 28, p.5.

Backman, M. (1999), *Asian Eclipse: Exposing the Dark Side of Business in Asia*, Singapore: Wiley.

Balazs, E. (1964), *Chinese Civilization and Bureaucracy*, New Haven: Yale University Press.

Bateson, A. (2003) "InterGen's China Plant at Impasse in Talks", Dow Jones International News, April 18.

BBC News (2003), "SARS could cost Asia $28bn", May 9.

Becker, J. (2000), *The Chinese*, New York, NY: The Free Press.

Biers, D. (2001), "A Taste of China in Camden", *Far Eastern Economic Review*, March 29.

Biers, D. A., and K. Wilhelm (2000), "Telecoms — a Cautious Courtship", *Far Eastern Economic Review*, December 7.

Bradsher, K. (2003), "Chinese Computer Maker Plans a Push Overseas", *The New York Times*, February 22, p.B1, B3.

Bricklin, D. (2001), "Natural-born entrepreneur", *Harvard Business Review*, September, Reprint R0108B, p.4.

Briley, D. A., M. Morris and I. Simonson (2000), "Reasons as Carriers of Culture: Dynamic Versus Dispositional Models of Cultural Influence on Decision Making", *Journal of Consumer Research*, Vol. 27, p.157–78.

Buckman, R., B. Dolvenin and S. V. Lawrence (2003), "The chips are down for China's computer Legend", *Far Eastern Economic Review*, June 13.

Bureau of the Census, U.S. Department of Commerce, 2002.

Business 2.0 (2002), "What Makes a Great Leader?", August, p.72–75.

Business Times (of Singapore) (1997), October 17.

Business Today (1998), "India's Business Families: Can they Survive?", Sixth Anniversary Issue, January–February.

Business Week (1999), "Zhang Ruimin, CEO, Haier Group, China", June 14 (taken off the web).

Business Week (2001), "Q&A: From the Nexus of Lexus", September 3 (taken off the web).

Business Week (2002), "The Stars of Asia", July 8 (taken off the web).

Carver, A. (1996), "Open and Secret Regulations in China and their Implications for Foreign Investment", in Child, J. and Y. Lu, *Management Issues in China*, London: Routledge.

Chan, K. B. and C. Chiang (1994), *Stepping Out, The Making of Chinese Entrepreneurs*, Singapore: Prentice Hall.

Chan, W. T. (1963), *Chinese Philosophy*, Princeton, N.J.: Princeton University Press.

Chang, G. G. (2001), *The Coming Collapse of China*, New York: Random House.

Chang, K.-c. (1980), *Shang Civilization*, New Haven: Yale University Press.

Cheng, A. and H. Vriens (1996), "Superman vs. China", *Asia Inc.*, Vol. 5, #12, p.42–49.

China Business Information Network, Business Daily Update — China (2002), September 11.

China Business Review (2000), "Foreign Investors Wise Up", November, p.8.

China Business Review (2002), "Amcham Survey Highlights Issues for US Business in China", July/August.

China Economic Quarterly (2001), "The Best Multinationals in China", Volume 5, Issue 2.

China Online (2002a), "China — Grand Cherokee could be Beijing Jeep's Last Great Hope", February 26.

China Online (2002b), "China — Ban on Cross-Regional Direct Marketing Explained", April, 1.

Chinese University of Hong Kong Press Release (1999).

Choi, I., and R. E. Nisbett (1998), "Situational Salience and Cultural Differences in the Correspondence Bias and in the Actor-Observer Bias", *Personality and Social Psychology Bulletin*, Vol. 24, p.949–960.

Chu, C. N. (1992), *Thick Face, Black Heart: The Path to Thriving, Winning & Succeeding*, New York: Warner Books.

Chu, T. C., and T. MacMurray (1993), "The Road Ahead for Asia's Leading Conglomerates," *McKinsey Quarterly*, #3, p.117–126.

Clark, T. (1998), "Reinventing Japan, Inc. ", *Industry Week*, July 6, taken off IndustryWeek.com website.

Clendin, M. (2002), "China starting to lure back its best brains", *EE Times*, January 6.

Clifford, M. L., H. Filman and S. Reed (2000), "Li Ka-Shing Sneaks Back into the Wireless Game", *Business Week*, May 15.

Clifford, M. L., A. Reinhardt and K. Capell (2002), "Li Ka-Shing's Long Shot — or Sure Thing?", *Business Week*, September 30.

Collins, J. (2001), *Good To Great*, New York: Harper Collins.

Collins, J. (2003), "The Ten Greatest CEOs of All Time", *Fortune*, July 21, p.54–68.

Davis, M., R. E. Nisbett and N. Schwarz (2000), *Responses to Weak Argument on the Part of Asians and Americans*, Ann Arbor: University of Michigan.

De Bary, W. T. and I. Bloom (1999), *Sources of Chinese Tradition, From Earliest Times to 1600*, 2nd edition, New York: Columbia University Press.

De Bary, W. T. and R. Lufrano (1999), *Sources of Chinese Tradition, From 1600 Through the Twentieth Century*, 2nd edition, New York: Columbia University Press.

Dolven, B. (2002), "The Best little Airline in China", *Far Eastern Economic Review*, January 17, p.32.

Dolven, B., and S. V. Lawrence (2002), "Power — Playing by The Rules", *Far Eastern Economic Review*, January 31, p.52.

Doran, J. (2002), "China to own and operate US company", *The Times* (London), October 22, p.4.

Eckholm, E. (2002), "Order Yields to Lawlessness as Maoism Recedes in China", *New York Times*, Section A, p.1, May 29.

The Economist (2000), "Tangled Web", (from the Economist.com)
April 6.

The Economist (2001), "The best and the rest", (from the
Economist.com) April 5.

The Economist, "The Greatest Leap Forward", (from the
Economist.com) April 5.

The Economist, "From Bamboo to Bits and Bytes", Survey of Asian
Business, (from the Economist.com) April 7, p.8.

The Economist, "Legend in the Making", (from the Economist.com)
September 13.

The Economist (2002), "How Cooked are the Books?", (from the
Economist.com) March 14.

The Economist, "Asia's Superman Swoops Again", (from the
Economist.com) August 15.

The Economist, "Not in the Club," (from the Economist.com)
October 10.

The Economist, "Set them Free" (from the Economist.com).

The Economist (2003), "Strings Attached", (from the Economist.com)
March 6.

The Economist (2003), "The communist entrepreneur", (from the
Economist.com) March 27.

The Economist "Bush telegraph", (from the Economist.com) May 22.

Encyclopedia Britannica (2002), "Buddhism, Historical Development,
Central Asia and China", CD version.

Einhorn, B. (2002), "Learning to Play Fair in China," *BusinessWeek*,
May 7 (taken off the web).

Eisenhardt, K. M., and D. Sull (2001), "Strategy as Simple Rules",
Harvard Business Review, January, p.106–116.

Ernsberger, R., et al (2001), "The Spread of China Inc.", *Newsweek
International* (taken off website, 09/03/2001).

Fairbank, J. K. and M. Goldman (1999), *China, a New History*,
Cambridge, MA: The Belknap Press of Harvard University Press.

Feder, B. J. (2003), "Worldcom enabled huge fraud, investigations
find", *The New York Times*, June 10.

Fei, X. (1992), *From the Soil: The Foundation of Chinese Society*,
Berkeley: University of California Press.

Finn, D. (1983), "The Price of Ignoring Posterity", *Harvard Business Review*, May–June, p.137–44.

Ford, I. D. and C. Ryan (1981), "Taking Technology to Market", *Harvard Business Review*, #2, p. 117-126

Fukuyama, F. (1995), *Trust: The Social Virtues and the Creation of Prosperity*, London: Penguin Books.

Gamble, J. (2001), "Inside Track: The struggle to get nappies off the ground", *Financial Times*, May 14.

Gates, B. (1996), "What I learned from Warren Buffet", *Harvard Business Review*, January–February, Reprint 96105.

Ghosh, B. C., and C. O. Chan (1994), "A Study of Strategic Planning Behavior Among Emergent Businesses in Singapore and Malaysia", *International Journal of Management*, Vol. 11, #2, p.697–706.

Gidoomal, R., and D. Porter (1997), *The UK Maharajahs: Inside the South Asian Success Story*, London: Nicholas Brealy.

Gilley, B. (2001), "Henderson Land — The pitfalls of property," *Far Eastern Economic Review*, November 15.

Gilley, B. (2002), "Is Yang Bin the Richest Man in China?", *Far Eastern Economic Review*, October 1, p.30.

Gilley, B. (2002), "The Perils of Flower Power", *Far Eastern Economic Review*, October 10, p.30.

Gilley, B., J. McBeth, B. Dolven, and S. Tripathi (1998), "Ready, Set...",
Far Eastern Economic Review, February 19, p.46–50.

Grant, A., J. Buttle, S. McKenzie, and G. Veale (2002), "Corporate Social Responsibility: A Survey of Global Companies", Ernst & Young, Environment and Sustainability Services Group.

Haley, G. T. (1997), "A Strategic Perspective on Overseas Chinese Networks' Decision-making", *Management Decision*, Vol. 35, #8, p.587–594.

Haley, G. T., and S. M. Goldberg (1995), "Net Present Value Techniques and Their Effects on New Product Research", *Industrial Marketing Management*, Vol.24, No. 3, p.177–190.

Haley, G. T., and U. C. V. Haley (1997), "Making Strategic Business Decisions in South and Southeast Asia," *Conference Proceedings of the First International Conference on Operations and Quantitative Management*, Jaipur, India, Volume II, p.597–604.

Haley, G. T., and U. C. V. Haley (1998), "Boxing with Shadows: Competing Effectively with the Overseas Chinese and Overseas Indian Networks in the Asian Arena", *Journal of Organizational Change Management*, Vol. 11, # 4.

Haley, G. T., C. T. Tan and U. C. V. Haley (1998), *New Asian Emperors: The Overseas Chinese, their Strategies and Competitive Advantages*, Oxford, UK: Butterworth-Heineman.

Haley, G. T., and C. T. Tan (1996), "The Black Hole of Southeast Asia: Strategic Decision-Making in an Informational Void", *Management Decision*, Vol. 34, #9, p.43–55.

Haley, G. T., and C. T. Tan (1999), "East versus West: Strategic Marketing Management Meets the Asian Networks," *Journal of Business & Industrial Marketing*, Special Issue on "Business-to-Business Marketing in Asia".

Haley, U. C. V. (1997), "The Myers-Briggs Type Indicator and Decision-Making Styles: Identifying and Managing Cognitive Trails in Strategic Decision Making", in C. Fitzgerald & L. Kirby (Eds.), *Developing Leaders: Research and Applications in Psychological Type and Leadership Development*, Palo Alto, CA: Consulting Psychologists Press, p.187–223.

Haley, U. C. V. (2001), *Multinational Corporations in Political Environments: Ethics, Values and Strategies*, London: World Scientific Press.

Haley, U. C. V. (2002), "Here There be Dragons: Opportunities and Risks for Foreign Multinational Corporations in China", in Haley, U. C. V., and F.-J. Richter (eds.) *Asian Post-Crisis Management: Corporate and Governmental Strategies for Sustainable Competitive Advantage*, New York: Palgrave.

Haley, U. C. V. (2003), "Assessing Business Risks in China", *Journal of International Management*, Vol. 9, p. 237-252 .

Haley, U. C. V., and S. A. Stumpf (1989), "Cognitive Trails in Strategic Decision-Making: Linking Theories of Personalities and Cognitions", *Journal of Management Studies*, Vol. 26, #5, p.477–497.

Hamilton, G. G., and Z. Wang (1992), "Introduction", Fei, X., *From the Soil: The Foundation of Chinese Society*, Berkeley: University of California Press.

Hansell, S. (2002), "With Ad Revenue Down, Yahoo Tries to Win Agencies' Favor", *The New York Times*, Business Day Section, p.C3.

Heilbroner, R. L., and A. Singer (1984), *The Economic Transformation of America: 1600 to the Present*, 2nd edition, New York: Harcourt Brace Jovanovich Publishers.

Hofer, C. W., and D. Schendel (1978), *Strategy Formulation: Analytical Concepts*, St. Paul, MN: West Publishing Co.

Hofstede, G. (1994), "Cultural Constraints in Management Theories", *International Review of Strategic Management*, Vol. 5, D. E. Hussey (Ed.), West Sussex, UK: John Wiley & Sons, Ltd., p.27–47.

Hong, Y. (2000), *Tending the Roots of Wisdom* (Translated by White, P.), Beijing: New Word Press.

Hung, F. (2003), "As virus worsens, Asia looks to West for options", *Electronic Engineering Times*, April 28.

Jones, M. C. (2003), "And our survey said", *Brand Strategy*, March 20.

Joseph, D. R. (2001), *Wen and the Art of Doing Business in China*, Pittsburgh, PA: Cultural Dragon Publishing.

Kahn, J. (2002), "China Holds Capitalist Chief of North Korea Trade Zone", *The New York Times*, October 5, Section A, p.7.

Kahn, J. (2002), "Chinese company to buy and run a bankrupt US Battery maker", *The New York Times*, October 21, p.2.

Kahn, J. (2002), "The Pinch of Piracy Wakes China Up on Copyright Issues", *The New York Times*, November 1.

Kiley, D. (2002), "Mercedes Racks Up Problems in Quality Survey", *USA Today*, March 18, Section B, p.3.

Konrad, R. (2003), "Silicon Valley pushes technology to cope with SARS", Associated Press Newswires, April 25.

Kopytoff, V. (2002), "Search Engines in China Face Balancing Act", *The San Francisco Chronicle*, September 16, p.E-1.

Kroeber, A. R. (2001), "The Best Multinationals in China: Five Companies that Made It", *China Economic Quarterly*, Vol. 5, #2, p.17–30.

Kurlantzick, J. (2002), "Making it in China", *US News & World Report*, October 7, p.44.

Kynge, J. (2002), "Survey-Energy and Utility Business", *Financial Times*, April 11, p.4.

Lau, D. C. (1995), *Mencius Says*, Singapore: Federal Publications, Pte. Ltd.

Lau, D. C. (1963), *Lao Tzu: Tao Te Ching*, London: Penguin Books.

Lau, D. C. (1979), Confucius: The Analects, London: Penguin Books.

Lawrence, S. V. (2000), "Formula for Disaster", *Far Eastern Economic Review*, October 5.

Lawrence, S. V., and D. Murphy (2001), "Repression-Appearances can Deceive," *Far Eastern Economic Review*, December13, p.32.

Lee, C. S. (2002), "Acer's last stand", *Fortune*, June 10.

Legge, J. (1970), *The Works of Mencius*, New York: Cover Publications, Inc.

Leggett, K., D. Bilefsky and T. Zaun (2003), "Foreign firms face setbacks as SARS cases mount in China", *Wall Street Journal*, May 25, Section B, p.1 and 4.

Leggett, K., and P. Wonacot (2002), "China-Trade — Burying the Competition", *Far Eastern Economic Review*, October 17, p.30.

Liu, M., and P. Mooney (2002), "Why China Cooks the Books: The Reputation of the People's Republic as an Economic Powerhouse is Based in Part on Pure Bunk", *Newsweek International*, Atlantic edition (obtained through Dow Jones International), April 1.

Liu, Y. (1998), *Origins of Chinese Law: Penal and Administrative Law in its Early Development*, Hong Kong: Oxford University Press.

Lu, Y. (1996), *Management Decision-Making in Chinese Enterprises*, New York: St. Martin's Press.

Lubman, S. P. (1999), *Bird in a Cage: Legal Reform in China after Mao*, Palo Alto, California, US: Stanford University Press.

Lynch, D. J. (2002), "Chinese success story has plot twist", *USA Today*, October 16, p.3B.

Magretta, J. (1998), "Fast, global and entrepreneurial: Supply Chain Management, Hong Kong style", *Harvard Business Review*, September–October 1998, HBR OnPoint, Product No. 2020.

Maine, H. (1930), *Ancient Law*, Oxford, UK: Oxford University Press.

Meredith, R. (2003), "The Counterfeit Economy" and "Microsoft's Long March," *Forbes*, February 17 p.78–86.

Meyer, D. E. (1995), "Adaptive Executive Control: Flexible Multi-Task Performance Without Pervasive Immutable Response-Selection Bottlenecks", *Acta Psychologica*, Vol. 90, p.163–90.

Meyer, D. E., and D. E. Keiras (1997a), "A Computational Theory of Executive Cognitive Processes and Multiple-Task Performance: I, Basic Mechanisms", *Psychological Review*, Vol. 104, p.3–65.

Meyer, D. E., and D. E. Keiras (1997b), "A Computational Theory of Executive Cognitive Processes and Multiple-Task Performance: II, Accounts of Psychological Refractory-Period Phenomena", *Psychological Review*, Vol. 104, p.749–91.

Mintzberg, H. (1987), "Crafting Strategy", *Harvard Business Review*, July/August, p.66–75.

Mintzberg, H. (1994), "The Fall and Rise of Strategic Planning", *Harvard Business Review*, January/February, p.107–114.

Mintzberg, H., and J. Waters (1985), "Of Strategies, Deliberate and Emergent", *Strategic Management Journal*, # 6, p.257–272.

MOFTEC, People's Republic of China.

Moore, G. E. (1965), "Cramming more components onto integrated circuits," *Electronics*, Vol. 38, No. 8, April 19.

Nicholas, K. (2002), "High Prices Encourage Software Piracy", *Australian Financial Review*, September 4.

Nikkei Report (2003), "Foreign firms mull changes in Chinese Investments: Survey", April 23.

Nikkei Weekly (2003), "Firms mull future of China operations", April 28.

Nisbett, R. E., K. Peng, I. Choi, and A. Norenzayan (2001), "Culture and Systems of Thought: Holistic Versus Analytic Cognition," *Psychological Preview*, April, Vol. 108, No. 2, p.291–310.

Pan, C. C. H. (1984), "Confucian Philosophy: Implication to Management" in TanChin Tiong (ed), *Proceedings of the 1984 AMA Conference, Singapore*, p.777–781.

Pande, P. S., R. P. Neuman and R. R. Cavanagh (2000), *The Six Sigma Way: How GE, Motorola and Other Top Companies are Honing Their Performance*, New York: McGraw-Hill.

Parikh, J. (1999), *Managing Relationships: Making a Life While Making a Living*, Oxford, UK: Capstone Publishing.

Patton, R. (2003), "When a Dash Becomes a Siege", *The New York Times*, Op-Ed Section, p.A-27, April 5.

PBS (Public Broadcasting System), Wideangle debate between Usha Haley and Mark Clifford at http://www.pbs.org/wnet/wideangle/shows/china/debate.html

Peng, K., and R. E. Nisbett (1999), "Culture, Dialectics and Reasoning About Contradiction", *American Psychologist*, Vol. 54, p.741–754.

Piore, A. and P. Mooney (2002), "China's Statistics are Fishier than its Oceans", *Newsweek International*, January 21, p.46.

The Travels of Marco Polo, edited and revised (2001) from William Marsden's translation by Manuel Komroff, New York: The Modern Library.

Pomeranz, K. (2000), *The Great Divergence: China, Europe, and the Making of the Modern World Economy*, Princeton, N. J.: Princeton University Press.

Powell, B. (2002), "The Legend of Legend", *Fortune International*, September 16, taken off the web.

Prahalad, C. K. and G. Hamel (1990), "The Core Competence of the Corporation", *Harvard Business Review*, May/June, pp.79–91.

Rawski, T. G. (2002), "Beijing's Cooked Books", *The Asian Wall Street Journal*, April 19, p.A9.

Redding, S. G. (1986), "Entrepreneurship in Asia", *Euro-Asia Business Review*, Vol. 5, #4, p.23–27.

Redding, S. G. (1995), "Overseas Chinese Networks: Understanding the Enigma", *Long Range Planning*, Vol. 28, #1, p.61–69.

Roberts, D., and M. L. Clifford (2003), "Beijing Calls in Troubleshooter", *Business Week*, May 12.

Rosen, D. H. (1998), *Behind the Open Door*, Washington DC: Institute for International Economics.

Rosenthal, E. (2003), "From China's Provinces, a Crafty Germ Breaks Out", *The New York Times*, April 27, p.1 and 18.

Servan-Schreiber, J. J. (1968), *The American Challenge*, New York: Scribner.

Shao, Z. (2002), "New Practice to Better Protect Investors", *China Daily*, February 26.

Shi, Z. (1997), "The Dual Economic Function of Confucianism", in Yu et al, *Economic Ethics and Chinese Culture, Chinese Philosophical Studies, XIV*, Washington, D.C.: The Council for Research in Values and Philosophy.

Shih, S. (1996), *Me-Too is Not My Style*, Taipei: Acer Foundation Publishing.

Shilling, A. G. (2003), "Broken China", *Forbes*, May 12, p.156.

Soap Perfumery & Cosmetics (2002), April 1.

South China Morning Post (2002a), "Fresh Curbs on Direct Selling Might Carry Political Slant", July 8.

South China Morning Post (2002b), "Amway Learns Key Lessons on Direct-Sales Obstacle Course", August 13.

South China Morning Post (2002c), "Corporate credibility crunch", October 23, p.2.

Sprague, J. (2002), "Haier Reaches Higher", *Fortune International*, September 16, taken off the web.

Sprague, J. (2002), "China's manufacturing beachhead", *Fortune*, October 28.

Starr, J. B. (1997), *Understanding China: A Guide to China's Economy, History, and Political Structure*, New York: Hill and Wang.

Sterman, J. D. (2000), *Business Dynamics: Systems Thinking and Modeling for a Complex World*, New York: Irwin/McGraw-Hill.

Stewart, T. A. (2002), "How to Think with Your Gut", *Business 2.0*, November, p.98–104.

Straits Times (of Singapore) (2001), "Singapore Portal gets World Links", September 18.

Studwell, J. (2002), *The China Dream*, New York: Atlantic Monthly Press.

Yoon, S-K. (2002), "Telecoms — Cheap Talk in China", *Far Eastern Economic Review*, January 31, p.38.

Tanzer, A. (1997), "The Amazing Mr. Kuok", *Forbes*, July 28, p.90.

United States Intelligence Agency, *World Factbook, 2002*.

Wack, P. (1985a), "Scenarios: Shooting the Rapids", *Harvard Business Review*, November–December, p.2–14.

Wack, P. (1985b), "Scenarios: Uncharted Waters Ahead", *Harvard Business Review*, September–October, p.73–89.

Wall Street Journal (2002), "Soda and Suckers in China", August 26.

Wang K. H. (2000), *Chinese Commercial Law*, Oxford, UK: Oxford University Press.

Webb, S. (2002), "Heard in Asia", *The Asian Wall Street Journal*, October 24, p.M1.

Wheelen, T. L., and J. D. Hunger (1998), *Strategic Management and Business Policy*, 6th ed., Reading, MA: Addison-Wesley.

Wild, O., "The Silk Road" at http://www.ess.uci.edu/~oliver/silk.html, taken June 1, 2003.

Wilford, J. N. (2002), "Under Centuries of Sand, a Trading Hub", *The New York Times*, Science Section, July 9, p.D1 and D9.

Wonacott, P., C. Hutzler and K. Chen (2003), "In SARS Shake-up, China Shows it's not alone in the World", *Wall Street Journal*, April 21, p.1.

World Markets (2002), "China: Pepsico Troubles Highlight Worst-Case Scenario for Joint-Venture Enterprises", August 21.

Yan, R. (1998), "Short-Term Results: The Litmus Test for Success in China", *Harvard Business Review*, September/October, Reprint # 98511.

Yi, M. (2001), "Land rush to the East", *San Francisco Chronicle*, October 29, p.G-1.

Zerega, B. (2002), "A tough call", *Red Herring*, November, p.38–41.

Zhang, Q. (1997), " Marxism and Traditional Chinese Philosophy", in Yu et al, *Economic Ethics and Chinese Culture, Chinese Philosophical Studies, XIV*, Washington, D.C.: The Council for Research in Values and Philosophy.

In addition to the above, numerous articles in the following publications have provided background and depth:

Asia, Inc.
Asia Pacific Economic Review
AsiaWeek
Asian Business
Asian Wall Street Journal
Business Times (of Singapore)
BusinessWeek
China Economic Quarterly
China's Wired/China Business Monthly
Far Eastern Economic Review
Financial Times
Forbes
Fortune
International Herald Tribune
Los Angeles Times
New York Times
Newsweek
Next (of Hong Kong)
San Francisco Chronicle
The Australian
The Economist
The Straits Times (of Singapore)
Time Magazine
Wall Street Journal

INDEX